Other Books of Related Interest in the Opposing Viewpoints Series:

AFRICA

OPPOSING VIEWPOINTS®

David L. Bender & Bruno Leone, *Series Editors*

Carol Wekesser, *Book Editor*
Christina Pierce, *Assistant Editor*

OPPOSING VIEWPOINTS SERIES ®

Greenhaven Press, Inc.   PO Box 289009   San Diego, CA 92198-0009

Library of Congress Cataloging-in-Publication Data

Africa—opposing viewpoints / Carol Wekesser, book editor. Christina Pierce, assistant editor.
     p.   cm.—(Opposing viewpoints series)
    Includes bibliographical references and index.
    Summary: A collection of articles debating the economic, social, and political problems of Africa. Includes critical thinking activities.
    ISBN 0-89908-186-X (lib.) . —ISBN 0-89908-161-4 (pap.).
    1. Africa. 2. Critical thinking. [1. Africa.] I. Wekesser, Carol, 1963- . II. Pierce, Christina, 1972- . III. Series: Opposing viewpoints series
(Unnumbered)
DT6.5.A35   1992
960—dc20   91-42292

"Congress shall make no law . . .
abridging the freedom of speech,
or of the press."

First Amendment to the U.S. Constitution

The basic foundation of our democracy is the first amendment
guarantee of freedom of expression. The Opposing Viewpoints
Series is dedicated to the concept of this basic freedom and the
idea that it is more important to practice it than to enshrine it.

Contents

Chapter 3: Can Western Aid Help Africa?

Chapter 4: What Form of Government Would Benefit Africa?

Chapter 5: How Will the Dismantling of Apartheid Affect South Africa's Future?

Why Consider Opposing Viewpoints?

"It is better to debate a question without settling it than to settle a question without debating it."

Joseph Joubert (1754-1824)

The Importance of Examining Opposing Viewpoints

The purpose of the Opposing Viewpoints Series, and this book in particular, is to present balanced, and often difficult to find, opposing points of view on complex and sensitive issues.

Probably the best way to become informed is to analyze the positions of those who are regarded as experts and well studied on issues. It is important to consider every variety of opinion in an attempt to determine the truth. Opinions from the mainstream of society should be examined. But also important are opinions that are considered radical, reactionary, or minority as well as those stigmatized by some other uncomplimentary label. An important lesson of history is the eventual acceptance of many unpopular and even despised opinions. The ideas of Socrates, Jesus, and Galileo are good examples of this.

Readers will approach this book with their own opinions on the issues debated within it. However, to have a good grasp of one's own viewpoint, it is necessary to understand the arguments of those with whom one disagrees. It can be said that those who do not completely understand their adversary's point of view do not fully understand their own.

A persuasive case for considering opposing viewpoints has been presented by John Stuart Mill in his work *On Liberty*. When examining controversial issues it may be helpful to reflect on this suggestion:

The only way in which a human being can make some approach to knowing the whole of a subject, is by hearing what can be said about it by persons of every variety of opinion, and studying all modes in which it can be looked at by every character of mind. No wise man ever acquired his wisdom in any mode but this.

Analyzing Sources of Information

The Opposing Viewpoints Series includes diverse materials taken from magazines, journals, books, and newspapers, as well as statements and position papers from a wide range of individuals, organizations, and governments. This broad spectrum of sources helps to develop patterns of thinking which are open to the consideration of a variety of opinions.

Pitfalls to Avoid

A pitfall to avoid in considering opposing points of view is that of regarding one's own opinion as being common sense and the most rational stance, and the point of view of others as being only opinion and naturally wrong. It may be that another's opinion is correct and one's own is in error.

Another pitfall to avoid is that of closing one's mind to the opinions of those with whom one disagrees. The best way to approach a dialogue is to make one's primary purpose that of understanding the mind and arguments of the other person and not that of enlightening him or her with one's own solutions. More can be learned by listening than speaking.

It is my hope that after reading this book the reader will have a deeper understanding of the issues debated and will appreciate the complexity of even seemingly simple issues on which good and honest people disagree. This awareness is particularly important in a democratic society such as ours where people enter into public debate to determine the common good. Those with whom one disagrees should not necessarily be regarded as enemies, but perhaps simply as people who suggest different paths to a common goal.

Developing Basic Reading and Thinking Skills

In this book, carefully edited opposing viewpoints are purposely placed back to back to create a running debate; each viewpoint is preceded by a short quotation that best expresses the author's main argument. This format instantly plunges the reader into the midst of a controversial issue and greatly aids that reader in mastering the basic skill of recognizing an author's point of view.

A number of basic skills for critical thinking are practiced in the activities that appear throughout the books in the series. Some of the skills are:

Evaluating Sources of Information. The ability to choose from among alternative sources the most reliable and accurate source in relation to a given subject.

Separating Fact from Opinion. The ability to make the basic distinction between factual statements (those that can be demonstrated or verified empirically) and statements of opinion (those that are beliefs or attitudes that cannot be proved).

Identifying Stereotypes. The ability to identify oversimplified, exaggerated descriptions (favorable or unfavorable) about people and insulting statements about racial, religious, or national groups, based upon misinformation or lack of information.

Recognizing Ethnocentrism. The ability to recognize attitudes or opinions that express the view that one's own race, culture, or group is inherently superior, or those attitudes that judge another culture or group in terms of one's own.

It is important to consider opposing viewpoints and equally important to be able to critically analyze those viewpoints. The activities in this book are designed to help the reader master these thinking skills. Statements are taken from the book's viewpoints and the reader is asked to analyze them. This technique aids the reader in developing skills that not only can be applied to the viewpoints in this book, but also to situations where opinionated spokespersons comment on controversial issues. Although the activities are helpful to the solitary reader, they are most useful when the reader can benefit from the interaction of group discussion.

Using this book and others in the series should help readers develop basic reading and thinking skills. These skills should improve the reader's ability to understand what is read. Readers should be better able to separate fact from opinion, substance from rhetoric, and become better consumers of information in our media-centered culture.

This volume of the Opposing Viewpoints Series does not advocate a particular point of view. Quite the contrary! The very nature of the book leaves it to the reader to formulate the opinions he or she finds most suitable. My purpose as publisher is to see that this is made possible by offering a wide range of viewpoints that are fairly presented.

David L. Bender
Publisher

Africa

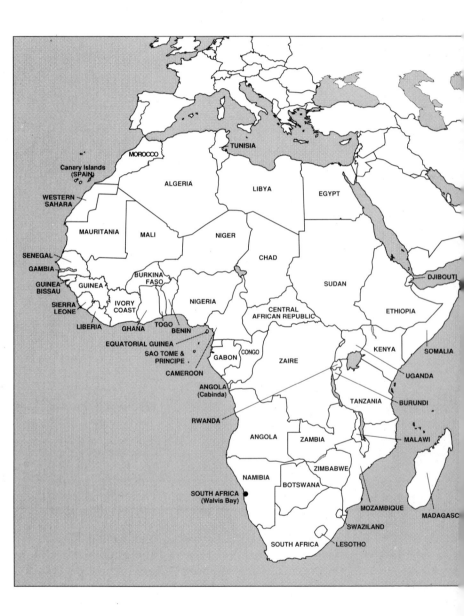

Introduction

"The problem of writing about a place as remote as Africa and getting it right is more than academic. Events on that continent come at us like intermittent dispatches from a distant front. . . . No causes, no connections, no patterns."

George Parker, *The Nation,* January 25, 1986

For centuries Africa has been a "Dark Continent" for many Europeans and Americans. Given the vastness of the continent (three times the size of Europe) and its proximity to Europe, it is remarkable that so little was known about this land for so long.

Although Africa first came to the attention of Christian Europe during the Middle Ages, much of what medieval Europe knew was based on legend. For more than three hundred years, Europeans thought a fabulously wealthy Christian named Prester John had established a kingdom somewhere in Asia or Africa. People believed he had led a crusade to the Holy Lands and then had gone farther into uncharted territory to establish his kingdom. As Europeans explored and learned more about Asia, they realized his kingdom could not be there and decided it must be in Africa. After hearing a Christian empire existed in what is now Ethiopia, Portugal's king sent a letter there, addressed to Prester John. Eventually, as European contact with Africa increased, Europeans realized Prester John was a myth, and the legend died.

During the Age of Discovery, Europe's interest in Africa was spurred by a more practical factor: Europeans needed a source of cheap labor to build and maintain their colonies in the New World. In 1518, Europeans began capturing, buying, and shipping Africans as slaves to the colonies. But although Europeans came to depend on Africa for labor, they still learned little about the continent; they simply picked slaves up at seaports and seldom ventured inland to explore. Slave traders took advantage of the weak empires and political factions in Africa by using Arab traders and other Africans to capture people in inland areas and bring them to the coast.

It was not until the Victorian era, after the slave trade had ended, that Westerners began exploring the interior of the continent. Many of the explorers were searching for the source of the Nile River. Before these explorations, the interior of Africa was unmapped, and Europeans had known virtually nothing of the people living there nor of the huge lakes, rivers, and spectacular waterfalls of central Africa. These explorations renewed interest in Africa and paved the way for the missionaries and colonial administrators who came shortly after to bring European ideas and beliefs.

Current Western knowledge of Africa is still limited in scope. Many people hear about tragic events—devastating famines, violent coups and riots, and oppressive dictators—without understanding the context in which these things happen. For example, the graphic media attention given to the horrors of the famines in the 1980s led to a massive relief effort for Africa. Many Westerners felt compassion for the suffering in Africa, and willingly donated money, time, and supplies to help end the famine. When famine struck again several years later, however, many in the West were surprised. They had thought the famine of the mid-1980s was unique; they were not aware that famine in that region is a recurring problem that requires long-term solutions. This lack of comprehension concerning the causes of famine is only one example of Western ignorance of Africa.

No single book can make up for the oversights of the past and give its readers a complete understanding of Africa. *Africa: Opposing Viewpoints* is meant to help readers clarify some of the images they currently have by giving them more background to events in Africa. The questions debated in *Africa* include: What Are the Causes of Africa's Problems? How Can Famine in Africa Be Reduced? Can Western Aid Help Africa? What Form of Government Would Benefit Africa? How Will the Dismantling of Apartheid Affect South Africa's Future? The book presents a wide range of viewpoints, enabling readers to gain a broader understanding of the diverse continent of Africa.

What Are the Causes of Africa's Problems?

Chapter Preface

In 1957, Britain freed Ghana from colonial rule, making Ghana the first sub-Saharan nation to be granted independence. Both Africans and Western experts predicted a promising future for Ghana and other African nations, and believed that once Africa was freed of the yoke of colonial rule, the continent would prosper.

But thirty years later, this promising future had failed to materialize. Africa remained a continent mired in poverty. This lack of progress was especially evident in the 1980s: between 1979 and 1985, the number of Africans below the poverty line grew by nearly two-thirds. A United Nations report described Africa as a deteriorating region characterized by political instability, repeated droughts, and a threatened environment. The report stated that "the unending crisis . . . threatened the long-term development prospects of the region as a whole."

What is the cause of this continuing lack of prosperity? Many scholars believe the lasting effects of colonialism are to blame. They cite the fact that the colonial powers established national borders without heeding Africa's traditional ethnic rivalries. Hence, many African nations are comprised of opposing ethnic groups that are either unable or unwilling to unite to solve the region's problems.

In addition, the imposed borders left some nations rich in resources while others were stranded in desert regions with few resources. Indeed, geography plays a key role in sub-Saharan Africa's poverty. Nearly all of the nations of this region lie in the zone between the tropics of Cancer and Capricorn, an area susceptible to unpredictable weather and frequent crop failures.

But other analysts contend that not all of Africa's problems can be attributed to the legacy of colonialism or the quirks of geography. They believe much of the blame lies with African leaders. Ghana, whose history is similar to that of many sub-Saharan nations, is an example of a nation ruined by poor leadership. Ghana was rich in resources in 1957. It boasted gold mines and a foreign exchange surplus of $400 million. Just a decade later, however, Ghana's people worked for the lowest minimum wage in Africa, and the nation had a foreign debt of $858 million. This decline can largely be attributed to Kwame Nkrumah, Ghana's leader after colonialism, who established a corrupt government that quickly impoverished its people.

While leadership, geography, and the legacy of colonialism all have had an impact on African nations such as Ghana, other factors have also contributed to Africa's problems. The authors in the following chapter debate why many African nations continue to struggle with hunger, poverty, and political unrest.

"The independent African states got their own national flags but they inherited economic dependence."

Colonialism Made Africa Poor and Dependent

Mai Palmberg

Most African nations gained political independence during the 1960s, yet their economies are still shaped in part by their past experience as European colonies. Under colonialism, the country which owned the colony exported its raw materials to Europe where the raw materials were made into manufactured goods. Some of the goods were then shipped back to the colonies for sale. The same pattern occurs in much of Africa now: African countries have weak domestic economies which are kept afloat by exports. In the following viewpoint, Mai Palmberg terms this relationship neocolonialism and explains how it continues the exploitation that colonialism began. Palmberg edited *The Struggle for Africa* and works with the Africa Groups of Sweden who support black liberation movements in southern Africa.

As you read, consider the following questions:

1. How are African countries kept dependent on the West, according to the author?
2. How does the author define "growth without development"?
3. What point does the author make by using the example of the mahogany tree sold in Europe?

From *The Struggle for Africa* by Mai Palmberg, published by Zed Books, 1983, London. Reprinted with permission.

Neocolonialism is not a sign of strength in imperialism, but a sign of its weakness. (LeDuan, Vietnam)

The then Prime Minister of England, Harold Macmillan, in a speech in Cape Town on 3 February 1960, said that 'a wind of change' was blowing over the continent and that the main question now was whether the peoples of Asia and Africa would turn to the East or to the West, to Communism or to 'the free world'. In December of the same year Charles de Gaulle, then President of France, spoke to army officers in Blida in Algeria. He asked them to try to understand what was happening in the world, to understand that the old methods of direct control, based on arms and the colonial state apparatus, had become impossible to practice, the new ways had to be found so that 'the activities of France in Algeria can continue'. In March 1961 the US President John F. Kennedy launched what was called 'The Alliance for Progress' for the Latin American states. To prevent the revolutionary example of Cuba becoming contagious the Latin American states were to embark on some social and economic reforms with the aid of US dollars.

These three speeches show how the leaders of the Western world understood that new forms for imperialism had to be created when direct colonial control was no longer politically possible. The question was how to continue the exploitation of the Third World as cheaply and as easily as possible, and also to prevent the 'loss' of more countries than China, that is, a change in a Socialist direction. Independent Africa became a field of experiments for neo-colonial policies. . . .

Economic Dependence

The independent African states got their own national flags but they inherited economic dependence. This dependence could be used by the imperialist forces to further their aims. The dependence rests on two pillars, a continued colonial division of labour and foreign control of key sectors of the economy. This pattern can be summarized in three points:

1. As in colonial times a large part of production is sold for export.

2. Most of the goods exported are a few unprocessed raw materials. Six raw materials constituted more than half of the exports from Africa in 1968: oil, copper, cotton, coffee, cocoa and ground nuts. In 1969, less than 10% of all exports from Africa were manufactured goods.

3. More than four-fifths of Africa's exports is directed to the imperialist states. Three-fourths of Africa's imports originate there. Western Europe still dominates, but the United States, and to a lesser extent Japan, are also important trade partners. There is almost no trade between the African states themselves.

18

The big private companies which have dominated the exploitation of African raw materials are powerful actors on the African scene. For many of them their annual turnover is far larger than the total state budget of the countries where they invest their capital.

They carefully guard the secrets of their trade. The technical development in modern industry is almost entirely controlled by big multinational companies, which own industries in a large number of countries, and often have near-monopoly in their fields of production.

Reprinted by permission of Zed Books, London.

Only a small part of the foreign investments from the imperialist states goes to independent Africa. But in the countries where they operate the companies often hold a dominant position in the economy, because domestic production is weak.

Today the big companies' interest in Africa is not only geared towards exploitation of raw materials. Some agricultural products are processed for export.

Assembly plants can be found in most African countries, because it can be profitable for the foreign companies to have this work done in countries where there is cheap labour. Green and Seidman, two economists, have, for example, written about how electric-light bulbs are 'produced locally' in Asia and Africa. As a matter of fact the only local component—besides labour—is the vacuum in the bulb. . . .

Investments and trade are not the only form of dependence. 'Development aid' has become an important instrument for the neo-colonial policies. The words 'development aid' give an impression that it is an unselfish sacrifice from the rich to the poor. But only if we look at it as part of the total economic relations between underdeveloped countries and industrialized capitalist states can we judge the real function of development aid. . . .

An overwhelming part of all development aid goes to *infrastructure*, that is to the preconditions for modern production. Infrastructure means, on the one hand, economic investments, such as communications, telecommunications, airports, harbours, energy supply, irrigation projects etc., and, on the other hand, social investments such as schools, hospitals and administrative buildings. Of course, such projects need not be worthless for the receiving country. But, in the first place, they are designed to reinforce export dependence instead of furthering domestic use of the raw materials. In the second place, these investments are, to quote [L.D. Black], a North American spokesman for development aid, 'an indispensable precondition for the capacity to attract foreign private investment'.

Development aid also means insight into the control of the receiving country's economy. Very often the most important economic decisions in the independent states are taken by foreign experts. Both the knowledge they gain and the decisions they take further the search by the 'donor countries' for markets for goods, services, and technology.

Unequal Exchange

To all this must be added the losses incurred by the Third World countries from deteriorated terms of trade. This means that most raw materials which as we have seen make up the major share of the exports from underdevelopd countries, have decreasing prices on the world market, whereas the prices of manufactured goods which the underdeveloped countries import steadily rise. . . .

This 'unequal exchange' means that for the Third World the loss is often more than what is 'given' in development aid. Another difficulty for the economy of Third World countries is the fact that they do not control the sale of their raw materials, but this is subject to speculation on the raw materials exchanges in New York and London. . . .

During the past few years prices have risen for almost all kinds of goods. But the basic pattern remains—the developing countries on the whole pay more for their imports than they receive for their exports. For example, between 1970 and 1975 the prices of foodstuffs that the developed countries exported to the developing countries rose by 138%. But the price of foodstuffs exported by the developing countries themselves rose by only 98% during the same period.

An Exploitative Relationship

The main aim of colonialism was to facilitate the expansion of European capitalism. Africa became a cheap source of raw materials and a market for excess industrial output. Apologists for colonialism often point to the development and education that came with European influence. But these advances were the result of the exploitative relationship between Europe and its African colonies.

Eugene Nyati, *World Press Review*, November 1990.

There is one important exception to this pattern of deteriorated terms of trade. Through their producer organization, OPEC, the big oil-producing countries have, jointly, been able to force large increases in the price they get for crude oil (more than 500% during 1970-75). The big Western oil companies started to speak of an 'oil crisis' and were able to increase the consumer prices above the crude oil prices, and thus avoid a loss of profits. . . .

Growth Without Development

The core of the problem for those advocating a capitalist path for Africa lies in the very definition of 'development' they use.

Economic development has been the explicit primary goal for all independent African regimes. How it would be achieved was described by an American economist, Walt Rostow, in a book called *'Stages of Economic Growth: A Non-Communist Manifesto'*. The African societies had by becoming independent come through the stage of 'traditional societies'. Now preconditions were to be created for 'take-off'. After 'take-off' there would be 'development towards maturity' and, lastly, entrance into 'the age of mass consumption'. *Life* magazine illustrated this process by a picture where the developing countries were depicted as aeroplanes taking off into higher altitudes.

Now more than 20 years afterwards, there has not yet been one example of 'take-off' on the Rostowian model, despite the fact that a large part of the development aid is based on this idea. It was not a scientific model but an ideology for the defence of the expansion of capitalism in the underdeveloped countries. It ignored the fact that African underdevelopment was not a lack of development, but distorted development, created by colonialism. Underdevelopment would last as long as this system of dependence would last. In the 19th century, Japan had started from a traditional economy but had become a highly industrialized country with mass consumption. But unlike Africa, Japan had been allowed to control its own economy.

No Support for Western Development Theories

The theory was still that all that was needed for Africa was to create its 'entrepreneurial class', which would become the core of an indigenous bourgeoisie, and then industrialization would automatically follow—with some aid from the generous Western countries. But not even the most pro-Western African states could provide any support for this development theory. Liberia was a country which had had an African elite imitating Western norms long before other African states became independent, Liberia did have statistics showing a rapidly growing production, but even conservative US advisors had to state in a report on Liberia that there was 'growth without development'. They wrote that there had been:

> an enormous growth in raw materials, produced by foreign companies for export, but unaccompanied by either structural changes, which could lead to the growth of other sectors, or by institutional changes which could spread the increase in income among all layers of the population.

Another often-quoted example of the success of the capitalist road to development is the Ivory Coast in West Africa. Here, too, statistics show a considerable growth, based on the export of coffee, timber, palm oil, and cocoa. There is a growing African middle class, for example, among the plantation owners. But they are completely dependent on the European bourgeoisie which take the largest profits from the riches of the Ivory Coast. No industrialization has been started, but what has happened is that the ruthless exploitation has left a few more crumbs in the country than in some other neo-colonial, dependent states. Timber export, for instance, is controlled by French interests, which lease forests at a low cost and take out enormous profits. The big hardwood trees are cut down with no thought for regrowth. Profits must be brought out fast in those African countries which still let foreign capital ravage freely. In a Swedish TV film in February 1977 one could see how one mahogany tree was sold in Europe with about £1,700 profit. The French company that sold it had then left in the Ivory Coast £11 in tax and £1.5 in wages to timbermen, loaders, truck drivers and sorters in the harbour.

The basis for the enormous profits in the Ivory Coast is free access to cheap labour. One million Africans come to the Ivory Coast from surrounding countries to find work. The Ivory Coast shows what happens when the capitalist model for growth without development is accepted—not only increased inequalities between a few countries with rapid growth and the great majority in poverty.

More and more African leaders and intellectuals realized soon after independence that the inherited colonial economy could not be the basis for an independent economy. Some saw the solution in close economic cooperation between the African states. When the Organization for African Unity (OAU) was founded in 1963, utopian statutes were adopted about a common economy, army, and government for a 'United States of Africa'. The OAU never became an instrument for an economic union. But it has had a certain role as a platform for political declarations against apartheid and colonialism.

Popular Control of the Economy

Closer economic co-operation without common political objectives has proved impossible. In such countries as the Ivory Coast the privileged elite has nothing to gain from economic co-operation to reduce neo-colonial dependence. The conservative governments have also served as mediators in the imperialist attempts to have 'responsible' regimes in power in southern Africa. . . .

As long as the majority of the Third World countries believe that changes can be made in co-operation with those industrialized countries which have created and maintained the Third World's underdevelopment, the neo-colonial policies have not completely lost the day. . . .

Political organization is decisive for development in the progressive states. Only through a popular basis and control of political life can the people decide what will be produced and for whom.

"Colonial rule has not been the cause of Third World poverty."

Colonialism Is Not Responsible for Africa's Problems

P.T. Bauer

Part of the controversy concerning colonialism is the term's meaning. In the following viewpoint, P.T. Bauer, a professor at the London School of Economics and Political Science, defines colonialism as simply one country controlling another country's political system. Based on that definition, he argues that colonialism in Africa ended in the 1960s and cannot be held responsible for Africa's current problems. Furthermore, Bauer believes that the wealthiest Third World countries are those which had contact with the West, because the West set up productive economies which are still generating wealth. Bauer wrote the book *Equality, the Third World, and Economic Delusion*.

As you read, consider the following questions:

1. Which Third World societies does Bauer argue are the poorest and why are they poor?
2. How does the author define "colonialism," and why does he disagree with the terms "economic colonialism" and "neo-colonialism"?
3. Why do people in the Third World buy imports, according to Bauer, and why do they produce goods for export?

From *Equality, the Third World and Economic Delusion* by P.T. Bauer. Reprinted with permission of the publisher, George Weidenfeld & Nicolson Limited, London.

> *Come, fix upon me that accusing eye,*
> *I thirst for accusation.*
>
> W.B. Yeats

Yeats' words might indeed have been written to describe the wide, even welcome, acceptance by the West of the accusation that it is responsible for the poverty of the Third World (i.e. most of Asia, Africa and Latin America). Western responsibility for Third World backwardness is a persistent theme of the United Nations and its many affiliates. It has been welcomed by spokesmen of the Third World and of the Communist bloc, notably so at international gatherings where it is often endorsed by official representatives of the West, especially the United States. It is also widely canvassed in the universities, the churches and the media the world over.

Western Guilt

Acceptance of emphatic routine allegations that the West is responsible for Third World poverty reflects and reinforces Western feelings of guilt. It has enfeebled Western diplomacy, both towards the ideologically much more aggressive Soviet bloc and also towards the Third World. And the West has come to abase itself before countries with negligible resources and no real power. Yet the allegations can be shown to be without foundation. They are readily accepted because the Western public has little firsthand knowledge of the Third World, and because of widespread feelings of guilt. The West has never had it so good, and has never felt so bad about it. . . .

About ten years ago a student group at Cambridge published a pamphlet on the subject of the moral obligations of the West to the Third World. The following was its key passage:

> We took the rubber from Malaya, the tea from India, raw materials from all over the world and gave almost nothing in return.

This is as nearly the opposite of the truth as one can find. The British took the rubber *to* Malaya and the tea *to* India. There were no rubber trees in Malaya or anywhere in Asia (as suggested by their botanical name, *Hevea braziliensis*) until about 100 years ago, when the British took the first rubber seeds there out of the Amazon jungle. From these sprang the huge rubber industry—now very largely Asian-owned. Tea-plants were brought to India by the British somewhat earlier; their origin is shown in the botanical name *Camilla sinensis*, as well as in the phrase 'all the tea in China'. . . .

Far from the West having caused the poverty in the Third World, contact with the West has been the principal agent of material progress there. The materially more advanced societies and regions of the Third World are those with which the West established the most numerous, diversified and extensive contacts: the cash-crop-producing areas and entrepot ports of South-East Asia, West Africa and Latin America; the mineral-producing areas of Africa and the Middle East; and cities and ports throughout Asia, Africa, the Caribbean and Latin America. The level of material achievement usually diminishes as one moves away from the foci of Western impact. The poorest and most backward people have few or no external contacts; witness the aborigines, pygmies and desert peoples. . . .

Explaining Backwardness

Considering that colonial rule ended well over a century and a half ago in Latin America, 36 years ago in south-east Asia, and more than two decades ago in Africa, and considering also the vast transfer of funds from the industrialised into the poor countries in recent years, "colonial exploitation" clearly is not a sufficient explanation for today's economic backwardness.

G.M.E. Leistner, *Africa Insight*, vol. 13, no. 3, 1983.

Large parts of West Africa were . . . transformed . . . as a result of Western contacts. Before 1890 there was no cocoa production in the Gold Coast or Nigeria, only very small production of cotton and groundnuts and small exports of palm oil and palm kernels. By the 1950s all these had become staples of world trade. They were produced by Africans on African-owned properties. But this was originally made possible by Westerners who established public security and introduced modern methods of transport and communications. Over this period imports both of capital goods and of mass consumer goods for African use also rose from insignificant amounts to huge volumes. The changes were reflected in government revenues, literacy rates, school attendance, public health, life expectation, infant mortality and many other indicators.

Massive Transformation

Statistics by themselves can hardly convey the far-reaching transformation which took place over this period in West Africa and elsewhere in the Third World. In West Africa, for instance, slave trading and slavery were still widespread at the end of the nineteenth century. They had practically disappeared by the end of the First World War. Many of the worst endemic and epidemic diseases for which West Africa was notorious throughout the nineteenth century had disappeared by the Second World War. External contacts also brought about similar far-reaching changes over much of Latin America.

The role of Western contacts in the material progress of Black Africa deserves further notice. As late as the second half of the nineteenth century Black Africa was without even the simplest, most basic ingredients of modern social and economic life. These were brought there by Westerners over the last hundred years or so. This is true of such fundamentals as public security and law and order; wheeled traffic (Black Africa never invented the wheel) and mechanical transport (before the arrival of Westerners, transport in Black Africa was almost entirely by human muscle); roads, railways and man-made ports; the application of science and technology to economic activity; towns with substantial buildings, clean water and sewerage facilities; public health care, hospitals and the control of endemic and epidemic diseases; formal education. These advances resulted from peaceful commercial contacts. These contacts also made easier the elimination of the Atlantic slave trade, the virtual elimination of the slave trade from Africa to the Middle East, and even the elimination of slavery within Africa. . . .

Wherever local conditions have permitted it, commercial contacts with the West, and generally established by the West, have eliminated the worst diseases, reduced or even eliminated famine, extended life expectation and improved living standards.

Marxist Misconception

Many of the assertions of Western responsibility for Third World poverty imply that the prosperity of relatively well-to-do persons, groups and societies is achieved at the expense of the less well-off. These assertions express the misconception that the incomes of the well-to-do have been taken from others. In fact, with a few clearly definable exceptions, which do not apply to the relations between the West and the Third World, incomes whether of the rich or of the poor are earned by their recipients. . . .

In recent decades certain readily recognizable influences have reinforced the notion that the prosperity of some group means that others have been exploited. The impact of Marxist-Leninist ideology has been one such influence. In this ideology any return on private capital implies exploitation, and service industries are regarded as unproductive. Thus, earnings of foreign capital and the incomes of foreigners or ethnic minorities in the service industries are evidence of forms of exploitation. Further, neo-Marxist literature has extended the concept of the proletariat to the peoples of the Third World, most of whom are in fact small-scale cultivators. In this literature, moreover, a proletariat is exploited by definition, and is poor because it is exploited.

The idea of Western responsibility for Third World poverty has also been promoted by the belief in a universal basic equality of people's economic capacities and motivations. This belief is closely related to egalitarian ideology and policy which have experienced a great upsurge in recent decades. If people's attributes and motivations are the same everywhere and yet some societies are richer than others, this suggests that the former have exploited the rest. Because the public in the West has little direct contact with the Third World, it is often easy to put across the idea that Western conduct and policies have caused poverty in the Third World.

The recent practice of referring to the poor as deprived or underprivileged again helps the notion that the rich owe their prosperity to the exploitation of the poor. Yet how could the incomes of, for example, people in Switzerland or North America have been taken from, say, the aborigines of Papua, or the desert peoples or pygmies of Africa? Indeed, who deprived these groups and of what?

Cause of Backwardness

Ever more political and intellectual leaders of Black Africa are acknowledging that they have deluded themselves with regard to the causes of their countries' backwardness as well as the means to achieve higher levels of material well-being.

For decades they had willingly and uncritically accepted the notion that colonialism more than anything else was responsible for the "balkanisation" of Africa . . . and generally for Africa's low rating in world politics and economic relations.

Erich Leistner, *Africa Insight*, vol. 14, no. 3, 1984.

The principal assumption behind the idea of Western responsibility for Third World poverty is that the prosperity of individuals and societies generally reflects the exploitation of others. Some variants or derivatives of this theme are often heard, usually geared to particular audiences. One of these variants is that colonialism has caused the poverty of Asia and Africa. It has particular appeal in the United States where hostility to colonialism is traditional. For a different and indeed opposite reason, it is at times effective in stirring up guilt in Britain, the foremost ex-colonial power.

Colonialism Is Not at Fault

Whatever one thinks of colonialism, it cannot be held responsible for Third World poverty. Some of the most backward countries never were colonies, as for instance Afghanistan, Tibet, Nepal, Liberia. Ethiopia is perhaps an even more telling example (it was an Italian colony for only six years in its long history). Again, many of the Asian and African colonies progressed very rapidly during colonial rule, much more so than the independent countries in the same area. At present one of the few remaining European colonies is Hong Kong—whose prosperity and progress should be familiar. It is plain that colonial rule has not been the cause of Third World poverty.

Nor is the prosperity of the West the result of colonialism. The most advanced and the richest countries never had colonies, including Switzerland and the Scandinavian countries; and some were colonies of others and were already very prosperous as colonies, as for instance North America and Australasia. The prosperity of the West was generated by its own peoples and was not taken from others. The European countries were already materially far ahead of the areas where they established colonies.

In recent years the charges that colonialism causes Third World poverty have been expanded to cover 'colonialism in all its forms'. The terms 'economic colonialism' and 'neo-colonialism' have sprung up to cover external private investment, the activities of multinational companies, and indeed almost any form of economic relationship between relatively rich and relatively poor regions or groups. . . . This terminology . . . regularly confuses poverty with colonial status, a concept which has normally meant lack of political sovereignty. . . .

According to Marxist-Leninist ideology, colonial status and foreign investment are by definition evidence of exploitation. In fact, foreign private investment and the activities of the multinational companies have expanded opportunities and raised incomes and government revenues in the Third World. Reference to economic colonialism and neo-colonialism both debase the language and distort the truth.

International Trade

The West is now widely accused of manipulating international trade to the detriment of the Third World. This accusation is a major theme of the demands for a New International Economic Order. In particular, the West is supposed to inflict unfavourable and persistently deteriorating terms of trade on the Third World. Among other untoward results, this influence is said to have resulted in a decline in the share of the Third World in total world trade, and also in a large volume of Third World foreign debt. These allegations are again irrelevant, unfounded and often the opposite of the truth.

The poorest areas of the Third World have no external trade. Their condition shows that the causes of backwardness are domestic and that external commercial contacts are beneficial. Even if the terms of trade were unfavourable on some criterion or other, this would only mean that people do not benefit from foreign trade as much as they would if the terms of trade were more favourable. People benefit from the widening of opportunities which external trade represents. . . .

It is often implied that the West can somehow manipulate international prices to the disadvantage of the Third World. But the West cannot prescribe international prices. These prices are the outcome of innumerable individual decisions of market participants. They are not prescribed by a single individual decision-maker, or even by a handful of people acting in collusion. . . .

Third World Debt

The external debts of the Third World are not the result or reflection of exploitation. They represent resources supplied. Indeed, much of the current indebtedness of Third World governments consists of soft loans under various aid agreements, frequently supplemented by outright grants. With the worldwide rise in prices, including those of Third World exports, the cost even of these soft loans has diminished greatly. Difficulties of servicing these debts do not reflect external exploitation or unfavourable terms of trade. They are the result of wasteful use of the capital supplied, or inappropriate monetary and fiscal policies. Again, the persistent balance of payments deficits of some Third World countries do not mean that they are being exploited or impoverished by the West. Such deficits are inevitable if the government of a country, whether rich or poor, advancing or stagnating, lives beyond its resources and pursues inflationary policies while attempting to maintain overvalued exchange rates. Persistent balance of payments difficulties mean that external resources are being lent to the country over these periods.

Decolonization

The rapid decolonization of Africa has been, and still is, a traumatic experience for the continent's own black population as well as the millions of white settlers, immigrants, and colonials who were uprooted, displaced, and forced to leave the parts of Africa they had built up and believed to be their own.

Karl Borgin and Kathleen Corbett, *The Destruction of a Continent*, 1982.

The decline of particular economic activities, as for instance the Indian textile industry in the eighteenth century as a result of competition from cheap imports, is habitually instanced as an example of the damage caused to the Third World by trade with the West. This argument identifies the decline of one activity with the decline of the economy as a whole, and the economic interests of one sectional group with those of all members of a society. Cheap imports extend the choice and economic opportunities of people in poor countries. These imports are usually accompanied by the expansion of other activities. If this were not so, the population would be unable to pay for the imports. . . .

The allegations that external trade, and especially imports from the West, are damaging to the populations of the Third World reveal a barely disguised condescension towards the ordinary people there, and even contempt for them. The people, of course, want the imports. If they did not the imported goods could not be sold. Similarly, the people are prepared to produce for export to pay for these imported goods. To say that these processes are damaging is to argue that people's preferences are of no account in organizing their own lives. . . .

The exponents of Western guilt further patronize the Third World by suggesting that its economic fortunes past, present and prospective, are determined by the West; that past exploitation by the West explains Third World backwardness; that manipulation of international trade by the West and other forms of Western misconduct account for persistent poverty; that the economic future of the Third World depends largely on Western donations. According to this set of ideas, whatever happens to the Third World is largely our doing. Such ideas make us feel superior even while we beat our breasts.

"Overpopulation is the root cause of underdevelopment."

Overpopulation Is a Cause of Africa's Poverty

Daphne Topouzis

Africa has the fastest-growing population in the world. The continent's overpopulation has depleted the land, the environment, and the water supply, and has devastated the economy, Daphne Topouzis asserts in the following viewpoint. She believes that unless steps are taken to slow Africa's population growth, the region's problems will only worsen. Topouzis is a contributing editor to *Africa Report*, a bimonthly magazine.

As you read, consider the following questions:

1. How does overpopulation affect Africa's labor force, according to the author?
2. According to Topouzis, why don't many African women use contraception?
3. What does the author believe is the only way to "defuse the population bomb"?

Daphne Topouzis, "The Problem with People," *Africa Report*, March/April 1991. Copyright © 1991 by the African-American Institute. Reprinted by permission of *Africa Report*.

A demographic and environmental time bomb is looming over Africa, imperiling an already fragile economic future threatened by crushing debts, depressed commodity prices, shrinking investment, and austere structural adjustment programs. Positive signs of a growing African consensus on family planning are largely being neutralized by deteriorating health and education services, and many experts believe that changing attitudes, however encouraging, might prove to be too little, too late.

The clock is ticking away and time is not on Africa's side. The continent is growing more rapidly than any other part of the world, undergoing "the fastest growth rate in human history for an entire region," according to Dr. Nafis Sadik, executive director of the UN Fund for Population Activities (UNFPA). Growth was 3.2 percent per year for the period 1980-1985, compared to a world rate of 1.7 percent and 2.3 percent for Latin America, the world's next highest.

The continent's population has almost tripled from 224 million in 1950 to 648 million in 1991, and may reach 2.6 billion by the year 2030—a five-fold increase—as a result of high fertility and declining mortality rates. Nigeria is expected to triple its population to 300 million by 2025, while Ethiopia and Zaire (among the continent's poorest countries) will reach 100 million each. In broader terms, the continent will be doubling its population every 22 years, if present growth patterns continue.

Until recently, unchecked population growth was characteristic of underdeveloped regions. In the 1950s, Africa and Latin America had roughly the same pattern of demographic growth, with an average of 6.5 children per woman. Since then, however, Latin American women have succeeded in curbing their fertility rates to 3.6 children, according to *Le Monde Diplomatique*. But in Africa, fertility rates remain high: 8 children per woman in Rwanda, 7 in Senegal, Niger, and Kenya, and 6 in Cameroon and Togo.

In most of Africa, contraception is practiced by a mere 5 percent of the population and in some countries such as Uganda, only 1 percent of women use contraception. Algeria, Mauritius, Morocco, Egypt, Kenya, and Botswana boast a birth control rate of 15-40 percent, while Tunisia, Zimbabwe, and South Africa have a birth control rate of over 40 percent. Even these countries, which remain the exception, are still far from the 75 percent mark necessary to achieve population stability.

Population Pressures

Rapid population growth will place tremendous pressure on the land, the environment, water supply, and employment. More ominously perhaps, it will exacerbate ailing economies and shake fragile political systems.

One of the most critical problems will be the absorption of millions of new entrants into the labor force. Africa's labor force will be no less than 650 million by 2025, more than the total number of workers in the developed world. Nearly half of Africa's population are children under 15 years of age. In 20 years or so, youngsters will become part of an explosive crisis which is already under way, with most African countries facing roughly 50 percent unemployment and underemployment rates compounded by sharp declines in the standard of living.

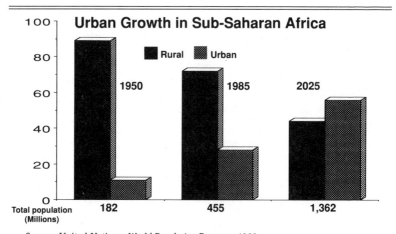

Urban Growth in Sub-Saharan Africa

Source: United Nations, *World Population Prospects 1988.*

Another major problem will be the extraordinary growth of Africa's urban centers: Between 1990 and 2025, the continent's urban population will grow by more than 700 million, in other words, larger than the continent's present population, according to the estimates of the Washington-based Population Reference Bureau. Housing, sanitation, and water supply problems will be daunting. Perhaps most devastating of all, however, will be the irreversible damage to the environment—including massive deforestation, desertification, and depletion of resources—and by extension to human development as a whole.

Decisive action is imperative to reverse current trends, argues UNFPA, pointing out that slower population growth, "will be a crucial part of any strategy of sustainable development."

For or Against Family Planning?

Industrialized countries have long held the view that overpopulation is the root cause of underdevelopment and have thus concentrated on family planning as the main antidote. From the opposite perspective, developing countries, led by Algeria and China, argued in the mid-1970s that the real problem lies with underdevelopment, not population growth. By solving development problems, demographic growth would automatically fall, ran the argument. Thus, the famous slogan *"La meilleure pillule, c'est le développement"* (the most effective [contraceptive] pill is development).

The latter camp accused the Western world of imperialist designs to "weaken" the developing world and, as a result, family planning became a political issue. Since then, the two camps have achieved a rapprochement and the controversy has been somewhat defused. Now the argument for family planning is being raised again by the donor community more strongly than ever before.

"I believe that population growth is *the* development and environmental problem facing the world in the 1990s," said Lynda Chalker, Britain's Overseas Development Minister—a view that is shared by most developed countries. Controversy over whether family planning aid constitutes eco-imperialism continues, but more so from within the donor community. In the U.S., family planning has become increasingly sensitive and controversial for different reasons, and as a result of pressure from the Moral Majority, the government has suspended its grants to UNFPA and the International Planned Parenthood Federation.

Optimistic Signs

Despite the bleak outlook for Africa's future, a handful of initiatives are beginning to bear fruit and recent data indicate that fertility rates are declining in Kenya, Botswana, Zimbabwe, and Senegal.

A World Bank report entitled "Kenya at the Demographic Turning Point?" outlines the reasons behind Kenya's declining fertility rates from a record 4 percent in the early 1980s—the highest fertility rate in the world. Those include the rising cost of social services, particularly education, which has forced the government to introduce cost-sharing programs and has markedly increased the cost of raising children; the shift in government attitudes toward supporting family planning; changes in the provision of family planning services; the drought of 1984; the specter of AIDS; and the significant decline in infant mortality rates from 184/1000 in 1948 to 60-80/1000 in the late 1980s. From 7.6 average lifetime children per woman, the rate has dropped to 6.7.

Nigeria, which currently has an estimated 117 million people, has an annual population growth rate of 3.4 percent. By the year 2050, it will be the world's third most populous country with an estimated 564 million. In 1991, despite opposition from religious leaders. The government began a nationwide campaign to reach 80 percent of Nigerian women and urge them to have only four rather than six children which is presently the norm, according to *International Family Planning Perspectives.*

Egypt's family planning policies have also borne fruit and the total fertility rate has dropped from 5.2 to 4.7, "enough to help drop down the total fertility rate for the North Africa region as a whole, from 5.6 in 1989 to 5.2," reported *Population Today.*

Involving Men in Family Planning

Perhaps the most encouraging sign of the future effectiveness of family planning programs is the realization on the part of many donors that the key lies with making family planning a man's, just as much as a woman's, issue. "Unless men can be encouraged to change their attitudes—and behavior—population is likely to continue growing too fast for the earth's resources to sustain," argues the UNFPA report, pointing out that it is often males who are the deciding factor in the use of contraception.

Even though as many as 77 percent of married African women do not want more children, they do not use contraception. The obstacle is not only financial. Cultural, religious, and psychological barriers are also in the way. A Kenyan survey showed that even though men were more informed about family planning than women, only a third discussed contraception with their wives, who feared they would be beaten if they were caught using birth control methods. Women are also wary of discussing contraception from fear of being perceived as prostitutes.

As far as involving men in family planning, the *Christian Science Monitor* cited the National Family Planning Council in Zimbabwe, Africa's family planning success story, which is one of the few programs which targets men. The Council boasts that contraceptive use is as high as 38 percent of sexually active women and while there are not yet indications of its success, family planning officials claim that male attitudes toward contraceptives are changing rapidly.

Education Is Vital

As African governments request Western aid to introduce family planning programs, the question now is how to channel this aid effectively. While most of the emphasis has focused on the need for family planning programs, there is a growing consensus that given the correlation between high birth rates and poverty, the only way to defuse the population bomb is to invest in raising the standard of living of poor countries—a proposal which would necessitate massive investments and which is unlikely to be adopted by Western donors.

UNFPA argues that health and education should become a priority if Africa's population crisis is to be reversed, and the *State of the World's Population 1990* argues that development policies and aid should aim at increasing developing countries' spending on health and education to 5 percent of GNP [gross national product].

In addition, experts believe that African women, who are heavily involved in food production and processing, as well as in fuel gathering, have few alternatives at present but to have more children in hopes of sharing their work load. Finding ways of alleviating women's work, enhancing their access to education and health, and providing them with options will almost certainly curtail population growth.

Despite a handful of success stories, most of Africa continues to undergo a population explosion it cannot afford. The World Bank has argued that "given the insufficiency of family planning programs in the whole of sub-Saharan Africa, it is very unlikely that the reduction in fertility assumed by all current projections will materialize." African governments have taken the first step by adopting family planning policies, but neither the financial nor the logistic and technical backing is readily available. If anything, as education and health budgets are being cut year after year, accessibility to family planning is getting further and further away from rural Africans who make up the overwhelming majority of the population.

A Glimmer of Hope

What is hopeful is that African governments have recognized the need to check population growth, and the donor community is beginning to acknowledge the fact that family planning is not the only way to address the problem and that it should not be considered in isolation from the broader socio-economic context. Health, education, and the alleviation of women's workloads are all central to Africa's population crisis and in desperate need of continued support by development planners.

"[Africa's] problems consisted of internal divisions, élitism, tribalism, and other forms of disunity."

African Disunity Is a Cause of the Region's Problems

Basil Davidson

Basil Davidson is a journalist who has traveled extensively in Africa. He is the author of *Modern Africa* and the developer of the eight-part television series "Africa." In the following viewpoint, Davidson cites conflict among Africa's tribes, ethnic groups, and economic classes as a primary cause of the region's problems. When colonial powers established the boundaries of African nations, they forced together people of diverse cultures, languages, and histories. After independence, these Africans found it difficult to unite and successfully combat the continent's economic and political problems. Davidson believes Africans will conquer these problems only after they unite and regain a sense of community.

As you read, consider the following questions:

1. Why did Nigeria's first constitution fail, in the author's opinion?
2. What problems made it difficult for the Sudanese to unite, according to Davidson?
3. What role does the author believe elitism played in the downfall of some of Africa's governments?

From *Modern Africa: A Social and Political History*, 2d ed., by Basil Davidson. London: Longman, 1989. Copyright © 1989 Longman Group UK Ltd. Reprinted with permission.

All peoples, winning their freedom, have had to go on wrestling with the handicaps of their own history: with the legacy left to them by the past. The gains of independence, and the powers these have given, have had to be measured against the weight and drag of those handicaps. So the questions we need to ask, when looking at Africa's years since independence, have to refer to the struggle between old handicaps and new powers. . . .

The Weaknesses of Nationalism

The great struggle of the nationalists, before independence, was to overcome 'colonial tribalism' and to unite peoples into nations. . . .

Nationalism proved strong enough to win the political unity required to end colonial rule. But nationalism in Africa, like nationalism everywhere else, has shown itself a contradictory force. It may start well, but still end badly.

In Europe, the forces of nationalism during the nineteenth and early twentieth centuries were strong enough to liberate the Italians and then the southern Slav peoples from various European empires. Nationalism did this in the name of equality and freedom. But the liberated Italy of 1861 soon began to use its armies to invade and dispossess Africans; and its nationalism then degraded into the brutalities of Mussolini's fascist dictatorship during 1922-45. The Slav peoples liberated from the old European empires likewise turned to quarrels among themselves and the rise of their own dictatorships. In much the same way the nationalism which gave rise to a united Germany became a disaster to the Germans and everyone else when, in the 1930s, German nationalism became nazism and launched the holocausts of the Second World War of 1939-45.

In Africa, too, the liberating force of nationalism was not long in becoming a source of conflict. Here, then, was a general problem for Africans liberated from the European empires. . . .

Confronting Separatism

The means and methods of government left behind by the departing colonial rulers did not work. Why was that? Nigeria and Sudan offer examples from the British model.

Nigeria began independence under a constitution which divided this very large country, and its very numerous population, into three regions. Each was governed by a party representing the majority people in each region: Hausa-Fulani, Yoruba, Igbo; while smaller parties represented other peoples or ethnic groups. Each region also elected members of a federal parliament based in Lagos, the country's capital; and this had power over all-Nigerian matters such as foreign policy and national defence.

There were several reasons why this failed to work. One was that each leading party and its politicians, in each region, tended more and more to govern as though, in fact, its region was a separate country. Each regional government claimed more and more power to take decisions in matters such as commerce and industry; and there were politicians who played this game in order to promote their personal careers. For these and for other reasons, there came a sharp rivalry between the regions. The project of an all-Nigerian unity began to fade.

Another reason for dispute grew out of that rivalry. Who should control the all-Nigerian federal parliament in Lagos? This became a serious source of conflict. As things turned out, the Northern Region's chief party, the NPC, dominated the federal parliament because it had more voters, and therefore more members of parliament, than two other big parties in the east and west, the NCNC and AG. So these two parties had to be 'junior partners' in a federal government dominated by the NPC, or else go into opposition. As things turned out, this put the AG into isolation.

Boundaries Separated Families

Colonial boundaries were haphazardly drawn, often splitting up families and some tribes. Other tribes that were traditional enemies were lumped together within national boundaries. Little effort was made to promote understanding and tolerance between the new neighbors.

Eugene Nyati, *World Press Review*, November 1990.

Tensions came quickly to breaking-point. A first explosion occurred in the Western Region during 1962, only two years after independence. A split in the AG led to violent strife. The federal government under NPC control tried to end this conflict by further undermining the AG. It imposed a state of emergency in the Western Region, and ruled there through a federal administrator until the beginning of 1963. But this really solved nothing.

Regional rivalries continued to sharpen, especially after a national census of 1964. This produced returns which gave the Northern Region a voting force so big that northern control of the federal parliament seemed bound to become a fixture to the disadvantage of other regions. On top of that reason for southern dissatisfaction, the Western Region exploded again during a campaign for new general elections in November 1965. By this time there was great bitterness among large sectors of Nigerian public opinion. To make matters worse, some important politicians were widely accused of gross dishonesty and corruption. With continuing violence in the west, and more threatened elsewhere, the politicians now seemed helpless or discredited. In January 1966 the military stepped in and took over national government. For Nigeria, the first period of independence had ended.

What had happened? The answer is that the means and methods left behind by colonial government had encouraged regional rivalries, and personal ambitions, to the point where everything was in confusion. New experiments were urgently required. Nigeria must find its own way to peace and progress. . . .

Division in the Sudan

Another problem of regionalism and separatism, once more arising from past history and the legacy of colonial rule, brought much trouble to the republic of Sudan. Here, acute cultural differences were combined with a legacy of acute colonial division. About four-fifths of all the people of this large country were Muslims, as they are today. They live in the north, centre and west of the Sudan; and most of them speak Arabic. The remaining fifth live in the distant south. Few of these southerners are Muslims; many are Christians. They speak Dinka, Nuer, Shilluk, and other languages.

These differences in Sudanese culture and history are very old. They go back to the early times of Islam and its penetration into the lands of the middle Nile. They were sharpened by conflict at many times in the past, and especially during the period of Egyptian control in the nineteenth century. And when the British took over, after their defeat of the Mahdia, they gradually built a colonial system which more or less completely divided Arabic-speaking Sudanese from the peoples in the far south. Instead of being able to get to know and trust each other, these two populations were kept severely apart.

When independence came in 1956, the Muslim Sudanese naturally took control because they were far more numerous than the southern peoples. They were left with institutions, with means and methods of government, which they proceeded to use. But instead of helping the southern peoples to share in government on a federal basis, the northern Sudanese sent down officials to take the place of the British.

Yet here was a case where agreeing to some regionalism could help to avoid conflict and separation. If the southerners could run their own affairs within a federal Sudan, the old distrusts and differences between south and north might gradually be overcome.

As it was, the southerners believed they had good reason to fear northern domination. An 'army of liberation', called

41

Anyanya, took the field against the central government's police and army. Only years later, in 1972, could peace seem possible. This was when, in that year, the Sudanese government gave southerners their own parliament and government. *Anyanya* withdrew its demand for a separate southern state. The way to Sudanese federal unity seemed open. Once again, after the means and methods left by colonial government had broken down, a time of experiment and renewal had proved necessary. Unhappily, this produced no success. Repeated northern failure to meet the demands for federal self-government by southern peoples has brought new warfare and huge disaster.

No National Identity

Pre-colonial Africans lived as scattered ethnic entities. This, coupled with the divide-and-rule policies of the colonial powers, explains the "tribal politics" of the first African nationalists. Because of this lack of a developed sense of national identity, it seemed logical that aspiring leaders would appeal initially to their own tribesmen. Defeated and opportunistic leaders also took advantage of the fluid situation to fuel ethnic suspicion.

Eugene Nyati, *World Press Review*, November 1990.

Another big problem arose, after independence came, when new national leaders lost touch with the lives and interests of their peoples. This opened a gap between the leaders, who now enjoyed power and privilege, and the mass of voters who were living in the same way as before. Into that poverty gap, many troubles flowed. . . .

This problem of élitist government by a small privileged group was not of course confined to Africa. It has brought trouble to all nations everywhere. But in Africa it was linked to another part of the colonial legacy; and this made the problem worse. 'Elitism' became linked with 'tribalism'—with all that part of colonial influence which had pushed the idea of tribes. And the two together—élitism *plus* tribalism—could be very destructive. . . .

The Failure of Colonial Institutions

Many of the troubles of Africa, after independence, followed on breakdown of parliamentary and administrative institutions set in place, at the time of independence, by departing colonial rulers. Those institutions failed to meet the problems left by past history, but, especially, by the legacy of colonial history.

Often enlarged by failed leaders and foreign interventions, such problems consisted of internal divisions, élitism, tribalism, and other forms of disunity. Patriotic leaders set themselves to solve those problems; selfish or corrupt leaders simply made them worse.

To these political difficulties on the road to stability, all of which were built into the situation on the day of independence, others of an economic and social nature were added. For what the new governments were obliged to take over was not a prosperous colonial business, but, in many ways, a profound colonial crisis. There was poverty and hunger in wide rural areas. Towns and cities grew hugely in size as rural people flocked to them in search of food and jobs, and often could find neither. If a few persons managed to make money or get good jobs, the majority did not. Even before independence, the gap in living-standards between the few with money, houses, or good jobs, and the many who had none of those good things, was wide. It was also widely resented.

Yet the few with jobs and money were precisely that small minority who, as Chief Awolowo claimed in 1947, were 'destined to rule the country', because they had the necessary education and political knowledge. They duly took over power; but the gap in living-standards between them and the majority continued to widen. As it widened, so did popular discontent. And when that discontent exploded into strife or violence, the politicians proved helpless. . . .

The Future of Africa

Africa must find its own solutions to its own problems. Listening to Africans now, it appeared that this was a conclusion with growing strength behind it. One heard it argued for in many different places by many different persons, whether highly or lowly placed. Imported solutions had been tried, and they had failed. Such solutions, said King Mosheshoe of Lesotho had been 'a bonanza for the transnational corporations and for consumers in the industrialised countries', but had done 'very little to improve the living standards of most people in Third World countries (ex-colonies)'.

What Africa needed, said this democratic monarch, was 'to develop open and participatory forms of economic and political planning': forms within which 'people can take part in public debate about the main production and development issues, and then have a direct say in the final decision'. Here was the voice of tradition speaking to a new vision of the future, to a further decolonisation: a decolonisation, this time, of minds and attitudes. As our tumultuous century came drawing to a close, the prophecy and promise of this new vision seemed likely to find a widening acceptance.

"Economic progress . . . requires Africans . . . to return to their free market traditions. "

Abandoning Free Market Traditions Caused Africa's Problems

George B.N. Ayittey

Many scholars believe that Africa's tribes were traditionally communist—tribal members shared food and land and did not own private property. In the following viewpoint, George B.N. Ayittey disputes this belief. He argues that African tribes were capitalistic and believed in the value of free trade and private ownership. Ayittey maintains that Africa ceased to prosper when it abandoned these economic traditions for socialism. Ayittey, a native of Ghana, is a Bradley Resident Scholar at The Heritage Foundation, a Washington, D.C. think tank.

As you read, consider the following questions:

1. What evidence does the author give to show that African tribes practiced capitalism?
2. Why does Ayittey believe colonialism lasted a long time in Africa?
3. How can the U.S. help Africa, in the author's opinion?

George B.N. Ayittey, "Restoring Africa's Free Market Tradition," The Heritage Foundation *Backgrounder*, July 6, 1988. Reprinted with permission.

Africa is a resource-rich continent that by all rights should be economically prosperous. Yet Africa in fact is the poorest continent on earth, with millions of its inhabitants facing malnutrition and starvation. Why is Africa so poor today? Is it the fault of colonialism? Of the post-colonial world economic system? Of "adverse" terms of trade?

One theory, widely held, is that colonialism is the root of Africa's current poverty. According to this theory, before the coming of the white man, Africans enjoyed a benevolent tribal communism that allowed the natives to survive without exploiting each other. Then the Europeans introduced such supposedly alien institutions as property rights, free exchange, and the profit drive. When Africa finally gained independence from its colonial masters, according to this theory, modern socialism was the only system suited to Africa's traditional communist institutions. Poverty is said to persist because of the tremendous difficulties that the continent's new leaders have had in overcoming the damage caused by colonialism.

This view is a myth. The fact is, before European colonial rule most of Africa had local free markets where goods were bought and sold for mutually agreed upon prices. Trans-regional trade linked distant parts of the continent. And the colonial leaders did not do away with these institutions. Since independence, in the very late 1950s and early 1960s, Africans individually have shown that they can be as effective entrepreneurs as any people in the world. The problem is that their governments have imposed rigid systems of centralized economic control that drain most of their economic energy. It is this centralism, based on socialist models, that has contributed enormously to Africa's impoverishment.

Economic progress, in a sense, requires Africans to be allowed to be Africans, to return to their free market traditions. If the United States and other industrial nations genuinely want to help lift Africa out of poverty, they will devise policies that resuscitate indigenous African market economies.

The Myth of Primitive African Communism

Europeans began trading with Africa in the 15th century. By the late 19th century, most of the continent was ruled directly or indirectly by European powers. The underdeveloped conditions in Africa, when contrasted with the industrializing economies of Europe, led to much misunderstanding concerning the nature of African society. Contributing to the misunderstanding was the popularity in academic circles of Marxist economic theory, which maintained that pre-civilized societies were characterized by primitive communism.

As such, it has been widely presumed that before and during

45

much of the colonial period Africa was dominated by tribal communism. It is said that private property did not exist. Food and the necessities of life supposedly were produced through non-competitive cooperation and allocated to members of the tribal "family" on the basis of need. It is further believed that most tribes produced just enough for their own consumption and that the commodities produced by the various tribes were similar. And the continent's vastness, combined with environmental obstacles, meant that little trade took place among the Africans themselves.

This idyllic state supposedly was destroyed by Europeans who introduced trade and a market economy. Natives, it is said, were forced to abandon self-sufficient communal production and sharing of goods and instead to sell their labor for money and engage in production for exchange.

A Racist Explanation

Socialism has never brought prosperity anywhere in the world, and the explanation that Africans are somehow different seems ludicrous at best and racist at worst. . . .

Even in primitive tribes that did not recognize private ownership of land, the weapons used to hunt animals were owned by individuals.

Goods were exchanged in pre-colonial Africa through village markets, where entrepreneurs gathered to trade their wares, and through inter-regional markets located along major trade routes. Colonial rulers kept these institutions intact.

Edwin Meese, *Conservative Chronicle*, September 27, 1989.

These notions had become conventional academic wisdom in the West by the 1920s and 1930s, when many future African leaders were studying in Western universities. They accepted as fact that there never had been a free market tradition in Africa and that colonial powers had imposed an alien system on the continent. The obvious antidote to this, they concluded, was that only a socialist system would suit African social and economic traditions.

Africa's Free Market Tradition

To be sure, the economy of primitive Africa differed in many ways from that of Europe. Tribes that survived through hunting did not have a conception of individual property titles in land. Since the animals that provided food for such tribes roamed over vast tracks of land, there was little point in dividing the land into small, individual parcels. Yet even in these tribes important private property existed: the weapons used to hunt animals were owned by individuals.

In areas where Africans survived through agriculture, land was ultimately the possession of the tribe in the sense that exclusive title often could not be sold to individuals outside the tribe. (There were even exceptions to this rule.) But by custom, families occupying land had the right to farm the land, sell or trade the resulting produce, and pass the land down to later generations of the family.

Domestic free markets and inter-regional free trade were part of economic tradition in nearly every part of the continent, especially in West Africa.

Village markets were weekly or biweekly fairs, varying in length from two to eight days. Where there was a cluster of villages, market days were rotated among them. Individuals and tribes did not all produce identical goods. Thus markets offered opportunities for individuals, families, and tribes to acquire goods that they did not produce themselves. Since different regions and groups tended to specialize in different products, markets were usually situated on the border between such different geographic zones as deserts, savannahs, and rain forests, or between different ethnic groups, such as Kenya's pastoral Masai and the Kikuyus, a tribe that cultivated the land.

The markets were well structured and organized. Some specialized in certain product lines, such as agricultural produce or handicrafts, while others carried a more general variety of wares. But each market had its own customs and rules regarding the settlement of disputes and the quality of products offered for sale. Each also grouped vendors according to product. Example: all tomato sellers were seated together in one section of the market. The object of this was to promote competition.

Trading activity was dominated by women affectionately called in English "market mammies." Rules were generally enforced by the "market queen," who was usually elected by the market women, not appointed by chiefs, Africa's traditional rulers. Any African, regardless of tribal origins, was free to engage in trade if he or she obeyed the rules governing the particular market. Nigerian traders, for example, were and still are found in virtually every local West African market outside Nigeria today.

Price Gyrations

Prices in this market fluctuated in accordance with the forces of supply and demand. When tomatoes were "in season," for example, the price fell and vice versa. These price gyrations were understood by the peasants. Most of the chiefs of Africa did little to interfere with the day-to-day operations of the market, nor did they impose controls or other stifling regulations. The African village market, to all intents and purposes, was an open free market, however "primitive."

In addition to the exchange of goods, the market provided an indispensable avenue for social interaction: to meet people, to gossip, or to discuss and keep abreast of local affairs. Foreign observers often wondered why some vendors were content with the sale of a few bananas per day. The reason is that they went to the market mainly for social interaction.

In Africa there was also an important historical and cultural link between the place where free exchange of goods took place and where exchanges of opinion and, ultimately, governmental decisions occurred. The market area often served as the site for village assemblies convened by the traditional rulers. Among the Ibo of Nigeria, for example, the *Ama-ala*, the traditional Council of Elders, ruled by decree and proclamation. However, when disputes arose, the Council would convene a Village Assembly to place the issues before the people for debate and resolution. . . .

The Colonial Period

European countries began to trade with Africa in the 15th century. While some colonies were established early on, notably the Dutch colony at the Cape of Good Hope in southern Africa, it was not until the late 19th century that Belgium, Britain, France, Germany, Italy, Portugal, and Spain divided up the continent and established their sovereignty. Colonial political and economic institutions differed under the different sovereigns. Some ruled directly. Others ruled indirectly through the local chiefs.

While the Europeans often sought to control indigenous economic activities to their advantage, they failed as often as they succeeded. In any event, Africa's vast distances and underdeveloped communications and transportation networks would have made complete control of native economic activities by any colonial administrator impossible. The extraordinary cost in time and money for any sort of control was a main reason that the British adopted the colonial policy of indirect rule. This generally left intact the indigenous economic activities. . . .

Notably absent during that era were state or colonial government enterprises. A few large European firms and companies dominated the various sectors of the economy, but no indigenous economic activity was reserved exclusively for the colonial government or European companies.

Small village shopkeepers emerged. Native businesses competed with European firms. Many were successful. There were rich African shopkeepers, timber merchants, transport owners, and farmers during the colonial period. Given the opportunities and access to capital, the natives proved that they could compete with the foreigners. In fact, the success of native Africans was one reason why South African whites favored apartheid. Write Frances Kendall and Leon Louw of the Free Market Foundation of South Africa: "The freedom that characterized tribal society in part explains why black South Africans responded so positively to the challenges of a free market that, by the 1870's they were outcompeting whites, especially as farmers."

Myth, Not Reality

The argument that for communally oriented Africa, socialism is the natural way of life . . . is a myth, contradicted on every African streetcorner, and in the rural areas of Africa, where, as everywhere else, small farmers are most productive working their own land.

Herman Nickel, *The Wall Street Journal*, January 31, 1990.

One reason colonialism lasted so long in Africa was that it did little to upset violently the traditional way of life. Had it done so, its demise would have come sooner. Resistance to colonialism came largely from the educated class in the urban areas where economic disparities and discrimination were more glaring.

The Emergence of Socialism

After independence, free markets and free trade were viewed by African leaders, educated in the West and influenced by socialist and Marxist ideology, as alien institutions imported by the colonial powers as a means to exploit the natives. Post-colonial economics were formed by an emotional anti-imperialism, which saw Africa's salvation in complete state control of the economy. . . .

The results of socialism for Africa's economic development have been disastrous. African countries have progressed little since independence. Most are actually worse off. A 1985 World Bank study found that Africa's per capita Gross Domestic Product in 1983 was 4 percent below its 1970 level. Countries such as Tanzania and Guinea, which had been food exporters in colonial times, now rely on imports and still cannot feed their people. Agricultural production has dropped as governments deny farmers the right to sell their products at market prices, nationalize land, and divert resources into money-losing industrialization projects. On a human misery index developed by the Population Crisis Committee in Washington, 25 of the world's 30 worst off countries are African. . . .

Despite the myth to the contrary, Africa has a tradition of local free markets and trans-regional trade. Natives bought and sold goods with little interference from their chiefs long before the coming of the Europeans. Even under colonial rule, indigenous market institutions survived and many black Africans competed successfully with foreigners. With 20th century independence, however, Africa's socialist leaders proceeded to brutally destroy economic freedom. This was accompanied by political repression and a denial of basic human rights.

Foreign aid money has been wasted on money-losing state enterprises or stolen outright by corrupt politicians. This must be stopped and reversed. Today, the most effective aid that the U.S. and the world can give Africa is help to rebuild, reinstitute, and modernize Africa's indigenous institutions of political and economic freedom. These now-tattered institutions have demonstrated in the past that Africans are as capable as any people of earning their own living and trading freely with others. Paternalistic controls that treat Africans like children only serve to continue the worst aspects of the colonial attitude towards that continent. If Western nations truly wish to eliminate the poverty and misery that is the lot of most Africans today, they must insist that Africa's leaders begin pursuing policies to restore Africa's traditional economic and political freedoms.

a critical thinking activity

Evaluating Sources of Information

When historians study and interpret past events, they use two kinds of sources: primary and secondary. Primary sources are eyewitness accounts. For example, the journals of nineteenth century British explorers Henry Stanley and David Livingstone, who explored the Congo (now Zaire), would be a primary source. A *London Times* report on Stanley and Livingstone's explorations would be a secondary source. Primary and secondary sources may be decades or even hundreds of years old, and often historians find that the sources offer conflicting and contradictory information. To fully evaluate documents and assess their accuracy, historians analyze the credibility of the documents' authors and, in the case of secondary sources, analyze the credibility of the information the authors used.

Historians are not the only people who encounter conflicting information, however. Anyone who reads a daily newspaper, watches television, or just talks to different people will encounter many different views. Writers and speakers use sources of information to support their own statements. Thus, critical thinkers, just like historians, must question the writer's or speaker's sources of information as well as the writer or speaker.

While there are many criteria that can be applied to assess the accuracy of a primary or secondary source, for this activity you will be asked to apply three. For each source listed on the following page, ask yourself the following questions: First, did the person actually see or participate in the event he or she is reporting? This will help you determine the credibility of the information—an eyewitness to an event is an extremely valuable source. Second, does the person have a vested interest in the report? Assessing the person's social status, professional affiliations, nationality, and religious or political beliefs will be helpful in considering this question. By evaluating this you will be able to determine how objective the person's report may be. Third, how qualified is the author to be making the statements he or she is making? Consider what the person's profession is and how he or she might know about the event. Someone who has spent years being involved with or studying the issue may be able to offer more information than someone who simply is offering an uneducated opinion; for example, a politician or layperson.

Keeping the above criteria in mind, imagine you are writing a paper on economic development in Africa. You decide to cite an equal number of primary and secondary sources. Listed below are several sources that may be useful for your research. *Place a P next to those descriptions you believe are primary sources. Place an S next to those descriptions you believe are secondary sources.* Next, based on the above criteria, *rank the primary sources, assigning the number (1) to what appears to be the most valuable, (2) to the source likely to be the second-most valuable, and so on, until all the primary sources are ranked. Then rank the secondary sources, again using the above criteria.*

P or S		*Rank in Importance*
_____	1. A "Sixty Minutes" interview in which the owner of a coffee plantation in Sierra Leone discusses the local economy.	_____
_____	2. A *Time* magazine article on poverty in Africa.	_____
_____	3. A lecture by a University of Nairobi economics professor on how Kenya can increase its gross national product.	_____
_____	4. An African National Congress plan for raising per capita income in poor African nations.	_____
_____	5. A Public Broadcasting Service documentary on the plight of Ethiopian farmers.	_____
_____	6. A newspaper analysis of a speech by the leader of the South African Communist Party explaining why socialist economies would benefit African nations.	_____
_____	7. A Peace Corps volunteer's description of her two-year experience teaching irrigation techniques to rural tribespeople in Zambia.	_____
_____	8. A book on colonialism and economic development in Africa by a *New York Times* journalist.	_____
_____	9. A paper by a Harvard historian that discusses the political obstacles traditionally thwarting Africa's attempts at economic independence.	_____

Periodical Bibliography

The following articles have been selected to supplement the diverse views presented in this chapter.

Africa News	"Making Its Own Miracles," April 3, 1989.
Africa News	"The Scourge of Debt: Africa's Invisible Crisis," April 3, 1989.
George B.N. Ayittey	"Africa's Survival," *The World & I*, January 1989.
George B.N. Ayittey	"Beyond Apartheid," *Crisis*, July/August 1990. Available from the Brownson Institute, PO Box 1006, Notre Dame, IN 46556.
Peter Brimelow	"Exploitation or Benefaction?" *Forbes*, November 27, 1989.
Victoria Brittain	"Africa: Which Way to Go?" *World Marxist Review*, November 1989.
George F. Brown	"An African Challenge: Cut High Fertility Rate," *Forum for Applied Research and Public Policy*, Summer 1991. Available from the Executive Sciences Institute, 1005 Mississippi Ave., Davenport, IA 52803.
Richard Carver	"Reform or Repression?" *Africa Report*, July/August 1991.
Charles Creekmore	"Misunderstanding Africa," *Psychology Today*, December 1986.
Llewellyn D. Howell	"The Heart of Darkness," *USA Today*, September 1991.
Sousa Jamba	"The African Disease," *The Spectator*, September 9, 1989.
Richard Joseph	"Partnership Not Patronship," *Africa Report*, September/October 1990.
Edwin Meese	"Africa Can Prosper with the Right Policies," *Conservative Chronicle*, September 27, 1989. Available from PO Box 11297, Des Moines, IA 50340-1297.
World Press Review	"Soviet-Style Underdevelopment," April 1988.

How Can Famine in Africa Be Reduced?

Chapter Preface

Africa's Persistent Causes of Hunger

NIGER
Drought

SUDAN
War and drought

LIBERIA
Civil war

ETHIOPIA
Drought in
northern areas

SIERRA LEONE
Presence of Liberian
refugees; two successive
poor harvests

SOMALIA
War-related
presence of
Ethiopian
refugees

RWANDA
Drought, plant diseases,
lack of agricultural inputs

MOZAMBIQUE
Displacement
caused by war

ANGOLA
Drought and war

MALAWI
Mozambican refugees
require food aid

Horn in *The Christian Science Monitor* © 1990 TCSPC. Reprinted by permission.

People who are uninformed about African famines often attribute them to a single cause: drought. However, as the above map shows, the causes of famine are often more complex than many people realize. While drought often plays an important part in causing a food shortage, other factors, such as war, also contribute to the crisis. For example, recent famines in eastern Africa may have been minor food shortages had it not been for the civil wars that forced farmers to abandon their lands. Plant diseases and a lack of seeds and other agricultural resources also exacerbate famine.

The authors in the following chapter present varying views concerning how famine in Africa can be reduced.

"The real benefits [of a famine early warning system] in terms of the saving of human lives and of improvement of such lives as survive will be immense."

Early Warning Systems Could Prevent Famine

Meghnad Desai

Meghnad Desai is professor of economics at the London School of Economics. In the following viewpoint, Desai proposes that a well-designed early warning system could help predict and prevent famines in Africa. While such a system would require much planning and consideration of all of the factors that contribute to famine, it would save lives and decrease the devastating effects of famine.

As you read, consider the following questions:

1. Other than drought, what are some of the causes of famine, according to Desai?
2. Why does the author believe it is important to understand how factors affecting famine are linked?
3. What does the author mean when he refers to a nation's "non-food production system"?

From "Modelling an Early Warning System for Famines" by Meghnad Desai, © The United Nations University 1990. Reprinted from *The Political Economy of Hunger*, edited by Jean Dreze and Amartya Sen: vol. 2 *Famine Prevention* (1990) by permission of Oxford University Press.

Droughts are a natural phenomenon; famines are not. Rains fail periodically but cannot be caused or hindered . . . by social forces. Famines however are social phenomena. Droughts may lead to failure of harvests if certain supporting conditions are present: lack of foresight, lack of irrigation water, etc. Failure of harvests may in their turn lead to acute starvation if certain other supporting conditions are present: lack of stocks of foodgrains, lack of availability of foodgrains at prices people could afford, lack of activity outside food growing to generate adequate purchasing power widely distributed. If starvation occurs then the starving may undertake various actions: migration to other areas for instance. These may exacerbate the severity of famine if the result is to heighten the unevenness of the distribution of goods as well as of purchasing power.

But famines can also occur without a prior 'natural' disaster. A central proposition of *Poverty and Famines* (Amartya Sen, 1981) is that droughts or harvest failures are neither necessary nor sufficient for famines to occur. Famines can occur due to political shocks—wars, civil wars, drastic changes in legal rights that define entitlements (e.g. the collectivization campaign in Russia), etc. . . .

Our knowledge of the complex and dynamic interrelationship between various economic and non-economic variables that go into turning an initial shock (natural or socio-political) into a full-scale famine has improved tremendously in recent years, mainly thanks to the framework provided by Amartya Sen (1981), which has been used in many cases, criticized and expanded upon in others. . . . There have also been strategies to warn of impending famines, both historically and much more so in recent years. These 'early warning systems' are the concern of this [viewpoint]. . . .

Understanding Famine

Before we can understand famines, we must understand how the food production and food supply systems work in 'normal times'. These 'normal times' may witness some portion of the population going hungry or suffering from malnutrition and its attendant diseases. But we still regard them as 'normal' since we wish to study the pathology of the system which leads to famines. If we were interested in eradication of hunger and poverty, we might regard the normal system itself as pathological but our present interest is in famines. We need therefore a general model in which even after a shock has occurred, there is no certainty that a famine will occur. . . .

The economies which are vulnerable to famines are predominantly agrarian, poor ones. Thus a model must give prominence to this aspect whether in the normal or the pathological state.

Food production is thus a pivotal part of the system. To model its nature and its effect on the other sectors is virtually to model the entire economy. Bearing this in mind, the economic activities of the system can be thought to be food production and food delivery, the rest being non-food production. The latter can be rural or urban. Influencing these economic sectors are the non-economic forces. These can be natural or socio-political. The initial shocks to the economic system emanate from these non-economic forces. . . .

The Food Production System

In normal times the economic sectors are mutually and simultaneously dependent on each other but in famine times, the food production system becomes pivotal and recursive with respect to the non-food production system. Thus famine represents a disjuncture in the normal functioning of the system.

The system structure of the economy [includes] . . . three basic blocks, one of which has four subblocks:

1. the nature system;
2. the socio-political system;
3. the economic system;
   (a) the food production system;
   (b) the non-food production rural system;
   (c) the non-food production urban system;
   (d) the food delivery system. . . .

The nature system is primary in time. It affects food production via the amount, the timing, and the spatial incidence of rainfall. Although droughts are not the only reasons for famines, they often are major triggering factors. But the nature system will also affect the non-food production system. It can do this either via drought affecting outputs or via disease which may for example affect the livestock. The stock variables of the nature system will be the ecological conditions—land fertility and erosion, the distribution of forests as against clear land, etc. The mapping of the ecological state is an important step in any anti-famine strategy.

Parallel to the nature system . . . is the socio-political system. Of course, continued economic failure will affect the socio-political system. In this sense it is only weakly exogenous but we take it as given for the time being. Civil wars and rebellions, war conditions and external invasions, sudden changes in the taxation regimes—all these are external shocks to the economic system. They can often cause drastic changes in entitlements either by disputing the legality of existing claims (as when a region is under disputed sovereignty by one side or other in a civil war) or by changing the legal framework itself (as when a political revolution changes rights of ownership as happened after the October Revolution in rural areas of Russia). A third example is change in the taxation regime, say from money payments to compulsory requisition. All these would be shocks to the system which could trigger further changes. On the other hand the socio-political system will also provide a public relief system. This is the part that is at the heart of the response to any early warning system. . . .

The End of Famine

The demise of hunger may be attainable because for the first time in human history it is possible to contemplate the end of food scarcity, famine, and mass starvation. With the exception of its intentional creation or perpetuation as a weapon of war or genocide, a combination of effective famine early-warning systems, national and global emergency food reserves, and improved experience with distribution and food-for-work programs has brought the end of famine well within sight. Despite the continuing African famine experience, famine is already rare and becoming even rarer.

Robert W. Kates and Sara Millman, in *Hunger in History*, 1990.

The food production system supplies food to the food delivery system and inputs to the non-food production system. Such inputs may be used to produce other edible products e.g. bread from flour. The food delivery system pays the food production system a sum of money determined by the price. The non-food production system demands food from the food delivery system and provides it with inputs e.g. transport equipment, warehousing facilities. Within the non-food production system there is likely to be mutual exchange between the rural and urban for the food production system as well as final goods for consumption. . . .

Causes Other than Drought

A failure of the rains is not necessary for a famine to occur nor is a diminution of food supply. An exogenous shock to the non-food system (say spread of a cattle disease) may itself trigger a decline in non-food incomes and cause starvation. Wars, even small, local ones, are notorious for causing food shortages. Mistiming of release of stockpiles of food, the regional/national political machinations that may misdirect food supplies in relation to where they are needed, are other examples of variables sufficient for causing famines.

This lack of a strong necessity of the 'natural' sequence of events or, what is the same, *the variety of possible causal linkages which lead to famine makes the devising of an early warning system for famines tricky.* Since any of the links could fail they all have to be modelled with equal care to yield ways which will make them forecastable. But if a failure occurs at an early stage then an early warning system will help in triggering mechanisms for offsetting its effect at later stages but also in warning to make doubly sure that later blocks in the chain do not malfunction. Time in this sense imposes an asymmetry. If rains fail and we are forewarned then steps can be taken to offset likely effects. There may also be a willingness on the part of various agencies to take such action since they cannot be held responsible for the failure of nature. There need not be recriminations. But if failure occurs in one of the later blocks, despite good rains, then action is much more urgent since anticipation is difficult. But at the same time, there may be a political or bureaucratic resistance to recognizing that action is needed. Droughts are relatively easier to forecast than civil wars, or mismanagement of food stocks. An early warning system can thus rule out failures at earlier stages of the cycle but should never lead to complacency. This is why it is necessary to link the early warning systems for each block in the model with each other. Otherwise, disaster having been successfully ruled out at the natural stage, the need to continue to monitor the progress of food from seed to the mouths of recipients at all stages may be overlooked. Thus good rainfall may trigger premature drawing down (even exports) of food stocks, only to be followed by the discovery that harvests have failed because of locusts, or that breakdown of transport facilities lets harvested grain rot. The linkages of the blocks in the model should force a similar structured linkage in the early warning systems and systems reacting to early warnings. . . .

Forecasting Droughts

Droughts are 'extreme events' and hence appear to be random shocks, yet our ability to model their occurrence has improved considerably. There are now well-established patterns of long and short cycles in climate. Long cycle evidence is not so helpful in early warning although it can explain a fundamental ecological shift in a region. Thus for the Sahel there have been studies of the longer-run changes in rainfall pattern as well as of the recurring long cycle. Data are of course sparse but not entirely lacking and the field of climate history has made substantial advances here. Thus S.E. Nicholson's work on the Sahel climate spans both the last 200 years and the early geological records. Data on river and lake levels stretching back over two or three centuries can be obtained and these point to interesting cycles. Thus, there were numerous droughts in the 1820s and 1830s in Southern Africa as well as further north towards the Sahel. But if 1820-40 was a rainfall deficient period, 1870-95 was surplus, and 1895-1920 was again deficient. There are parallels in the rainfall pattern in the two successive drought years 1912-13 and again 1972-73 in the Sahel region. . . .

If a rainfall data series exists, modelling it will signal any forthcoming change. There are however other early warning signs within the climate year which could also be exploited. Thus it is possible to use data on climate in between the two rainfall seasons to improve our forecast. Thus, winter temperature is often a good leading indicator of subsequent rainfall. This would imply that by modelling the two seasonal variables—winter temperature and rainfall—*jointly* we could improve the forecasting ability. Again the techniques are available and are easy to implement. . . .

The Food Production System

The next block is the food production system. Clearly a lot is known about the input-output system in food production. For our purposes, an early warning system can be devised effectively only if the timing of the various operations between input and output are articulated in detail. Thus what we need is not the static production function but the stage-wise process starting with clearing, hoeing, planting, replanting in the case of rice, guarding the field from creatures which might attack the growing food plant, and finally harvest. The availability of water at the crucial stages in this cycle has to be marked. If water fails to arrive via rainfall, the availability of alternative water sources has to be specified. A failure of rain predicted by the nature system model can give us up to a year's advance warning. The response to this may be by encouraging a change in the cropping pattern and planting crops suitable for drier climates. If this were not possible, alternative rural activities could be prepared for in the meantime. Thus if the drought is successfully forecast, the early warning system can go into action with the longest gap we can expect to have. This is a relatively easy problem to tackle. If our nature system has failed to predict the drought correctly then it is at this stage that various warning systems should go into action. They should first alert to the need for alternative water supply to be made available (from reserves, etc.). If such water is not normally available, then the input-output system tells us that the harvest so many weeks hence will be poor. The water input-harvest output lag is thus a window of warning and gives the various agencies time to act before the failure becomes a panic in the food market. . . .

Parallel to the food production system will be the non-food system. This will differ according to country and nothing much can be said about it in general. Thus these activities may be pastoral, fisheries, non-agricultural labour, small industry, etc. The key question for the early warning system is to articulate the dependence of the non-food production system on rainfall or any other natural/meteorological variable. In each case where such dependence can be established, the impact of the various shocks would depend on the timing of the input-output sequence and the place of the natural variable in this time sequence. Thus rainfall will matter for a sweetwater fisheries economy. . . . A rainfall failure if forecast provides an early warning that the fish catch will be low if rivers are going to be depleted. Any further useful information will depend on a detailed study of each local economy. . . .

Conclusion

The problem of devising an early warning system is one of articulating the various blocks which translate a natural failure into an economic and social disaster. . . .

I would like to argue that [this] is both feasible and desirable. . . . It will of course demand resources, human as well as financial. It will also require much international cooperation and coordination in information gathering, in bringing together intimate knowledge of local conditions and theoretical expertise of meteorologists, economists, anthropologists, and systems analysts. But the real benefits in terms of the saving of human lives and of improvement of such lives as survive will be immense. If we can devise a system that gives a year's, six months', or even three months' early warning then the task would be worth it. It may be a false warning. If so, so much the better. In matters of life and death, the loss function is asymmetric; we may as well err on the safe side having failed to do so for so long.

> *"Early warning systems . . . have not yet truly been tested."*

Early Warning Systems May Not Prevent Famine

Michael H. Glantz

Some experts have proposed early warning systems as a way to anticipate and prevent famines. In the following viewpoint, Michael H. Glantz expresses his doubts concerning the effectiveness of these systems. The causes of famine are numerous and complex, making famines difficult if not impossible to accurately predict, the author states. In addition, even if a famine is predicted, the world's response may be insufficient to ease the suffering. Glantz is head of the Environmental and Societal Impacts Group at the National Center for Atmospheric Research in Boulder, Colorado.

As you read, consider the following questions:

1. Why was Ethiopia's early warning system ineffective, according to Glantz?
2. Why do experts disagree about the definition of famine, in the author's opinion?
3. What three questions does the author believe must be answered before famine in Africa can be eradicated?

Michael H. Glantz, "Why Are Famines Difficult to Predict?" This article appeared in the January 1990 issue of, and is reprinted with permission from, *The World & I*, a publication of The Washington Times Corporation, copyright © 1990.

Since the earliest times, people have been fascinated by the prospects of forecasting future events. Which army will win a battle? Will drought occur this year? Will there be an economic recession? Will it rain this weekend? Will a volcano erupt? When will the next earthquake take place?

Some forecasts of future events, however, are more crucial to society than others. Forecasts of life-threatening situations obviously take precedence over others. And most recently, forecasting famines has become a particular focus of attention.

The Ethiopian famine of 1984-85 and the apparent failure to forecast it heightened emphasis on the importance of famine early warning systems to humanitarian responses. If one could forecast the emergence of famine or its precursors, action could be taken to avoid the actual outbreak of famine.

Questions Concerning Famine

Interest in famine early warning systems is not new. India has had famine codes since the 1870s; and the Sudan had them in the 1920s. Why, then, are societies still seeking to understand this age-old process? Why do we still have famines, given the great technological and industrial developments of the past few centuries? Of the 25 officially designated droughts in sub-Saharan Africa in the early 1980s, why did five of them still result in famines?

In fact, it was the devastating impact of famine in Ethiopia in the early 1980s that sparked resurgent interest in famine prevention through forecasting. This interest was generated less by official government concern than by citizen responses in developed countries. Despite pleas for food assistance by the Marxist Ethiopian government's Relief and Rehabilitation Commission (RRC) over a period of a few years, little assistance was forthcoming from the international donor community. Only after a BBC [British Broadcasting Corporation] camera crew filmed the horrible conditions in the Korem refugee camp located in north-central Ethiopia, and released it to the world media in October 1984, did people everywhere raise pressure on their governments to respond to the emergency.

Ethiopia has had a formal early warning system ever since the devastating famine of the early 1970s, which led to the military's overthrow of Emperor Haile Selassie's regime. Using the lack of responsiveness by the Selassie government to the victims of drought and famine as an excuse, a Marxist faction took power and jailed the emperor, who died in captivity in 1975.

As a first step, the new military government established a commission to investigate the famine and the role of the imperial government in it. Another early step was to establish the RRC, and within it, an early warning system. Many have come to agree that, despite its shortcomings, it was among the best such systems in sub-Saharan Africa. One of the weaknesses of the RRC, however, was that it was under the control of a Marxist regime, while the international food donors are industrialized noncommunist states. When, in 1983 and 1984, the RRC appealed to the international community for assistance, their pleas were met with skepticism. The Marxist government was spending huge sums celebrating its 10th anniversary in power. At the same time, the government was engaged in an internal war with liberation movements in the northern provinces of Eritrea and Tigre. Donor countries reasoned that withholding grain from Ethiopia might make its government fall. Donors also feared that if Ethiopia were given relief grain, the government would divert the grain to their army and it would not reach the targeted populations in the famine-prone parts of the country.

Today a different ethic prevails, both within Ethiopia and in the international community of food donors. Ethiopia is more receptive to food aid from noncommunist countries (the major donor being the United States) and has shown a greater willingness to accept donor restrictions on the transport and use of that aid. The Western donors, for their part, are less reluctant to assist Ethiopians with their short- and long-term food problems, realizing that the ultimate victims of famine in that country have been apolitical peasants trying to survive not only the vagaries of weather but also the plans of the military government. Herein lies the central reason for the renewed interest in establishing, in a spirit of cooperation, a reliable and credible Ethiopian early warning system. But with so much attention on the politics surrounding Ethiopian famines and responses to them, little attention has been focused on the question of whether such systems can work. What are the constraints that restrict their reliability, timeliness, and credibility?

Process Versus Event

Famine has scores of definitions, and how we view them determines how, when, and even whether we might identify a famine. Some people, such as those responsible for releasing grain from warehouses in donor countries, tend to view famine as an event. They require hard evidence or quantitative indicators to release emergency grain shipments. Their indicators include the number of deaths, the number of people in an emergency feeding center, or whether mass migrations are taking place in the countryside.

Others, such as those who deal with nutritional problems, see famine in a totally different light. They consider famine to be a process and include pre-famine conditions in their definitions of famine. They tend to sound alarms early in the process, so that the last stages of the famine process—mass starvation and death—can be averted. They consider different indicators to be important, including reduced crop yields, increased prices for grain, declining nutritional status of infants, reduced rainfall, the sale of personal items (jewelry, cooking utensils), and the increasing dependence on "famine" foods consumed only under duress.

Thus, when someone in the field suggests that a famine is emerging, and someone in Washington, Paris, or London wants a "body count," they are not communicating about the same phenomenon. The first issue that must be resolved is the need to broaden the definition of what constitutes a famine. For an early warning system, the broader the definition, the better the possibility of an early identification and an early response. . . .

The Failure of an Early Warning System

The value of . . . expensive and complicated early warning systems remains the subject of considerable debate. Although these systems do provide a unique perspective on continent-wide weather patterns, some chroniclers of the 1984-85 famine suggest that satellite observations may actually have delayed relief efforts in Ethiopia by causing actual crop conditions to be misread. They have pointed out that, drawing on a straightforward ground-level 'early warning system', the Ethiopian government had made early appeals for aid from the international community. The government's system was based on simple observation: starting in 1981, starving people had been migrating in search of food and work, and, as the drought continued, the migration had increased in urgency. Unfortunately these early warnings were ignored, and relief came too late for many famine victims.

Aklilu Lemma, in *Africa Beyond Famine*, 1989.

Many analysts tend to rely only on quantifiable indicators of famine: nutrition, prices in the marketplace, rainfall, acres planted, crop yields, and so forth. Yet, qualitative indicators, including anecdotal information, may also be important. If a truck driver sights unusual migrations from isolated villages, or he observes the sale of famine foods in the market, such information should play a role in early warning systems, even though they may not be readily quantifiable.

Controversial Famine Indicators

Indicators themselves also raise controversy. Which ones provide enough lead time to respond to the event? Which ones are concurrent with or lag behind the event to be averted? Some people consider drought to be the best early warning indicator of famine. Others disagree. Yes, rainfall is readily quantifiable, and it affects the health of crops. But there are instances when, although there has been a sharp reduction in rainfall, the rain that falls does so at the appropriate time for crop growth and development; as a result, crop yields do not decline. This reinforces the view that one must distinguish between meteorological and agricultural droughts.

Early Warning Systems

Nutrition is another controversial early warning indicator. By the time nutritional levels show a decline, the march toward famine has begun. While it is an easily quantified indicator, it may be better for monitoring changes in nutritional status or for reinforcing other early warning indicators than for prompting early response to deteriorating food security situations at the family or village level.

The "warning" part of the Ethiopian national early warning system worked in Ethiopia in the early 1980s. It was the response part of the system that failed. The most recent food emergency situation in Ethiopia occurred in mid-1987 and 1988. During these years, both the timely warning and timely response parts of the system performed well. One could argue, however, that early warning systems in Ethiopia—or in other drought-prone parts of sub-Saharan Africa—have not yet truly been tested. Warnings were issued in late summer 1987 and famine did not occur. Should this situation be viewed as an early warning success, or as the result of happenstance?

While 1986 was a good year for rainfall and for agricultural production in Ethiopia, this only proved to be a short break from the devastating drought and famine conditions of prior years. While rains during the short growing season (occurring from February to April) appeared to be near normal and favorable for good crop yields, the longer, more important growing season (May to September), during which about 85 percent of the annual food crops are grown, appeared to be headed for trouble.

At least three groups have claimed responsibility for successfully predicting severe food shortages: the United Nations' Food and Agricultural Organization, the U.S. Agency for International Development's Famine Early Warning System, and the Ethiopian government's RRC. However, close scrutiny of the critical July-August decision-making period shows that each missed the earliest signs of an impending food crisis. In fact, evidence suggests that the real alert came from a field trip of a World Food Program officer to the chronically food-deficient (and war-torn) provinces of Tigre and Eritrea, who alerted the world through FAO's release of his field observations to the news media. Fortunately, a quick response, once all the warning systems agreed that the situation was deteriorating, thwarted the occurrence of this potential famine. In addition, the international donor community wanted to make amends for its lack of response to the Ethiopian famine earlier that decade. As a result, donors were much more vigilant than they might prove to be in the future. Happenstance played a major role in averting this crisis.

Concluding Comments

Can famine early warning systems work? How can we truly test them? Sometimes the political nature of famines makes a proper response (as opposed to detection) more difficult to achieve. Often friendly governments do not want to embarrass their allies by publicizing their inadequacies in coping with food shortages, regardless of cause. A case in point was the general awareness of the international community (e.g., the United States, Sweden, even the International Red Cross) in the early 1970s that Haile Selassie's government was not responding to the drought-precipitated famine in its northern provinces. . . .

Can international responses to famine be put on a humanitarian plane? Can famine early warning and early response be permanently depoliticized? Can humanitarian concerns be made to automatically override political considerations? Only when these questions are answered affirmatively will African countries and the international community be in a position to cope effectively with severe food shortages. Only then will African and donor governments be able to rid the continent of famine.

"By the dawn of the 21st Century, 29 African nations will be unable to feed their populations."

Decreasing Africa's Population Will Reduce Famine

The Population Institute

The Population Institute is an organization dedicated to reducing population growth throughout the world. In the following viewpoint, the author argues that overpopulation is a primary cause of Africa's famines. Africa cannot feed its people because it has too large a population and too little fertile land to support it. The author advocates decreasing population growth to prevent widespread starvation in Africa.

As you read, consider the following questions:

1. List some of the reasons the author gives for Africa's stunted economic development.
2. For many years, the West pressured African nations to control their population growth. How did African leaders respond to this pressure, according to the author?
3. According to the author, how have actions by the United States harmed Africa's efforts to control population growth?

From The Population Institute's "A Continent in Crisis: Building a Future for Africa in the 21st Century," Number 8, 1988. Reprinted with permission.

For centuries, Africa has been the forgotten continent—neglected by diplomats, ignored by historians, patronized by politicians, even maligned and insulted by Hollywood filmmakers. Today, popular Western notions about Africa remain vague and misshapen by decades of fiction, racism, and Tarzan movies. In Western diplomatic offices, Africa has been relegated to the back burner, the token projects there understaffed, underfunded, and too often deprived of top-level leadership or interest. It is not an overstatement to say that U.S. policy toward Africa over the past eight years has consisted for all practical purposes of just three parts: South Africa, Egypt, and Libya, all rather exceptional cases. The vast majority of Africans whose countries lie in between have received little sustained international attention.

That state of affairs will soon change. Africa, so long brushed aside in the hustle of global relations, will step to the fore in the years immediately ahead. It will be put under the global spotlight because of the tragedy developing there—a crisis cutting across its social structure, economy, and environment—but the spotlight this time will not quickly fade, because how effectively we deal with this crisis will, in a very real sense, determine the kind of world we inhabit in the 21st Century. . . .

A Pattern of Starvation

A brief overview of Africa's situation makes clear why it cannot be ignored. Africa's population is now 630 million, and it is growing faster than any other region in the world. If its present growth rate is not altered, its population would triple by the year 2028. But while Africa's population grows by 3.1 percent annually, the continent's food supply increases by only 1.1 percent per year. That means that every year Africa's dependence on uncertain food imports grows more acute. And, in painfully practical terms, it means that each year more Africans will starve. The suffering that was triggered in Ethiopia by severe drought is becoming built into the demographic structure of the entire continent.

There is no simple explanation for why Africa's economic development has been stunted and why Africans today remain so grievously poor. Lack of capital and highly skilled personnel is a factor. As is ongoing civil strife, which, besides its human toll, tends to be disruptive and costly to long-term development schemes. Staggering external debts act as drags on many African economies. Historical policies of colonial exploitation (so often pointed to by Africans themselves) have surely played a role, as have the present-day mistakes and mismanagement by some African governments (so often pointed to by Western donors). Finally, the accelerating degradation of one of Africa's greatest economic assets—its natural resource base—has had a clear and ominous impact on the continent's hopes for a self-sufficient future. Somewhere in the mix of these factors is the wellspring of Africa's woes. But it is the added element of runaway population growth that aggravates each of these factors and makes the mix so very difficult to overcome.

A Deteriorating Continent

Despite wide-ranging economic reforms by African governments and key initiatives by the international community to support African recovery efforts, the continent's critical economic situation is still deteriorating. There can be no doubt whatsoever that this deterioration will continue unless reducing rampant population growth becomes a priority with all relevant government agencies, private organizations and with the nations of that beleaguered region of the world.

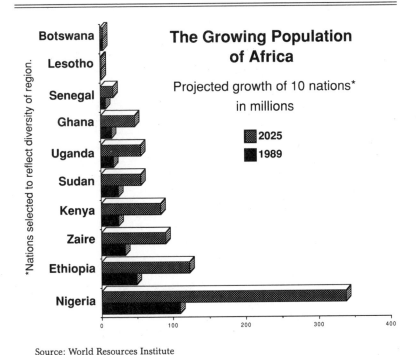

The Growing Population of Africa

Projected growth of 10 nations* in millions

■ 2025
■ 1989

*Nations selected to reflect diversity of region.

Source: World Resources Institute

The United Nations Population Fund, the multi-lateral agency that has worked longest and most extensively in Africa, reported in its Mid-Term Review of the United Nations Programme of Action for African Economic Recovery and

Development, that "half of Africa's people are under 14 years, and 70 percent are under 25. Many African countries are increasing their populations in 20 years or less. Their cities are growing even faster; some will double in size by the end of the century.

"The needs of these increasing numbers give added urgency to Africa's efforts for economic recovery," according to the report. "But the rate at which numbers increase will be one of the factors which will determine their success.

"In many countries, infant mortality has been cut by half in the past thirty years. Twenty years have been added to the average expectation of life. But while death rates have fallen over much of Africa, birth rates have hardly changed.". . .

It is important to take note of the large, sweeping, and dangerous ways in which population growth is reshaping Africa's future. We have already noted the growing food insecurity in Africa. Since 1978, per capita food production in Africa has fallen by 11 percent, and the United Nations Food and Agriculture Organization (FAO) predicts that by the dawn of the 21st Century, 29 African nations will be unable to feed their populations. It should surprise no one that UNICEF has found that childhood malnutrition is already on the rise in 10 African countries. During the first half of 1988, FAO provided emergency food assistance to 17 African nations, far more than to any other world region. The widening scarcity cannot be explained away simply by unfavorable weather cycles or crop failures. To keep up with its population growth, Africa would need to more than double its yearly gains in agricultural productivity. Recent history makes clear that that kind of rapid expansion is not possible. Meanwhile, Africa will need to feed an additional 20 million people, and after that an even larger increment. . . .

Rapid population growth is making Africa's economic problems dramatically worse by diluting the salving effect of foreign development assistance. With 32 out of 54 African countries doubling their populations within the next 25 years, foreign aid simply cannot keep up. Instead of paying for meaningful and lasting improvements in the African quality of life, our aid dollars right now are, in effect, subsidizing the rapid expansion of these populations. As population grows faster than national economies, quality of life declines for each person. In 1987, despite relatively favorable agricultural conditions, per capita income was stagnant or declined in 24 African nations. . . .

An Emerging African Consensus

Yet the African story is not exclusively one of despair by any means. In fact, it is the story of the remarkable convergence of great need with great opportunity. This is because leaders across Africa have increasingly come to recognize in recent years the direct links between population growth and their problems related to development, the economy, and the environment. Robert I. Rothberg, academic vice president at Tufts University and the author of *Africa in the 1990s: U.S. Policy Opportunities and Choices,* observes that there have been "steady indigenous responses to well-targeted local campaigns to limit family size" in Africa. "Reducing population growth in Africa is in our interest as a superpower," he says. "Africa's well-being increases our own."

As the needs of Africa have grown more acute with surging population growth, an emerging majority of African governments is now prepared for the first time to deal directly and humanely with the population issue. Their arrival at this consensus is no incidental achievement, for only 15 years ago most African leaders agreed that rapid population growth was a *spur* to economic development rather than a hindrance. In fact, in 1974 at the first U.N. World Population Conference, African delegates were virtually unanimous in their rejection of Western calls for reductions in population growth; some even suspected racist motivations for the sudden Western concern with African overpopulation.

The Third World Responds

That resistance has been steadily washed away, however, in the years that followed the 1974 Bucharest conference by the increasingly unmistakable impact of population growth on Third World societies. As populations swelled, schools overflowed, homelessness and unemployment soared, cities spilled out into the countryside in haphazard, unplanned growth, and per capita productivity and national wealth shrank. By the time the delegates met again 10 years later in Mexico City for the International Conference on Population, it was the Third World participants who spoke loudest about the need for an easing of population pressures. The African delegates reflected that new perspective, and throughout the 1980s more and more African governments have agreed that lasting development is possible only if population growth subsides. . . .

In the words of Under Secretary General Nafis Sadik, Executive Director of the United Nations Population Fund, "There is a growing consensus among African leaders that part of the cure for Africa's economic problems will be slower population growth and well-spaced, healthier families. This is the message they are bringing to their people. The evidence is that they are being heard.

"Family size is a personal decision. Women in Africa still want large families, compared with women in the rest of the world. Men still take pride in the size of their families. But more and more ordinary people are seeing that having many children means costs as well as benefits, and they are making their own decisions."

Ironically, however, just as the African nations have come to agree with the "Western" view taken at the 1974 Bucharest conference, the leading Western promoter of population policies has shown troubling hesitation to help. United States funding for population assistance has been slashed over the past eight years and U.S. contributions to the two leading international population aid programs—the United Nations Population Fund (UNFPA) and the International Planned Parenthood Federation (IPPF)—have been indefinitely suspended. Thus, just when the nations of Africa and the industrialized donor community should be working together at last to make their most important strides toward population stabilization and lasting development, U.S. equivocation is holding everyone back. That will have to change. The need is too urgent and the opportunities for a constructive partnership with the African leadership are too great to ignore.

> *"War, not overpopulation, is the major force disrupting economic life in Africa."*

Overpopulation Is Not the Cause of Africa's Famines

Jacqueline Kasun

Jacqueline Kasun is a noted economist and author of the book *The War Against Population: The Economics and Ideology of Population Control.* In the following viewpoint, Kasun maintains that Africa is not overpopulated, and that population growth is not the reason for Africa's food shortages. Kasun believes that war and economic mismanagement are to blame for famine. Only when these end will Africa be able to feed itself.

As you read, consider the following questions:

1. What actions by the Ethiopian government exacerbated the nation's famine, according to the author?
2. What comparison does Kasun make between Taiwan and Ethiopia?
3. How does the author show that slow population growth does not result in rapid economic growth?

Jacqueline Kasun, "Africa's Anguish: Is Overpopulation Really the Problem?" *A.L.L. About Issues*, November/December 1988. Reprinted by permission of the American Life League, Stafford, Virginia.

War, not overpopulation, is the major force disrupting economic life in Africa. In both Ethiopia and the Sudan, major civil wars have raged for years. Many farmers have become refugees or have had their crops destroyed in the fighting. Many were unable to plant or harvest. Others were unable to send their harvests through battle zones to the people who needed them. Means of transport have also been destroyed. Armed conflict is also occurring in most of the other countries of Africa.

In addition to war, most African countries are also suffering the consequences of incredibly bad economic policies on the part of their governments. In Ethiopia, for example, the government confiscated the people's food supplies in order to export them to the Soviet Union and Cuba in exchange for weapons and troops. The government of Ethiopia destroyed the indigenous network for storing food, which was the country's first line of defense against the recurrent periods of drought, and it confiscated farmer's tools and draught animals.

In Ghana, to mention another typical example, the government subsidized inefficient and corrupt state industries by creating huge amounts of new money and taxing farmers to the point where they couldn't afford to replant. The result was drastically falling output and rampant inflation, resulting in almost complete economic collapse. This debacle, like similar events in other African countries, had nothing to do with "overpopulation."

Untapped Resources

Agricultural scientists agree that Africa has the resources to produce a great deal more food than at present. A study by the Food and Agriculture Organization of the U.N. concluded that Africa could raise enough food for 10 billion people—seventeen times its present population and two times the present population of the entire world! What is lacking is not the agricultural resource base but the political climate that will protect and encourage peaceful production.

Throughout Africa rich agricultural resources go unused. In Kenya, for example, less than half of its agricultural land is in use.

Werner Fornos simply asserts, without proof or evidence, that "surging population" is the root of all evils in the Third World, and then proceeds to describe ways to reduce population growth. Any response should point out this lack of supporting evidence, and should point out the evidence, cited above, that war and bad economic policy are the real reasons for poverty and hunger.

It should also be noted that although the population of Africa may be growing more rapidly than the more developed nations (this can't be claimed with certainty because the published figures may not fully show the effects of war and famine), the size and density of the African population is still not very large: a population about a fifth larger than that of Europe scattered over a vast continent six times as large as Europe, at an average density of 50 persons per square mile, compared with the 262 per square mile in Europe.

The True Size of Africa

Is Africa over-populated? So much has been published about total population levels in starving countries that the true extent of the numbers affected has been forgotten. . . .

So many figures are tossed around without comparing them to anything recognizable that the average person is left with the view of Africa as a continent teeming with wall-to-wall human beings, all of them with swollen bellies and matchstick limbs. How many people can picture the true size of the African continent? Would you believe it's larger than the United States, Europe (excluding Russia), and China all put together—and China and the United States, each one alone, is twice the size of Europe (again, excluding Russia)? And how many people live in Africa? One-third as many as in the United States, Europe, and China combined. Over-populated? Not by any stretch of any reasonable person's imagination.

Population Renewal Office, *Out of Africa: Some Population Truths*, 1989.

Many very thickly populated countries enjoy great wealth and productivity—for example, the Netherlands (922 per square mile), West Germany (633), Japan (845), Taiwan (1412), Hong Kong (13,562), Singapore (11,536)—indicating that population is not a barrier to affluence.

Nor is rapid population growth a deterrent to economic progress. For example, between 1960 and 1986 the populations of Ethiopia and Taiwan both approximately doubled in size. As we know, Ethiopia experienced war, economic devastation, and famine. Taiwan, however, experienced rapid, peaceful economic growth and great prosperity. By 1983 Taiwan had a per capita output of almost $2700, compared with less than $150 in Ethiopia. Ethiopia is rich in resources, traditionally an exporter of agricultural products. Taiwan has only a scrap of rice land to support a population that is fifteen times as thickly settled as Ethiopia's.

Even more importantly, perhaps, slow population growth does not cause more rapid economic growth. Mainland China, for example, has used ruthless measures for years to try to reduce births, and has apparently succeeded in keeping population growth well below that of Taiwan. Its economic performance, however, has been dismal, and its per capita output is about one-seventh as large as Taiwan's—though Taiwan has five times as many people per square mile as China.

Birth Controllers: Feasting on the Famine

Those who have some understanding of economic development know that population growth has little to do with it. What really matters is whether ordinary people are allowed to provide for themselves and their families in peace, free from the devastation of war and oppressive governments. This is what the people of Ethiopia have not had.

It is tragic that, in addition to their other misfortunes, the people of Ethiopia should now be blamed for "overpopulating" by the special interest groups who hope to turn the famine to their own advantage by collecting millions of dollars in U.S. grants for birth control.

"The solutions to Africa's food supply problems can only be found in African villages. "

Africans Themselves Can Reduce Famine

Pierre Pradervand

Pierre Pradervand, an educator in Switzerland, has been active in the field of development for more than twenty-five years as a researcher, program administrator, publisher, and coeditor of *Famille et Developpement*, an African grassroots development magazine. In the following viewpoint, Pradervand expresses his belief that Africans have the skills and knowledge to reduce famine without outside aid. Rather than importing agricultural methods and seeds from the West, Africans can rely on traditional practices to increase productivity and decrease hunger.

As you read, consider the following questions:

1. How have some African farmers compensated for decreased grain production, according to Pradervand?
2. The author explains that many African farmers oppose the use of chemical fertilizers. Why?
3. Why does Pradervand believe it is important to not view Africans as victims?

Abridged from Pierre Pradervand, *Listening to Africa: Developing Africa from the Grassroots* (Praeger Publishers, New York, an imprint of Greenwood Publishing Group, Inc., 1989). Reprinted with permission of the author and Greenwood Publishing Group, Inc. All rights reserved.

In May of 1987, Paul T. Ilboudo, one of the fathers of the literacy program in Burkina Faso, and I were driving together to the village of Nomgana, where I was to meet the villagers. Burkina Faso is commonly cited as one of the poorest countries in the world. It faces colossal environmental problems, a stagnating economy, and a fairly heavy national debt. Its population, which is 90 percent illiterate, is growing fast (2.8 percent per year). At one point during the drive, I asked, "Paul, what are the hopeful developments you see in your country?" He had this amazing reply: "There are so many, I don't know where to start."

For the past 10 to 15 years, Africa has seen remarkable developments that can explain a reply as unexpected as that of Paul Ilboudo. New energies, new experiences, a burst of creativity, a courage defying explanation are being manifested by millions of people. In the villages, especially, a silent revolution is underway that is completely changing the continent's development landscape. In tropical Africa, literally millions of farmers have moved to take their future into their own hands and to reclaim the self-reliance that was theirs until the disruption of colonial occupation and the post-Independence era of rapid modernization. As the result of the tens of thousands of small village projects that they have initiated, these farmers are improving their own living conditions, sometimes with no outside help. In many areas, village self-help groups are joining together to create powerful organizations, which for the first time can speak out in their own interest.

Yet many people outside Africa have heard little of these changes, the awakening of this extraordinary and rich continent with its virtually untapped human and material resources. This has been written to stand as a record of this silent revolution that could be the greatest sign of hope in Africa today. It is an attempt to put aside clichés and to listen to Africa. Listen to these farmers describe their challenges and how they are meeting them. Listen to the optimism they express despite the obstacles they face. Listen to their desire to create their own patterns of development and to establish a new relationship with the rest of the world in a climate of mutual respect. Listen and learn of their courage and creativity, their integrity and resilience, their dignity, vitality, and their joy. . . .

The Food Supply

When I started off on my trip in 1987, I was certain that wherever I went, at least in the Sahel, I would find food scarce. Available statistics all pointed to a decrease in per capita food production over the past 15 years. I was astonished, then, by the number of villages where the facts ran counter to the information I had read and to my preconceptions.

"There has been a substantial improvement since people started eating vegetables. Before, we used to eat tô (tô is a millet-based staple common to many parts of Burkina Faso), tô, and still more tô, every day. Now, each day we eat something different," the members of the Naam group in Kongoussi explain. "The food supply has been greatly improved in our village. Families now have a regular supply of food, and vegetable gardening has enriched our diets," say the farmers of the Foyer de Kheune, in the Walo region of Northern Senegal.

Africans Educate Themselves

As the state has become increasingly irrelevant in the eyes of ordinary Africans, traditional institutions have begun to assume greater responsibility in facilitating the creative adaptation of the poor. In many communities, emphasis has shifted from production of export crops to foodstuffs. Farmers market their produce through their own channels, disregarding political boundaries and marketing boards. They also substitute local products for commodities formerly purchased from stores.

The importance of such local initiatives for building a more democratic state, responsive to the needs of peasants and workers, should not be underestimated. Through defining their own needs and designing and implementing their own projects collectively, ordinary Africans are educating themselves in organizational dynamics and self-government.

Fantu Cheru, *The Silent Revolution in Africa*, 1989.

With the help of the village groups, the farmers have compensated for the decrease in grain production by producing alternative foods and by making wiser use of available resources (e.g., the dried wild fruits of the 2 x F Committee). Unfortunately, these are never included in official statistics. The efforts of the village groups that started market gardening have resulted in real improvements. The decrease in grain production has been offset by the purchase of rice paid for with the income from the peanuts and garden produce. "The improvement is as much on the level of food variety as the quantity of food available," explained the members of the Kouté-Diomboulou AJAC group, in the Casamance region.

"Before, food was more abundant but much less varied," said the women of the Séguénéga Naam group. "Now we eat better than before [and here they gave me a list of the vegetables and other foods, such as pasta, that they had never eaten before the 1971-73 drought]. Before there was more millet to eat, but sauces were not as tasty. We ate more, but we also wasted a lot of food. Since then we have learned to manage available food supplies better."

The decrease in grain production has been partially compensated by an increase in vegetable production. During the famine year of 1984, the 54 Naam groups in the area around Ouahigouya produced 300 tons of vegetables, including 100 tons of potatoes. This vegetable production saved many lives. This result is all the more encouraging if one takes into account that as recently as 10 years ago most of these farmers knew nothing of market gardening and had to learn everything, from planting techniques to marketing, from scratch. . . .

Soil Conservation Strategies

At a meeting I attended in Thiès, Senegal, in January 1987, organized by FONGS, an umbrella organization of peasant federations in Senegal, 30 peasant leaders outlined, in about two hours, a soil conservation strategy for their regions. Such a strategy is crucial in attaining self-sufficiency in food supply in the Sahel. It corresponds to the experience and the convictions of the peasants themselves, and thus they are prepared to explain and defend it in their villages. Strategies imported from outside, which might be theoretically correct but without the whole-hearted backing of the farmers, have proven to be of little use.

The 30 peasant leaders decided that first farmers must limit the size of their fields and herds. This implies moving from an "extensive" to an "intensive" model of agriculture and livestock breeding. Organic manure and compost should be used whenever possible instead of chemical fertilizers (which, with the exception of Zimbabwe, are in any case far too expensive for most peasants). Only as a last recourse (and participants in the meeting insisted on this) was a moderate use of chemical fertilizer acceptable, but only when there was not enough natural compost available. "We have to use first of all what we know and give preference to what is natural," the participants stressed. Surprisingly, the strongest argument against the use of chemical fertilizers was that "the use of fertilizers encourages laziness." Making compost, on the other hand, can be a demanding task, especially when raw materials are hard to come by, and requires more of the farmer's time than the use of chemical fertilizers. Farmers were encouraged to undertake their own research on natural methods of protection against insects. Not only do chemical pesticides ultimately contaminate underground water, but they produce pesticide-resistant insects. They are also expensive (for African farmers, such costs are usually prohibitive).

Crop rotation should be introduced on a regular basis, as it enables a natural regeneration of the soil. Participants also stressed that farmers should make better use of open spaces and organize them more rationally. This means avoiding over-grazing (a common problem in Africa), and planting hedges to limit wind erosion. (It is ironic that in the still recent past, at least in some areas of the Sahel, agricultural technicians were telling the peasants to cut down their hedges, uproot all the trees and give top priority to monoculture, which explains why the soils are totally leached and sterile.) Participants at the meeting also insisted on reforestation, which must become a top priority everywhere in the Sahel, and many other areas of Africa. Also, peasant organizations must encourage farmers to allow their fields to lie fallow for a few years, so that the soil may regenerate naturally. This was widely practiced in precolonial times, but is now possible only if farmers return to more intensive methods of cultivation.

Villages Hold the Solutions

Faced with this down-to-earth peasant common sense, one cannot help thinking of a statement made by Wendell Berry (1981), the American farmer and writer, who in *The Gift of Good Land* wrote: "Solutions have perhaps the most furtive habits of all creatures; they reveal themselves very hesitantly in artificial light, and never enter air-conditioned rooms." One wonders how many high-level committees have met since the 1971-73 drought to discuss the issue of soil regeneration—probably the most pressing agricultural issue in Africa today; how many experts have traveled through the Sahel; how many reports have been written, and how many millions of dollars spent on documents, which, in the best of cases, have had only a marginal impact. Yet is it not logical that the solutions to Africa's food supply problems can only be found in African villages, in collaboration with the continent's top agricultural experts—the farmers who produce the food? . . .

No More Victims

We don't have any means of locomotion. We are fueled by courage.

Wandifa Sama, 2 x F Committee, Kenyeto

You may not be responsible for being down, but you are responsible for getting up.

Reverend Jesse Jackson, speaking to black school children in the United States

There is a tendency in a certain kind of development literature to present the Third World farmers as victims—victims of colonialism, of the tropical climate, of multinationals, of oppressive elites of their countries, of the terms of trade, and more. It is clear that none of these difficulties have made their plight easier.

What is remarkable is that growing numbers of peasant leaders are refusing the kind of analysis that would depict them as victims. For a victim is someone to be pitied, someone who needs a good Samaritan to help him. When someone is presented as a victim, it is easier to request aid for him and easier to present oneself as a savior. "Some Northern NGOs [nongovernmental organizations] see themselves as the saviors of Africa. That is one of the reasons they are not too pleased to see us appear in the field," comments a dynamic African woman, the founder of a native Sahelian NGO. It is this very paternalistic stand which has helped engender so many unhealthy attitudes toward the Third World. Yet such attitudes exclude *a priori* any possibility of creative partnership, because one cannot be the partner of a victim, only his savior.

Coping With Crises

The Northern media image of African people as helpless victims, passively accepting events around them, is false. It is an image which African people do not recognize and which draws their anger and disgust when used by Northern relief agencies to raise funds. Because of their experiences with their world, Africans have developed a variety of alternative means to deal with food and water shortages, with economic contractions and governmental neglect or abuse.

Bill Rau, *From Feast to Famine*, 1991.

Twice during my conversations with peasant leaders, they vigorously criticized the unjust mechanisms of international trade, which lead to the absurd situation where the least developed countries in the world are contributing to the growth of economies where waste has become the everyday norm. Yet, despite these leaders' awareness of the immense challenges African farmers have to meet, they simply refused to consider themselves as victims.

More and more, Africans are asking for a real partnership. Fortunately, at least some foreign NGOs have realized this and are changing. Even if, as an African in a responsible position in one of the world's largest Western NGOs told me, "converting the ways of thinking of the NGOs is much more difficult than converting the ways of thinking of the farmers." Partnership implies that the partners really consider themselves as equals. If that is to be more than simply a statement of intent, it means, for example, enabling the partner to spend funds in the way he deems best, even if it does not always correspond to the view of the donor. It implies that each one assumes the full responsibility, if not for the material conditions of his environment, at least of his response to these conditions. To paraphrase Jesse Jackson, one may not be responsible for being born into poverty, but one is responsible for either putting up with one's plight with resignation or deciding to do something about it. . . .

The Daring of Vision

We are very optimistic concerning the possibility we have of resolving our own problems. If we continue as in recent years, we will have eliminated hunger in seven to ten years, and we will by then be self-reliant in food production.

A farmer from the region of Diogo, Senegal

We will succeed in eliminating hunger because we have got together, and we are going to achieve all that we decide together.

Barry Minata of the Naam women's group in Séguénéga, Burkina Faso

Patiind Yaandé [We don't know failure]

—Name of a Naam peasant group

For many people in the world, ending hunger by the year 2000 appears to be totally utopian—or a possibility, but a possibility that may not be achieved because of widespread resignation, indifference, or apathy.

This is certainly not the opinion of the farmers I talked to, perhaps because they know what it means to be hungry. Hunger adds a certain urgency to the matter! For these farmers, the debate on ending hunger is not theoretical, but a real part of their daily struggle. As Barlo Diedhiou, one of the founders of the 2 x F Committee, put it: "If we really want to eliminate hunger, we can. It all depends on us—on our motivation, our commitment." Other peasant organizations in Africa also believe in the possibility of ending hunger by the year 2000. When asked about the possibility of reaching this goal, Mamadou Cissokho told me:

The year 2000? But that's too far away! Here in Bamba-Tialène, our food stocks already represent 30 percent of our yearly consumption. And the recent harvest will enable us to reach 60 percent. If rainfall is adequate, we can end hunger in the coming ten years, not only in our village, but in all the regions of Senegal that work with us. You see, we share the same philosophy: 50 percent of the harvest of communal fields is automatically stored [as buffer stocks], and past food aid is also added to food reserves, i.e. farmers reimburse in kind food aid received during the 1984-85 famine. In addition, each farmer has to contribute compulsory savings in cash.

In January 1987, less than three months later, I was again in Bamba-Tialène. In a region where in 1984 farmers had been eating their seeds and their bullocks and selling their plows to survive, I saw an amount of grain in the storage depot that corresponded to 60 percent of the village's annual needs. Bourama

Diémé, one of the managers of the Committee, commented that "with the peasant movement, nothing is impossible. It's all a question of patience."

A Bright Future

This optimism of the farmers struck me constantly. . . . For these peasant leaders, be it Tanyanuiwa Kusema in Zimbabwe or Abdoulaye Diop in Senegal, optimism is a pedagogical imperative: one can only mobilize people through hope, with a vision. As a leading Sahelian peasant leader explained:

> I believe in the end of hunger because I have no other choice. My whole being, all my people, are involved in this struggle. Without this vision of the end of hunger, it's not even worthwhile making any plans, marrying, having children. Your whole life is literally immobilized. Because I've known hunger, I have no reason to exist if I am not optimistic. The day I lose my optimism, I lose the very meaning of my struggle.

What if we accepted the goal of a world free from hunger by the year 2000? Our peasant partners from the Sahel are challenging us to accept it by the very fact of their holding it as an achievable aim. . . .

Are we, citizens of this planet, going to accept the challenge?

"[African] famines . . . are primarily human rights disasters."

Promoting Human Rights Can Reduce Famine

Alex de Waal

Africa's famines are caused less by nature than by wars and political oppression, Alex de Waal asserts in the following viewpoint. Wars in Ethiopia and other African nations have displaced thousands of people from their farms, causing widespread hunger in these nations. Only by promoting peace and human rights can Africa be freed from famine. De Waal is the author of *Famine That Kills: Darfur, Sudan, 1984-1985.*

As you read, consider the following questions:

1. Why does de Waal believe that freedom of the press is an integral part of ending famine in Africa?
2. How do arms sales contribute to Africa's famine, according to the author?
3. What caused Ethiopia's 1983-1985 famine, in the author's opinion?

Alex de Waal, "A Human Rights Agenda to Prevent Starvation in Africa," *Peace and Democracy News*, Summer 1991. Reprinted by permission.

Famine is preventable. Countries such as India and Botswana have shown that, even in the face of chronic poverty and repeated drought, famine can be prevented. With a measure of political will and technical and managerial skill, effective mechanisms for preventing mass starvation are relatively straightforward. Yet, year after year, famines still afflict the people of a dozen countries in Africa. Billions of dollars of relief and development aid have been poured into these countries, but relief agencies still show us distressing pictures of stick-thin children and their pathetic mothers and tell us that our money is needed to save their lives. Nature seems to have been particularly unkind to these countries, in denying them either the resources with which to sustain their populations or the human skills necessary to exploit those resources.

Journalists, relief agencies, and African governments continue to present these famines as natural disasters and humanitarian tragedies. Western donors—both governments and the general public—continue to respond with material and technical assistance. However, the problems still persist, and many observers are becoming extremely pessimistic, even to the extent of wondering whether it is worth keeping all these people alive if they are simply going to be thrown on our mercy time and again for the foreseeable future. This pessimism carries with it an implicit agenda: that far more draconian measures are needed, namely massive involuntary population control by means of compulsory family planning, forcible relocation, or simply leaving people to starve. Such actions (or willful neglect) would be not only unethical, but close examination of the causes and nature of famines shows that they would also be unnecessary and ineffective.

Why cannot the Indian or Botswanan success be repeated in, say, Sudan? Are the roads that much worse, the climate that much harsher, the overpopulation too great, or the people that much more apathetic? The answer to each of these questions is no.

Famine as a Human Rights Disaster

The truth is that these famines are not natural disasters, nor are they linked to so-called "overpopulation," and as a result, the assistance given has been consistently inappropriate. The famines in Ethiopia, Sudan, Angola and Mozambique are primarily human rights disasters. Blame lies with political and military systems. If this is recognized and the governments (and rebel movements contending for power) in these countries come to give a greater respect to human rights, famine prevention will become a much simpler task. The reason why solutions to famine in Africa have been so elusive is that our analysis of these famines has been grossly inadequate. A wrong diagnosis has led to a wrong prescription. Material assistance—and this includes not only short-term relief but long-term "development" aid—in such a situation is merely a bandage on a wound that continues to fester. The bandage will continue to be necessary, but medicine is also needed to treat the sickness that underlies famine: massive human rights abuse.

The human rights agenda for famine relief in Africa contains three main items: democratic accountability, arms expenditure, and the humanitarian laws of war.

Democracy and the Free Press

The first aspect of the human rights agenda in famine relief is democratic accountability. Governments which are held accountable by a free press and elected representatives do not allow famines to occur.

There is a lesson here from the history of India. In the days of the British Raj, the colonial government drew up the Indian Famine Codes, sophisticated procedures to be brought into effect when famine threatened. Relief was provided in the form of paid employment on public works, and the laborers then bought food on the open market; the size of India meant that food could be brought in from other famine-free regions. Free food was given to those unable to work. The whole system was triggered by a complex "intelligence" or "early-warning" system based upon careful observation of the harvest, food prices, migrations of people, and other indicators of social distress. This system worked well, except that in one notorious case (Bengal in 1943) the government did not implement it, and over one million people died.

At the achievement of independence, the Indian government kept the system essentially intact, with one major change. The early-warning system was dropped. It was no longer needed. Famine is a sensitive political issue in India. If a food scarcity threatens, the free press will alert the public to the fact and pillory any politician who fails to take heed. Elected representatives stand in danger of being voted out by their constituents if they fail to prod the government into action. India has not suffered a famine since independence, despite an average level of food consumption lower than many African countries. An open, adversarial political system with a free press has proved to be a far better means of warning of famines than the most sophisticated technically based data-gathering and processing system.

The African countries where famine has occurred have not been blessed with any such democratic political system. Ethiopia, for example, is a one-party state with total government control of the press and no freedoms of association or assembly allowed. The government department responsible for famine warning and relief is generally recognized as one of the most efficient in Africa—for instance, it warned of the 1984-5 famine two years in advance—but the government feels no compunction to act on the information provided. If the government does act, it turns the famine to its political and military advantage, using the weakened state of the rural people as an opportunity for forced removals and regroupings. Meanwhile, the estimates of food needs provided by the Relief and Rehabilitation Commission are simply turned over to Western donors in the hope that they will provide food; if they do not, the government does not mobilize any reserves of its own for humanitarian assistance.

© 1989 John Trever/*The Albuquerque Journal*. Reprinted with permission.

Sudan suffered famine in 1984-5, again in 1988, and is today facing a famine more severe and widespread than either. In 1984-5, then-President Nimeiri refused to recognize the existence of the famine and ask for assistance until four months after the huge scale of the crisis had been evident. Organizations such as the Sudan Doctors' Union, which tried to pressure the government to act, were suppressed. The 1988 famine occurred as a consequence of civil war in the south of Sudan. This was a time when Sudan was enjoying a parliamentary government with an uncensored press, and so would seem to be a counter-example to the rule suggested. However, press and parliamentarians were concerned only with the protection of the rights of northern Sudanese; famine in the rebellious southern Sudan was an issue of minor interest in Khartoum politics. The current famine has taken place during the repressive rule of a military government which exported the country's strategic food reserve in early 1990 and—in an echo of 1984-5—refused to declare a famine even when a food shortage of one million tons became evident in late 1990.

By contrast, African countries with a measure of democratic accountability have succeeded, against similar or greater odds, in avoiding famine. Cape Verde and Botswana are prime examples; Kenya, Tanzania and Zimbabwe also contain elements of the same safeguards.

Arms Expenditure

The second element in the human rights agenda concerns the economic bankruptcy that follows massive expenditure on armaments. This expenditure diverts money from basic development and health programs and ultimately renders the state insolvent, unable to provide even the most essential services, and politically unstable. During the 1980s the Ethiopian government consistently spent more than half of its annual budget on prosecuting the war and ran up billions of dollars of debt to its major arms supplier, the USSR. Other governments spend smaller but also massive amounts. Another case is Sudan, where the economic crisis brought on largely by war brought down an elected government in 1989, to be replaced by a military dictatorship. The military rulers then proceeded to export its grain reserve to obtain hard currency with which to intensify the war.

Counter-Population Warfare

The third item on the agenda concerns the respect for human rights in war. War is the most important cause of famine in Africa. This observation is often made, but less often refined. Some wars create famine, others do not. Wars fought between well-defined regular armies may cause upheavals for civilian life, and civilian casualties as a result of people being caught in the crossfire, but they do not generally create famine. The wars between Ethiopia and Somalia in 1977-8 and Tanzania and Uganda in 1979 are two examples.

Counter-population wars (usually civil wars), on the other hand, do create famine. In some cases, insurgent groups deliberately destroy economic infrastructure, terrorize civilian populations, and lay siege to towns, creating famine conditions. RENAMO in Mozambique is a good example of such a movement. More commonly, government counter-insurgency strategies are aimed at making it impossible for popularly based rebel movements to operate, by strictly controlling the activities and movements of the people or by removing them from the insurgency zone. Such counter-insurgency methods have been associated with the most severe famines Africa has seen.

The classic example of this is the famine in southern Sudan, which reached its nadir in 1988. The first signs of famine were seen in government-controlled towns in 1985-6, as a result of the activities of the rebel Sudan People's Liberation Army (SPLA), which cut off these towns from external supplies. However, the major cause of the famine was the government policy of arming militias from among the tribes sympathetic to the government and encouraging them to go and attack the civilian population believed to be sympathetic to the SPLA. From 1985 to 1988 there was massed militia raiding, in which tens of thousands of people were killed. Crops were destroyed and grain stores burned. Fruit trees were cut down. Cattle were stolen. Children were taken into slavery.

With their economic base destroyed, hundreds of thousands of people were forced to leave their homes to seek work or charity in the towns of northern Sudan: this meant traveling into the territory of the raiders themselves. The militia robbed the famine migrants of the last of their possessions and prevented them from following the "survival strategies" that rural people normally follow in order to survive hard times: collecting wild foods from the bush, collecting and selling firewood, working for money on farms, seeking out charity. The army also prevented food aid from reaching the famine victims: internationally donated relief grain stood idle in railway wagons, sometimes only a mile away from the starving migrants. In the summer of 1988, death rates in some of the famine camps reached the extraordinary levels of one percent per day: had not the population been replenished by a continual inflow of new migrants, the camps would simply have become graveyards.

These astronomic death rates contrast with the levels of mortality which occurred in the same region during the famine of 1984-5, caused largely by drought. In this famine, the rural Sudanese were able to husband their resources, market their animals, travel to find work and charity, collect wild foods, and return to their farms to plant when the rains came. Death rates were more than twice as high as normal, at between four and six percent per year. One percent per day is about 60 times as high as these levels.

Drought Cannot Be Blamed

The Ethiopian famine of 1983-5 is another example of a counter-insurgency famine, though in this case there was also a severe drought at the same time. To understand why the drought cannot be labeled as the sole culprit, we must recall what occurred in Sudan at the same time. In Sudan the drought was more severe, but the death rates were kept down largely by the rural people's own skill and tenacity. We should also note what happened after the severe drought of 1987 in northern Ethiopia: famine was predicted, meager amounts of aid were delivered to the affected area, but famine did not materialize. The reason was that in 1987-8 the rural people of northern Ethiopia were able to utilize their time-honored strategies of traveling to find work and food in the adjoining areas of the Ethiopian highlands—which always produce a surplus, even in the driest year. The reason why they were able to do this in 1987-8 was that by this time the Ethiopian army was no longer able to mount counter-insurgency operations in the countryside, for it was on the defensive in the face of rebel advances.

Political Phenomena

Much of the world seems to have fatuously accepted the official claim that Ethiopia's famine and the one million deaths were, as Ethiopia's ambassador to the United Nations puts it, "adversities caused by environmental factors." This stems from deeply rooted contemporary belief that world hunger is primarily a product of natural failures: too little rain, too many people, mysterious "desertification," bad soil, bad luck.

Yet it took willful acts of men to turn acts of nature into calamity. Absent a larger, overriding political breakdown, environmental factors do not now cause people to suffer and die from malnutrition. . . .

Today (and it has been true for most of this century), famine deaths are political, not natural, phenomena. And it is political change that will end and prevent them.

Karl Zinsmeister, *Reason*, June 1988.

It was the Ethiopian government's counter-insurgency tactics in 1983-5 that turned a drought, which would have created hardship, into a severe famine, in which hundreds of thousands died. The first signs of serious famine appeared in March 1983. This came as something of a surprise, since the harvest which was gathered in at the end of 1982 was the best in years. There were pockets of drought, as there always are in the Ethiopian highlands, and it was assumed that the drought-affected farmers would be able to migrate for work in the surplus areas or sell animals and buy grain from traders. But in February 1983, the government launched a huge military offensive into the largest surplus-producing district of northern Ethiopia (Shire in western Tigray). About 100,000 surplus-producing farmers were forced to abandon their homes, and the migrants who had come looking for work had to turn round and go home—or go to relief camps.

At the same time, a set of restrictions was imposed upon migrants in general and petty traders in particular. Thousands of donkey traders should have been active buying grain in surplus areas and selling it in deficit areas. In the name of controlling rebels, the traders were not allowed to move. The inhabitants of the deficit zones had no alternative but to sell their possessions—including disposing of precious plough oxen, which amounts to a form of agrarian suicide—and buy the scarce food that was available at increasingly high prices.

Thus was the famine set in motion. It was intensified by drought and by a tightening of restrictions, bombing of marketplaces, and further military campaigns. The notorious program for compulsory resettlement of 600,000 farmers from the northern highlands to southern Ethiopia was only one of a number of measures which deterred rural people from traveling to towns to buy food or receive relief. Ironically, the great majority of the aid provided by Western governments and relief agencies went to the isolated pockets of the famine-stricken area were controlled by the Ethiopian army (indeed, much also went to the soldiers and militiamen themselves), allowing the government to exert even closer control over the hungry rural population. The famine period saw the Ethiopian army expand the area under its control. When counter-attacking, the rebels showed little compunction in attacking relief convoys along with military targets.

A Code of Conduct

War-created famine will cease if wars cease. Unfortunately, Africa's protracted wars appear to be exceptionally difficult to resolve. In the meantime, a code of conduct for war, akin to the Geneva Conventions, is needed to prevent armies and guerrillas from perpetrating the kind of counter-population warfare that creates famine. . . .

When relief agencies and Western governments at last correctly identify famines as human rights disasters, a new and much more effective agenda for famine prevention will become clear. The conquest of famine in Africa will suddenly become much closer than was realized.

Recognizing Statements That Are Provable

We are constantly confronted with statements and generalizations about social and moral problems. In order to think clearly about these problems, it is useful if one can make a basic distinction between statements for which evidence can be found and other statements which cannot be verified or proved because evidence is not available, or the issue is so controversial that it cannot be definitely proved.

Readers should be aware that magazines, newspapers, and other sources often contain statements of a controversial nature. The following activity is designed to allow experimentation with statements that are provable and those that are not.

The following statements are taken from the viewpoints in this chapter. Consider each statement carefully. *Mark P for any statement you believe is provable. Mark U for any statement you feel is unprovable because of the lack of evidence. Mark C for any statement you think is too controversial to be proved to everyone's satisfaction.*

If you are doing this activity as a member of a class or group, compare your answers with those of other class or group members. Be able to defend your answers. You may discover that others will come to different conclusions than you do. Listening to the reasons others present for their answers may give you valuable insights into recognizing statements that are provable.

P = *provable*
U = *unprovable*
C = *too controversial*

1. Nineteen eighty-six was a good year for rainfall and for agricultural production in Ethiopia.

2. The economies that are vulnerable to famines are predominently agrarian and poor.

3. Part of the cure for Africa's economic problems will be slower population growth and healthier families.

4. An early warning system will prevent famine and save countless human lives.

5. The 1988 Sudanese famine occurred as a consequence of civil war in the south of Sudan.

6. India has not suffered a famine since independence, despite an average level of food consumption lower than many African countries.

7. Droughts are a natural phenomenon; famines are not.

8. The political nature of famines makes a proper response more difficult to achieve.

9. Popular Western notions about Africa remain vague and misshapen by decades of fiction, racism, and Tarzan movies.

10. In many African countries, infant mortality has been cut by half in the past thirty years. Twenty years have been added to the average expectation of life.

11. Rapid population growth is making Africa's economic problems dramatically worse.

12. There were numerous droughts in the 1820s and 1830s in southern Africa.

13. U.S. funding for population assistance has been slashed over the past eight years.

14. Africa has the resources to produce a great deal more food than it produces at present.

15. The Ethiopian government confiscated food supplies to export them to the Soviet Union and Cuba in exchange for weapons and troops.

16. India and Botswana have shown that, even in the face of chronic poverty and repeated drought, famine can be prevented.

17. Donating grain to famine-stricken Ethiopia in the 1980s would have brought down its government and caused a military coup.

Periodical Bibliography

The following articles have been selected to supplement the diverse views presented in this chapter.

Edward B. Barbier	"Sustaining Agriculture on Marginal Land," *Environment*, vol. 31, no. 9, November 1989.
Nick Cater	"The Forgotten Famine," *Africa Report*, May/June 1991.
Carole Collins and Steve Askin	"What About Africa?" *The Progressive*, June 1991.
Fabrizio del Peiro	"Satellite Help Against Famine," *The World & I*, September 1990.
Michael J. Dover and Lee M. Talbot	"Feeding the Earth: An Agroecological Solution," *Technology Review*, February/March 1988.
Thomas J. Goliber	"Africa's Expanding Population: Old Problems, New Policies," *Population Bulletin*, vol. 44, no. 3, November 1989. Available from the Population Reference Bureau, Circulation Department, 777 14th St. NW, Washington, DC 20005.
Hans Hurni, interviewed by Silvia Honer	"Helping Africa End Its Famine," *World Press Review*, July 1991.
Kathy McAfee	"Why the Third World Goes Hungry," *Commonweal*, June 15, 1990.
Colleen Lowe Morna	"Beyond the Drought," *Africa Report*, November/December 1989.
Bede N. Okigbo	"Finding Solutions to the Food Crisis," *Africa Report*, September/October 1988.
David Osterfeld	"Africa and the Difference Between Growing Food and Eating It," *The Freeman*, May 1988. Available from the Foundation for Economic Education, Irvington-on-Hudson, NY 10533.
Tom Post	"Disaster Fatigue," *Newsweek*, May 13, 1991.
Richard F. Schubert	"Africa, Famine, and Compassion Fatigue," *Vital Speeches of the Day*, June 1, 1988.
Jill Smolowe	"Death by Starvation," *Time*, January 22, 1990.
Irwin Tang	"The Forgotten," *The Nation*, September 30, 1991.
Karl Zinsmeister	"All the Hungry People," *Reason*, June 1988. Available from PO Box 526, Mt. Morris, IL 61054.

Can Western Aid Help Africa?

Chapter Preface

The United States annually provides African nations with more than one billion dollars in aid. Of this, approximately 75 percent is economic aid, 16 percent is food, 6 percent goes to the Peace Corps, and 3 percent is military aid. Other Western nations and organizations also donate food and financial aid to Africa. While those who give aid may have good intentions, the effect of aid on Africans is a controversial subject: Some experts believe aid decreases Africa's poverty, but others believe it exacerbates the region's problems.

Those who favor Western aid say it eases hunger and bolsters African economies by helping develop industry and business. The U.S. State Department, for example, argues that "Aid programs in Africa are reaping huge dividends," including Africans well educated in new agricultural technologies. They also cite the fact that aid provides education and health care to African women and children, and consequently improves their quality of life. Some African experts believe aid also leads to effective restructuring of the region's economies by encouraging Africans to develop a free-market system and private enterprise instead of depending on state-run economies. Once these are created, some aid experts believe, Africans will be on their way to bringing themselves out of poverty.

Others are less enthusiastic about the long-term effects of aid. "Money alone has not solved Africa's problems and, in many instances, may actually have made things worse," states Jessica Tuchman Mathews, vice president of the World Resources Institute. Mathews and others argue that aid money is often misdirected into projects that do not help Africans. For example, some aid projects encourage African farmers to adopt Western crops and farming techniques. Unfortunately, these crops and techniques have sometimes proved to be unsuitable to the soil and climate of Africa. Aid is also criticized for helping Africans only in the short term, not teaching them how to make changes that would allow them to sustain themselves in the future. Heritage Foundation analyst Michael Johns states: "Foreign aid and credits sent to Africa, while good intentioned, have failed to spark economic growth. . . . African economies have actually shrunk."

While many Western nations and organizations want to assist Africa, the effects of this assistance are controversial. Critics of aid argue that it only pushes Africa deeper into poverty, but supporters believe that without aid, Africa would be even poorer. The authors in the following chapter debate the consequences of foreign aid to Africa.

"Food aid could make a significant contribution to turning Africa back from crisis."

International Aid Can Reduce Famine

Hans Singer

Providing food to famine-stricken regions of Africa is a necessary and effective way of reducing hunger, Hans Singer argues in the following viewpoint. Food aid not only provides Africans with food, it also gives them a commodity to sell. With the profits from selling food, African nations can finance development projects that will strengthen their economies and help prevent future famines. Singer is professor emeritus at the University of Sussex in England and Fellow of the Institute of Development Studies.

As you read, consider the following questions:

1. What comparisons does Singer make between famine in India and famine in Africa?
2. Why does the author believe it is feasible to increase food aid to Africa by eight million tons?
3. What does Singer mean when he refers to "triangular transactions"?

From "The Role of Food Aid" by Hans Singer, in *Towards Economic Recovery in Sub-Saharan Africa*, James Pickett and Hans Singer, eds. Reprinted by permission of Routledge, London.

Increasing food insecurity has been a disturbing feature of the economic malaise in sub-Saharan Africa. The evidence is more fragmentary and less robust than could be wished, but there is reason to believe that the number of people without enough to eat, on minimal nutritional standards, is growing absolutely and relatively. Moreover this hunger shows every sign of becoming chronic unless significant and specific countermeasures are put into effect. Identifying some of these, particularly under the rubric of food aid, is the main purpose of this [viewpoint]. Before doing so, however, it is important to be sure that the food crisis has not spontaneously subsided, that it would not disappear if—other things being equal—there were to be a sustained period of good weather. This is a significant point, so that it deserves to be spelled out. Most agriculture in sub-Saharan Africa is rain-fed, and output is positively correlated with the weather. The present contention, however, is that, as things are, a growing number of Africans are dangerously hungry, even in years when rainfall is timely and adequate.

In this regard the first point to establish is that the African food crisis goes back at least twenty-five years. It did not start with the Ethiopian emergency in 1984, with the harrowing pictures on television and the harrowing stories on radio, and when the general public suddenly became acutely aware of the fact that many people, and particularly many children, were actually starving to death. The turning point can in fact be located in 1962. Until then sub-Saharan Africa had been a net food exporter. In that year the region became a net importer, and since then the net import requirements of food in sub-Saharan Africa have steadily increased. If present trends continue, they are projected to reach 35 million tons by the year 2000, which is only a decade or so away.

A Comparison to India

To understand the enormity of this change, consider the contrast with India. In 1960 sub-Saharan Africa and India both produced 50 million tons of food grains. Today India produces 150 million tons—having trebled its food production since 1960, largely as a result of the green revolution, and of associated technological improvements in agriculture. But while Indian food production has trebled, African food production is still stuck at little more than 50 million tons. Thus, from a position of parity twenty-five years ago, sub-Saharan food production has declined relatively to such an extent that it is but one-third of Indian output.

This single ratio shows starkly the seriousness of the African predicament. Nor is it possible to believe that agricultural stagnation reflects changes in comparative advantage. On the whole there has been no corresponding increase in resource-based or manufactured exports. The African countries have not increased their capacity to get by trade what they have failed to provide in production. That this is so is confirmed by the growing share of aid in food imports. Thus, in 1974, 23 per cent of cereals brought into sub-Saharan Africa took the form of food aid. By 1986 this share had risen to 42 per cent.

1985 International Food Aid to Selected African Countries

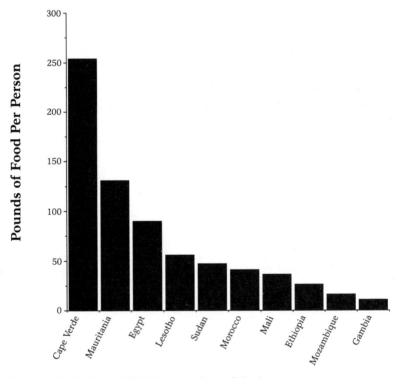

Source: United Nations and USDA Economic Research Service.

In Africa the average farmer grows 600 kg of cereals a year; in the US and Canada the output per farmer is 80,000 kg of cereals. The average North American farmer thus produces 130 times as much cereal as the average African farmer. The emergency, which was so apparent in Ethiopia, the Sudan, Angola, Mozambique, Somalia and a number of other countries in 1984, comes and goes with the weather. But the emergency is a symptom, and the lack of rainfall is but a most proximate cause. The real food crisis in Africa springs from the steady decline in food production per capita, from the failure of agricultural productivity to keep pace with population increase.

Since 1961 the average annual production growth of major food crops in sub-Saharan Africa has increased by 1.6 per cent, but the population has increased by 2.8 per cent. Thus food production has consistently lagged behind population growth now for over twenty-five years, and food production per capita has been declining at an annual rate of 1.2 per cent. If it is assumed that Africa south of the Sahara had food security in 1960, then (other things being equal) by 1985 the degree of security would have been reduced by 50 per cent. But Africa was not food-secure in 1960. Even then large numbers of people—particularly the so-called 'vulnerable groups', and specifically the children—were already undernourished; food supplies were grossly insufficient for proper nutritional requirements. If the basic food supply of people who were already on the margin of subsistence is cut in half the consequence is bound to be widespread starvation, at least in the absence of unlimited foreign exchange for food imports, or unlimited food aid. . . .

In these circumstances it is not surprising that food imports into sub-Saharan Africa have been growing by more than 7 per cent per year. Part of the imports has come as food aid, but the remainder has required the expenditure of scarce foreign exchange. As a result this has not been available to finance imports of fertilizer or agricultural machinery or other imports needed to increase the output of food. Even the significant diversion of scarce foreign exchange has not been enough to ensure food security. As has been seen, a growing proportion of food imports has come as aid. Without this there would, from the mid-1970s, have been large-scale starvation over much of sub-Saharan Africa. . . .

Food and Development

Food aid now accounts for close to 50 percent of all sub-Saharan African food imports. Without food aid, the sub-Saharan countries would be able, with the present availability of foreign exchange for the purpose, to import only half the food they import now. Some of the foreign exchange used to pay for commercial food imports may in fact also represent foreign exchange set free by food aid. Moreover, many African countries depend directly for their revenue and therefore for the local finance of development projects on the budgetary support which they get from the sale of food aid. Although emergency food aid looms large in the public mind, most food aid is in fact supplied in bulk for local sale. When food aid is mentioned most people immediately think of children in Ethiopia and food supplied to the camps there in which hungry people congregate, but actually that is only a relatively small part of total food aid. Most food aid is supplied as so-called 'programme aid' or balance of payments support. In other words the countries are being given food aid supplied in bulk. It is then sold to the people, with the proceeds from the sale, the so-called 'counterpart funds', being used for financing development projects, either approved national projects or the local finance part of aid projects. . . .

Increased Aid Is Needed

Although African needs are very great, they do not weigh heavily in the context of total food availability in the donor countries. The latest estimates of the US Department of Agriculture and of the FAO [Food and Agriculture Organization of the United Nations] of the needs of sub-Saharan Africa differ slightly, since they use different methods for estimating food aid needs, but they converge on an estimate of some minimum 4 million tons of additional food aid in terms of cereals. This leaves out of account other food and non-food items, which can be very important, and also the cash contributions which must go with the food: the cost of transporting and distributing it can be greater than the value of the food itself. This 4 million tons of additional cereals is needed simply to prevent the present condition from getting worse, to hold the status quo. In order to produce an improvement in the nutritional position—particularly among children, and pregnant and nursing women, as the most vulnerable groups—much larger food supplies would be needed, estimated by the US Department of Agriculture at an additional 7-8 million tons.

Moreover, even if our real targets are only the poorest and most vulnerable groups, for example children, a certain amount of 'leakage' or spread cannot be avoided. In many ways the welfare and nutrition of children cannot easily be separated from the nutrition of their family. The children are part of the family, especially the young children. A certain amount can be done by concentrating food aid on school meals and distribution through rural mother-child health clinics, but again it is not certain to reach the poorest people. The poorest people very often do not send their children to school. So in order to deal with the most acute nutritional needs of children and mothers and to prevent at least the worst irreversible malnutrition, which leads to permanent harm to the people suffering from it, the estimates of additional food aid needed vary between 7 and 8 million tons.

This sounds a lot. The present volume of food aid is something like 11 million tons altogether (for the whole world, not just for Africa), so 8 million extra tons for sub-Saharan Africa seems like a big expansion. But it might be politically acceptable to the donors concerned and it would certainly be technically feasible. Total world cereal production is no less than 1,650 million tons, and total world exports are 220-240 million tons, varying of course from year to year. Thus an additional 8 million tons, although it sounds a great deal in terms of present food aid, is only 0.5 per cent of world production and 3-4 per cent of world exports. If properly administered—admittedly a big if, involving problems which there is no time to deal with here—it could lay the basis for solving the immediate malnutrition problem. If further combined with good policies by the recipient countries, good policy dialogue or control by the donor countries, and above all also combined with sufficient aid, it could also lay the foundations for dealing with the long-term African food crisis. . . .

Seven Measures

What, then, should be done to make food aid an effective means of helping solve the African food crisis? Seven measures are suggested.

Aid Makes a Difference

Aid from "outsiders" can help. Northern and Southern NGOs, international donors, concerned individuals, development professionals, relief specialists—all can make difference. . . .

Outsider aid symbolizes central and important human concern and empathy. In terms of humaneness, the world would be poorer without it. It is, therefore, incumbent on us to find ways to ensure that aid is truly supportive of development. It is essential that every act of assistance contribute to the goal of enabling people to gain self-sustaining economic and social security. It is also essential that we see this goal as immediate and attainable, not as some "pie in the futuristic sky" dream which we really have no genuine hope of or responsibility for achieving.

Mary B. Anderson and Peter J. Woodrow, *Rising from the Ashes*, 1989.

---

1. First, we must broaden our concept of emergency. We must not imagine that we are doing enough when we give food aid when starving people concentrate in the refugee camps and we see pictures of starving children. Our food aid stops the moment the people drift away from the camps and go back to their villages or perhaps, as in Ethiopia, are transferred by the government to other parts of the country. Emergency food aid is not controversial, but we must have a much broader concept of emergency. As I have argued, the African emergency is a chronic, long-term emergency. We must broaden our sense of moral commitment beyond helping to keep people alive when the emergency strikes. We must have early warning systems

and use them to forestall the acute phase of the emergency. The nutritional status of children is the best single component in a system of early warning of impending food crisis, although there are others. We must have a safety net in the form of reserve stocks of food built up in the recipient countries, to enable us to take timely action to prevent the emergencies. We must have the transport and distribution facilities to deliver food in the villages so that people do not drift away from their farms to refugee camps in the first place. Later we must give food aid for rehabilitation. When people have been away from their farms and go back they need seeds, they need food, they need storage facilities. So the first condition is to broaden our concept of emergency, backwards towards prevention and forward towards rehabilitation. That would already take us a long way.

2. The second recommendation is actively to promote triangular transactions in food aid. There are food surpluses available in Africa which can be transported between countries and within countries. Promoting triangular transactions, we can use our food aid, for instance, to buy maize from Zimbabwe, which normally has a surplus, in that way encouraging food production in Zimbabwe, and deliver it to Zambia, which has a food deficit. This is not only much cheaper in terms of transport costs; it also delivers the kind of maize that African people prefer, rather than surplus Western food, which may not be the food they want. The Japanese food aid programme already depends to a high degree on triangular transactions of this kind; the British food programme similarly. The position of these two countries is similar in this respect owing to the fact that they have no major food surpluses to give direct. Britain differs in this respect from other EC [European Community] countries, which all have actual food surpluses. Although the discussion has been limited to Africa, triangular transactions also apply elsewhere; for instance, Thailand and Burma—and increasingly also Indonesia—have potential export surpluses of rice that could be delivered, say, to Bangladesh and other deficit areas in Asia as well as Africa. For countries like Japan and the UK which are not tied to surplus disposal, and have no major surpluses to give away, this kind of transaction is particularly indicated.

Linking Aid to Structural Adjustment

3. I would advocate increasing the links of food aid with the structural adjustment programmes which nowadays practically all African countries are forced to undertake, often under the auspices of the IMF [International Monetary Fund] and World Bank. The supply of additional food aid as part of the structural adjustment lending of the the World Bank and the IMF can reduce some of the worst effects of the present adjustment policies, particularly on poorer sections of the population, which

make these adjustment policies often politically unacceptable, or impossible to implement if accepted. Very often there are food riots when food prices are increased as part of austerity programs, governments may be overthrown or as in Zambia, are quickly forced to renounce the agreement with the IMF and World Bank and follow the same old policies as before. To avoid this the proper combination of additional food aid with structural adjustment lending can be particularly useful in giving adjustment a more 'human face'. At the same time the policy reforms should ensure that food aid is given in the context cf proper priorities for local food production, avoiding disincentive effects.

Additional Steps

4. Use food aid as balance of payments support, when it displaces commercial imports and releases foreign exchange, thus making possible more expansionary policies increasing the demand for local food.

5. Concentrate the additional food on the poor, who previously had no effective demand for food, and concentrate income increases made possible by food aid on the poor, with their high income elasticity of demand for food. This would also increase political-humanitarian support for food aid as part of a 'basic needs' strategy, and can be crucial in terms of adjustment stresses.

6. Use the additional resources obtained by the government and the leverage of food aid donors on measures benefiting local food producers: improvements in the rural infrastructure, producer subsidies (e.g., by operating a dual price system), improved supplies of fertilizer or other agricultural inputs (including consumption items acting as incentive goods), rural credit. The best mechanism for doing this would seem to be tying food aid (preferably linked with financial aid, and with all donors acting in coordination) to sectoral food strategies by means of a 'policy dialogue'—both currently 'trendy' approaches.

7. Use as much as possible of food aid, either directly or indirectly through 'monetization' and the use of counterpart funds, for labour-intensive public works and other forms of income generation in rural areas. This also increases the cost-effectiveness of income transfers through food aid, avoids the local transport costs of food aid, and makes it possible to follow a policy of simultaneously assisting the urban and rural poor by different means appropriate to both.

Given such developments on healthy lines, an expanded volume of food aid could make a significant contribution to turning Africa back from crisis and help it to solve its food and development problems.

"Food aid . . . has often helped destroy people's ability to feed themselves. "

International Aid Worsens Famine

Gayle Smith

Gayle Smith has been working on development and relief efforts in Africa for more than a decade. In the following viewpoint, Smith maintains that international economic and food aid only increases Africa's dependence on developed nations and exacerbates famine. Rather than giving Africans aid, Smith concludes, developed nations should find ways to encourage self-reliance in African nations.

As you read, consider the following questions:

1. How do northern nations view development in Africa, according to Smith?
2. What personal example does the author give to show that Western nations are willing to donate food, but unwilling to help Africans become self-sufficient?
3. What kinds of crops must Africans produce if they are to become self-sufficient, in Smith's opinion?

Gayle Smith, "The Hunger," *Mother Jones*, September/October 1991. Copyright © 1991 by Foundation for National Progress. Reprinted by permission.

April 1991 was a spectacular month for the disaster business. Just a few weeks after Iraq's defeat provoked the flight of over one million Kurds, a savage cyclone killed more than one hundred thousand people in Bangladesh. In the midst of these crises, aid agencies struggled to point out to the media that yet another famine was ravaging the African continent. But the aid agencies are wrong, for Africa is not starving again. It is starving still.

My own introduction to famine came in 1982. Farmers in Ethiopia told me then that a famine was coming, that after only two years of drought, they had already begun to sell off their oxen. Faced with another poor harvest a year later, those same farmers explained that they had no alternative but to sell their tools and eat their seeds. By 1984, farmers in the tens of thousands were abandoning their land to search for food. By 1985, most of them were dead.

The images of famine stay with you forever. I watched women who had raised ten children grovel on the ground to eat dirt in a final act of desperation. I saw white-bearded village elders trudge for six weeks through the mountains, only to die in the massive feeding camps of eastern Sudan.

The Uncaring Media

But what was at least as disturbing as these scenes of desperation was the sight of literally hundreds of journalists pushing and shoving to get the best angle on a mother holding her dying child. As the news of the famine broke, the flurry of advertisements by aid agencies, each promising to save more Ethiopians than the next, left an even more bitter taste in my mouth.

Few reporters pushed to cover the famine before it reached epic proportions, and the number of aid agencies operating in Ethiopia swelled to well over fifty only after famine had been declared in the headlines. It was as though a dense cloud had descended over Ethiopia during the night—and when it lifted in the morning, over seven million people were starving to death.

And now it's happening again. UN officials have announced that as many as thirty million Africans are threatened with starvation. Although the world's media will cover the famine as news, the disasters that continue to strike Africa are normal fare for much of the South. These seemingly endless disasters are not "natural"; they are not really caused by drought, hurricanes, earthquakes, or floods. Consider, for example, that although California has been plagued by drought for five years running, there are not thousands of starving Californians gathering in camps. But in the late eighties, two years of drought in Sudan killed 250,000 people.

The famine in Ethiopia was not an instant phenomenon, and

instant solutions will not fix it. As with the famines now plaguing Sudan, Angola, Mozambique, and pockets of West and Central Africa, the roots of the crisis go way back.

The Roots of Famine

Key to Africa's condition is "development," a term that means distinctly different things to those being developed and those doing the developing. In the northern sense of the word, Africa's development began some five hundred years ago with the internationalization of trade. As Europeans gained control of the world's waterways, they saw the "dark continent" as a source of raw materials and the gold to underpin their growing money economy. Between 1500 and 1870, Europeans ripped the heart out of the continent, taking some 22.9 million able-bodied farmers out as slaves. By the late 1800s, Africa was divided into spheres of European influence based not on the equitable development of the African economy, but on Europe's interests.

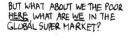

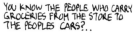

Punchline by Christian. Reprinted with permission.

Early in the twentieth century, Africans began to demand control over their own political futures. Country by country, they fought for and won political independence from European colonists—but economic independence proved harder to gain. The structure of African economies, which had been "developed" not to feed Africans, but to meet the needs of Europe, remained intact.

Sudan, Africa's largest country, is a good example of the kind of development that has made Africa the "Third World's Third World," a site of recurring famines and unpayable debt. Although never wealthy, the Sudanese had maintained the ability to feed themselves for centuries. When Britain governed the country, it decided that Sudanese farmers should grow cotton, to supply burgeoning British mills. Using the latest in agricultural technology, the British developed huge cotton-growing schemes on Sudan's most fertile land.

When Sudan became independent in 1956, the new government, encouraged by "development" banks and foreign donors, continued to emphasize cotton production. Two things happened: over time, the world market price of cotton fell, and Sudan's supply of foreign currency plummeted. Since agricultural resources were tied up in cotton, food production kept steadily declining. With no foreign currency, the country had to take out loans to import food. The mills of northern England, however, still had a constant supply of cheap Sudanese cotton.

Not all of Africa's problems, of course, began or ended with colonialism. Local struggles for power, unjust and corrupt regimes, and inter-African wars have played major roles in the continent's economic decline. But the North has had its own agenda for developing Africa—one that sees the continent as the source of supply for its production and a market for its goods. Ironically, it is the foreign aid ostensibly provided to ease Africa's suffering that is often the instrument for carrying out this agenda.

A Variety of Aid

The aid that goes to Africa from the North—from governments, from nongovernmental organizations (NGOs), and from multilateral lending agencies—includes military, economic, development, and relief aid.

Military aid is the most obvious culprit in the wreck of Africa. The expanding international arms industry has had a field day in Africa, which spends more than fourteen billion dollars a year on weapons and ammunition. During the cold war, the continent became a chessboard. When I first arrived in Sudan, soldiers were still carrying AK-47s supplied to Khartoum by the Soviet Union in the early seventies. By the mid-eighties, their Kalashnikovs had been replaced by U.S. M16s—part of the millions in military hardware that superpowers supplied to each of the Horn's countries in turn. It is no coincidence that over the last decade, some of the largest recipients of U.S. and Soviet military aid in sub-Saharan Africa—Sudan, Ethiopia, Mozambique, and Angola—have been nations where war and

111

famine are the most common.

Economic aid is provided by investors, including USAID and the World Bank, in the form of loans that yield interest to the donor. (Though it presents itself as a development agency, it is important to remember that the World Bank is a bank, and lends money to make a profit.) These northern investors urged African governments to take out huge loans in the seventies—right before two oil-price hikes and a drastic fall in world market prices for Africa's commodities crashed the Third World's economies. OPEC countries invested the profits from these price hikes in northern banks, which then made another round of loans to African governments. Many of the loans went to projects that ten years later loomed as vast monuments to stupidity, and millions in loaned project money were spirited out of Africa into foreign bank accounts by corrupt rulers. The debt still stands—and the interest payments keep growing.

Development aid is usually provided in the form of grants by governments and NGOs. While activists in the South have been somewhat successful in insisting on "appropriate" development—small-scale projects oriented toward local conditions and needs—the "bigger is better" mystique still persists in many cases. The tomato-paste processing plant built in an area of Sudan where no tomatoes were grown and the milk-powder factory in an area where cows could not survive are classic examples.

And development aid includes food aid—which helps the United States deal with its own agricultural surplus, and looks good on television, but has often helped destroy people's ability to feed themselves. During the 1984-85 Ethiopian famine, I worked with the Relief Society of Tigray, an agency operating in Ethiopia's northern Tigray region. We obtained food aid with relative ease. Then, at the height of the famine, REST launched an agricultural rehabilitation project designed to help farmers feed themselves. For less than two hundred dollars, a farming family could be provided with seeds, tools, and oxen—the means for subsistence. Offers of food aid still poured in, but getting money for rehabilitation was like pulling teeth. By the end of the year, we had raised less than 21 percent of the money for the project, and tens of thousands of families remained dependent on external food aid.

The Ineffectiveness of Food Aid

Finally, there's relief aid. If relief aid is what comes in when all other kinds of aid have failed, then there's ample evidence that failure has come to Africa. Since 1980, Africa has received billions in foreign aid, most of it from the United States. During this period, the continent has charted a course of steady decline. Africa today produces less food, has more starving people, and owes more money than it did ten years ago. At best, the aid programs of the past are not very effective; at worst, they have been part of the problem

Aid programs of the future don't look to be much better, if northern development experts succeed in setting the priorities of the nineties. High on their list are managing the African debt and establishing free-market systems. This means "structural adjustment," in the lingo of the World Bank—a package of deregulation and economic reforms designed to further develop Africa's export crops, in order to generate sufficient hard currency to pay off debt and import the goods that countries can't produce.

Aid Is Ineffective

In the context of Africa's food crisis, food aid has become a vital component for the maintenance of stability by governments, not for saving lives. The type of food aid most commonly given to Africa is not that provided in emergency situations, as in Ethiopia in 1983-84, but regular food aid programmes of the U.S., the EEC [European Economic Community] and the World Food Programme. From the supply side, these programmes were designed to rid 'donor' countries of surpluses and to create markets for commercial sales. From the demand side, food aid offers governments a financially inexpensive way to meet internal demands for select commodities. . . . The official approach in Sierra Leone, and many other African countries, to dealing with the 'food crisis', which becomes defined in terms of urban demand, is to import the food that non-nationals have produced. Local farmers are then by-passed and government is able to postpone dealing with the numerous constraints to production for peasant farmers which would provide them with a reasonable return for their efforts.

Bill Rau, *From Feast to Famine*, 1991.

Ghana, a cocoa-producing country on Africa's west coast, is often held up by the Bank as an example of successful adjustment. Ghana first adopted an adjustment program in 1983, and by the late 1980s, World Bank statistics showed that the country's cocoa producers were making more money.

But statistics can show anything. Upon further scrutiny, it was discovered that 94 percent of the gross income from cocoa had gone to the richest producers. Poor farmers remained poor. At the same time, Ghana's food self-sufficiency declined. The Bank then advocated, and the government agreed to, an emphasis on large-scale commercial fishing. Local fishermen, unable to obtain the credit and equipment made available to commercial enterprises, were squeezed out. Cheap fish, the primary source of protein for Ghana's people, began to disappear from local markets.

To obtain the aid needed to solve its economic problems, according to current "development" wisdom, an African country must enter into an adjustment program. But by doing so, it essentially signs on for another round of the export-led-growth approach that has plagued Africa from the beginning.

A New Way of Thinking

Breaking this famine-breeding cycle requires a fundamental shift in how we think about development and how we think about Africa. The first step is to realize that development is something done by people, not to them. As it stands now, development policies are designed by "experts" who sit in capital cities of the North. To change the often destructive impact of these policies, the North has to listen to, and support, Africa's priorities for its own development. High on the list among the community organizers and development workers I talk with is "self-reliance."

Central to self-reliance is food production aimed not at external markets but at local consumption. This seems basic common sense; yet during the 1984-85 famine, Ethiopia was exporting green beans to England. For famines to end, Ethiopia and countries like it will have to shift away from the capital-intensive, import-dependent agribusiness promoted by the North toward producing grains and vegetables for their own people.

The technical components required to make this shift aren't complicated. Most of them can be found within Africa, based on traditional agricultural methods. But this orientation would also require northern donors to extend credit privileges to local rather than commercial producers, and to make fertilizer, seeds, and tools widely available to small, poor farmers, particularly women.

Accepting that Africans should be the ones to set their development priorities means that the North will have to shift its own. Dumping food aid on Africa would no longer be a way to solve the problem of our overproduction. Foreign-aid programs would have to be uncoupled from political machinations and reoriented toward development. Northern governments and banks would have to accept radical debt-relief measures. When, in 1988, France canceled the $170 million debt of the twenty poorest African countries, even though the amount was a tiny part of the $230 billion the continent owed, it showed other northern nations that debt cancellation is possible. But chances are that unless northern development priorities change, new debts will continue to accrue.

Breaking the cycle of famine would also mean abandoning the charity mentality that prevails in the aid industry. Donors should insist that aid go for rehabilitation projects, not just for emergency food. And we need to remember that white northerners do not have the answers for Africa. Our aid organizations and NGOs need to listen more carefully to what their African counterparts are saying.

The North Must Respond

Finally, African development needs to be seen in a political context. In 1991, popular protest led to fundamental political changes in some thirty-two African governments. More countries have made moves toward democracy than in the last twenty-five years combined. The U.S. government sees "democratization" as scheduled elections and free markets. Those of us who understand the limitations of this—and the high cost that free-market economics has already exacted from Africans—can push for alternative models by supporting small, grass-roots democracy projects, like those backed by many African NGOs. But we cannot support the changing relationship between Africans and their governments without democratizing, as well, the relationship between Africa and the rest of the world. From the sixteenth century onward, Africa has supported the North—with its labor, its resources, and the money its hungry people send to northern banks. It is time for the North to play fair.

In the short term, however—this month, this year—an immense wave of famine is sweeping the continent, and real people are dying in frightening numbers. Aid must be forthcoming. But I hope that when Americans write their checks this time around, they'll think about why they're keeping Africans alive. I hope they'll write their checks to African organizations and to the few northern organizations that follow the leadership of African development activists, and that they'll call the networks to complain about the endless images of helpless African children. I hope that relief agencies will match, dollar for dollar, the aid that goes for emergency relief with aid targeted for basic agricultural rehabilitation. And I hope that after this famine recedes, people will remember that the fight for Africa's future is a long one.

> *"Reforms are changing the structure of African economies so the countries will have a real shot at long-term growth."*

Western Aid Reforms Can Strengthen Africa's Economies

U.S. Agency for International Development

The U.S. Agency for International Development (AID) carries out economic assistance programs designed to help the people of developing countries best use their human and economic resources, increase their agricultural and industrial production, and promote economic and political stability. In the following viewpoint, U.S. AID argues that reduced government involvement and other economic reforms already undertaken in some African nations have been successful, and should be employed throughout the continent to achieve economic growth.

As you read, consider the following questions:

1. In the author's opinion, what factors might make a structural adjustment program attractive to African governments?
2. According to the author, what specific improvements have structural adjustment programs made in Africa?
3. Why does the author think that structural adjustment programs are difficult to initiate?

U.S. Agency for International Development, "Africans Initiating Economic Reforms," *U.S. AID Highlights*, Summer 1989.

After nearly a decade of economic stagnation, famine and pestilence, there's good news out of Africa today. And that good news may well grow as more countries join those already walking away from their old approaches to economic management.

African farmers increased their production each year from 1984 to 1988 by about 4%. In the 15 years before that, production had grown only 1.25% a year. Since 1985, Africa's gross national product (GNP) has grown by about 3% a year, excluding oil producing countries. While that only matches the rate of population growth, it means that for the first time this decade the average African is no longer getting poorer.

Assessing the Situation

A growing number of economic experts believe the improvement in Africa's economic statistics, beginning in 1985, is a result of economic reform and adjustment programs adopted by many African states. Over 30 African countries are now participating in International Monetary Fund (IMF) or World Bank policy reform programs that favor increased efficiency in reallocating resources to productive activities.

Those reforms are changing the structure of African economies so the countries will have a real shot at long-term growth.

Policy reform is not without critics. It is a difficult process, requiring some very basic changes in economies such as reducing government employment and cutting subsidies of food and energy.

No one would argue that this kind of fundamental change is not painful, but the alternative appears to be a relentless decline in everybody's standard of living.

Taking Stock of Reform

Though economic reforms are being adopted across much of the African continent, they still are being rejected by some countries—and the results are telling.

According to a study by the World Bank and the U.N. Development Programme, policy reform in Africa is beginning to produce real gains in production and economic growth. The report compared the economic performance of African countries instituting strong reforms to those with weak or no reform programs. It found that those with reform policies had stronger gross domestic product (GDP) growth and export growth along with solid improvements in agricultural production.

The report was optimistic that Africa's recovery has begun, but it issued a warning: Increased productivity will not come overnight. Africa will continue to need outside help to sustain its reform-driven recovery.

It could be many years before African countries that choose to carry out strong policy reforms and structural adjustment programs are able to give their citizens the standard of living others in the developing world expect from their own economies. For example, if average incomes in 10 of Africa's poorest countries would continue to rise by 1% a year, it would take 50 years before incomes would reach the current level of the average person in India. Economic reform is a matter of urgency in these countries to achieve the rising levels of growth necessary to sustain an improved standard of living.

Structural Adjustment Reforms Include:

- Reducing government control over the economy;
- Allowing the price of agricultural produce to rise or change with market demands;
- Reducing the budget deficit;
- Reducing consumer demand for imports;
- Keeping interest rates above the inflation rate;
- Reducing the rate of growth in the money supply;
- Lowering overvalued exchange rates for a country's currency.

Today, Africa is a land of about 40 countries with vastly diverse cultural and economic heritages. The region as a whole is among the poorest and least developed areas of the world partly because of long-standing problems that hampered growth and compounded social problems. But, it is also poor because some government policies discouraged individual initiative and entrepreneurship.

Distrust of the Private Sector

As many African countries gained independence in the 1960s, they consciously decided that development had to be guided and directed by the state. There was no indigenous formal private sector. Most private firms were controlled by multinationals and by citizens of other countries. Distrusting the private sector and building on colonial institutions, which also emphasized state control, young African governments took control of marketing and production. This state control of their economies ultimately led to distorted prices and markets. The governments often subsidized food to lower consumer prices. That action amounted to a tax on farmers—a tax that benefited city dwellers by helping them to eat at prices below the cost of producing the food. Often food was imported, creating taste dependencies for foodstuffs such as wheat flour that African countries may never be able to produce competitively.

At independence, most of Africa wanted to build an educated urban middle class. What developed instead was a small urban elite living at the expense of their country's farmers. This resulted in widespread rural poverty made worse by drought and, in many cases, civil strife. Many farmers got so little money for their produce that they left their farms and headed for the cities, further straining the social services provided by governments and decreasing the amount of food available for city dwellers.

The old economic system sought to provide services and employment alongside heavy industry. Eventually, the expense of this approach led to great inequity in African societies.

Over-valued currencies in many countries discouraged exports by making things too expensive to sell abroad.

In Sudan, for example, the official government exchange rate made it virtually impossible to export gum arabic, so plantation workers chopped down the gum arabic trees and used them to make charcoal to sell. This not only eliminated a resource, it damaged the environment as a whole.

Africa's internal economic problems were exacerbated when fundamental changes wracked the international economy in the late 1970s and the 1980s. World prices for many commodities traditionally exported by Africa fell sharply. The result was overall economic decline and a 20% drop in per capita income from 1980-85.

Though per capita growth had been slow in the 1970s, it worsened drastically in the '80s, turning into negative growth. Two major droughts, followed by famine, also struck the continent in the '80s. Even a plague of locusts laid waste to large areas of the Africa's Sahel. Populations grew faster than African economies. The oil shocks of 1973 and 1979 made imports cost much more for most countries in Africa. At the same time, the rest of the world, falling into recession, bought fewer African goods, causing their prices and profits to drop. The nations of Africa began to borrow heavily to maintain their levels of consumption. Continued borrowing grew into today's major debt crisis.

African governments realized something drastic had to be done to put their economies back together. What they found were the IMF and World Bank programs of structural adjustment and policy reform that were supported by the U.S. Agency for International Development (USAID).

Making Reform Work for People

In Mali, as part of its Economic Policy Reform Program, the government decided to improve the country's economic climate for private enterprise and to reduce the drain of the public sector on the rest of the economy. To do this, Mali had to reduce the size of its government payroll. With help from USAID and other donors, an innovative and completely voluntary early retirement program was developed to lower the government's salary expenditures without throwing people out of work.

The Effects of Policy Reform

Here is the human side of policy reform as explained by Americans who worked in Mali:

When Mali's Mohammad Amin raises the steel shutters to his kiosk (a small sidewalk shop) along the dusty avenue across from Bamako's market place, he remembers the years he used to sit, drinking tea, doing almost nothing at his job in the ministry.

When he could, Mohammad would even slip away early and drive a rented taxi to make extra money. When he couldn't get away from his government job, he drove the taxi at night. The first job paid most of the rent for his two-room apartment; the second kept his family of eight from hunger. His hours were long. He rarely saw his family.

Then, the Mali government, as part of its overall program of economic reform, offered Mohammad and many other government employees incentives for early retirement. He left his poorly paid government job and used the retirement fund to help him secure a loan that he used to buy a kiosk near the market where the farmers come to sell their produce. The partially guaranteed loan program was yet another facet of the Mali Economic Policy Reform Program.

At first, his friends told him he was crazy to leave the security of government. Worse still, he was buying a shop to sell things to farmers. Everyone knew farmers were too poor to buy anything but the barest of essentials. The government marketing board paid them so little for their crops.

All that has been changing since 1985. Now the farmers have money. The government, with assistance from USAID and other donors, stopped regulating the price of commodities three years ago. Since then, farmers are free to sell their goods at whatever price the market will bear. Now, it pays to grow more than just enough to feed their own families. The farmers are spending some of their money at Mohammad's kiosk before returning home. He feels things are finally getting better—slowly to be sure—but better just the same.

Of course, Mohammad and the others who were part of the program don't think of it as a structural adjustment and policy reform program, but they know their lives have begun to improve. The government, too, is benefiting. As a result of the early-out program alone, it has some $.5 million more to spend on infrastructure each year.

Though Mohammad Amin is a composite of the 210 people the USAID staff assisted in Mali's early retirement program, the story is based solidly in fact and reflects the 80% satisfaction rate of those who participated.

The Benefits of Structural Adjustment

• GDP growth in the countries practicing reform policies increased from an average of 1% in 1980-84 to nearly 4% in 1986-87.

• GDP for non-reformers grew at only 1.5% for the same period.

• Export growth rates rose 5-6% in countries that initiated economic reforms.

• Non-reformers managed an export growth rate of only 1-2%.

• Agricultural production grew twice as fast in countries practicing policy reform as it did in those that did not.

Aided by adequate rain, in 1988 Mali's farmers exported 100,000 tons of grain after satisfying the needs of their own country. In 1983, Mali was a grain importer.

What is happening in Mali and throughout Africa is part of a growing worldwide movement recognizing that the command economy experiment, that is, the system where the government dictates the terms of production, has failed. Letting people make their own economic decisions based on global economic realities has proven much more effective.

Under policy reform in Zambia, for example, currency devaluation caused a dramatic increase in the use of the more effective ox plow over the old, short-handled hoe. USAID projects had been encouraging this switch for many years but with only limited success. The farmers, it was later learned, were saving to purchase imported tractors. When currency reform made the tractors too expensive, the farmers opted for the ox-drawn plow instead. Farm productivity then began making real gains.

Making Hard Choices

In spite of favorable evidence showing the long-term benefits of policy reform programs, the familiar and comfortable old ways of multiple currency exchange rates, subsidized interest, guaranteed jobs for all college graduates and heavily subsidized food are not always readily abandoned. They serve a politically powerful segment of Africa's populace.

But, deep in debt and with their currencies buying less and less, many African countries are facing up to this most unwelcome dilemma. The money has run out. There is no longer any way to continue the social subsidies many have known all their lives. Righting their economies after so long will be a painful experience for Africa's political elites and other privileged groups. In order to encourage farmers to grow enough to feed the nation and have some left over for export, the domestic price of food must rise to realistic world market levels. Where the old system was designed to serve those with political influence, economies in reform programs may reduce the living standards of some while raising those of the poorest sectors in society.

That, of course, can be politically dangerous because it strikes at the pocketbooks of the very class that Africa's leaders created, the bedrock of their political support. These are the people the government employs in its offices and industries—industries protected by import restrictions—industries which turn out products people buy only because there is no other choice. Economic policy reform creates opportunities for people to make their own choices. Choices like what to buy, at what price, from what merchant. Policy reform is the right to decide what to plant and when, and at what price to market the fruits of one's labor.

Letting people make these choices allows a nation's economy to respond more quickly to the ever-changing world economy and even to take advantage of the opportunities that change may offer.

"SAPs [Structural Adjustment Programs] have afflicted the African people and societies in ways that threaten their very future."

Western Aid Reforms Are Harming Africa's Economies

Adebayo Adedeji

In the following viewpoint, Adebayo Adedeji asserts that the economic reforms that the World Bank has demanded of Africa have damaged the continent's economies by slowing government-led development, increasing foreign debt burdens, and discouraging indigenous reform and technical advances. He advocates the Lagos Plan of Action (LPA) and the African Alternative Framework for Structural Adjustment Programs (AAFSAP), plans that increase exports and government income, as alternatives to traditional World Bank policies, which require decreasing imports and government spending. Adedeji serves as undersecretary-general of the United Nations, and as executive secretary for the Economic Commission for Africa.

As you read, consider the following questions:

1. The author describes specific results of SAPs. Explain what these results are.
2. What alternatives to SAPs does Adedeji propose?
3. Why might the World Bank and the International Monetary Fund (IMF) be reluctant to give up their demands for SAPs, according to Adedeji?

Adebayo Adedeji, "Economic Progress: What Africa Needs," *Transafrica Forum*, Summer 1990. Reprinted with permission.

Reviewing the development challenges of the 1980s, one cannot but sadly surmise that for Africa it has been a decade of lost opportunities and diminished achievements.

Throughout the 1980s Africa experienced a vicious and unremitting socioeconomic crisis. All the major indicators point to significant and sometimes precipitous retrogression to the extent that Africans are worse off in 1990 than they were in 1980. Output and income growth, capital formation and export growth have declined. Deficits in the balance of payments and inflation rates have accelerated, while the debt and debt-servicing burdens have reached unmanageable levels. The productive and infrastructural facilities have crumbled, while the basic social services—especially education, health and housing—have been rapidly deteriorating. Piling on top of the recurrent drought and chronic food deficit phenomena, these problems have contributed to uninterrupted economic decline and falling standards of living of the African people.

Statistics of Decline

Throughout the decade, per capita income also declined unabatedly in Africa—the only continent where such a development took place. Average per capita income, already abysmally low, fell from $752 in 1980 to $545 in 1988, declining by 2.6 percent annually. . . . With regard to the debt problem, Africa owed $48.3 billion in 1978. This figure multiplied by more than five times to $257 billion in 1989 with debt-servicing obligations accounting for 40 percent of export earnings on the average and going beyond 100 percent for many countries.

This economic decline has had a devastating impact on the well-being of millions of Africans. Since 1980, per capita private consumption has fallen by one-fifth. . . . Unemployment has reached crisis proportions: the unemployed in the formal wage sector are estimated to number over 30 million. . . . Some 10,000 children die in Africa every day of causes linked to malnutrition and to the non-availability of rudimentary health care. . . .

It cannot be overemphasized that Africa cannot afford to have a repeat performance in the 1990s—a decade which promises to bring even greater challenges, not least of which is a literal population explosion. It is imperative, therefore, that one must pause to consider why, in spite of all efforts, the economic performance has been so disappointing. . . .

The Causes of Decline

A careful and reasoned analysis of the African economic problematique can only lead to the conclusion that its underlying causes are the lack of structural transformation and the pervasive low levels of productivity. . . . Endogenous aggravating factors include the structural imbalances evident in the great disparities in urban and rural development and in income distribution, rapid population growth, the inadequacy and/or misdirection of human and financial resources, poor economic management, inappropriate economic policies, political instability and the prevalence of social values, attitudes and practices detrimental to development. More serious exogenous aggravating factors are the formidable constraints posed by the intertwined problems of the heavy debt burden, diminished export earnings and declining real resource flows.

Reality of Structural Adjustment

Of course, as we look back at the 1980s, very few of us can doubt that we were, in one way or another, affected by the Structural Adjustment Programmes (SAPs) that many of our countries have been pursuing. In some cases the impact of such programmes has led to riots because of the tremendous suffering they impose on the people: loss of jobs, reduction in social services, impossible increases in prices, generalised poverty and the constant threat of destabilising society as a whole. Indeed, these programmes continue to be formulated and implemented as if people do not matter. As such these programmes have failed to recognise that all of us—poor or rich, young or old, educated or not—are all part of the social and economic reality in our countries.

United Nations Economic Commission for Africa, *African Alternative Framework to Structural Adjustment Programmes for Socioeconomic Recovery and Transformation, 1991.*

Therefore, left to itself, the African economy has a built-in tendency to generate crises from within and to assimilate others from abroad. Unless these fundamental structural problems and bottlenecks are dealt with, the African economy cannot right itself and break away from the vicious cycle of underdevelopment. This phenomenon has significant implications for the strategies, policies and programmes directed towards revitalizing the African economy. . . .

The Focus of Economic Policies

The donor community, particularly the Bretton Woods institutions, has refused to accept and support Africans' perception of their development objectives and strategies. Instead, the institutions proposed their own strategies for the development path that they thought would be good for Africa. . . .

The main preoccupation of most African policymakers became crisis management for economic survival. The focus of economic policies shifted to short-term concerns resulting mainly from external shocks. Long-term development objectives were put on hold. In their place were devised Structural Adjustment Programmes (SAPs), by the Bretton Woods institutions, which these countries were required to adopt if they were to qualify for external support and, in particular, have access to the desperately needed foreign exchange.

The reality that the badly needed external financial resources could be forthcoming only within the framework of SAPs has literally shackled African countries to these programmes. They have thus been pressurized into accepting solutions that may at best cope with the symptoms of the crisis and not with its root causes. . . .

It should be evident by now that policy reforms aimed merely at improvements in financial balances and price structures are unlikely to succeed in bringing about socioeconomic transformation and sustained development.

Over the past years, numerous assessments have been conducted to determine whether SAPs have led to a sustainable basis for development. Beyond these assessments, the ECA [Economic Commission for Africa] has also had the benefit of personal contact with Africans from all walks of life, be they entrepreneurs, traders, or ministers.

Despite the view of the Bretton Woods institutions—that countries which have imposed structural adjustments perform better economically than those without such programmes—there is increasing evidence that economic performance has not rebounded in any sustainable fashion as a result of these programmes. Studies by the ECA as well as by the World Bank itself show that main economic indicators have actually worsened following the adoption of SAPs. Indeed, one authoritative review after another has demonstrated the inadequacy of SAPs.

Taking Stock of Structural Adjustment

Much worse, SAPs have afflicted the African people and societies in ways that threaten their very future. The Khartoum Declaration is illuminating. It was adopted by the ECA-sponsored International Conference on the Human Dimension of Africa's Economic Recovery and Development. The gathering included over 200 African ministers, high-ranking officials and senior experts from government, UN agencies, representatives of international and regional development and financial organizations, donor agencies and NGOs [nongovernmental organizations], African and non-African scholars and the mass media who met in Khartoum in March 1988. The Declaration states that:

> The severity of the African crisis is such that country after country has been putting in place structural adjustment programmes in their effort to halt their economic degradation and achieve a turn-around. Unfortunately, far too many of these

programmes—whether nationally conceived or in collaboration with the World Bank, the International Monetary Fund and the donor community—are rending the fabric of the African society. . . .

In his report to the UN General Assembly on the mid-term review of UN-PAAERD [United Nations Programme of Action for African Economic Recovery and Development], the Secretary-General drew attention to the fact that:

> The implementation of structural adjustment programmes has given rise to general concerns. The limited objectives and short-term perspectives of those programmes are sometimes viewed, by African countries and others, as being at variance with the objectives of more balanced long-term development. Their human and social costs have often been seen as out of proportion with their real or intended benefits. The most vulnerable population groups, in particular women, youth, the disabled and the aged, have been severely and adversely affected, directly and indirectly, by such measures as the withdrawal of subsidies on staple food items, the imposition of limits on wage increases at or below the inflation rate, the retrenchment of civil servants and private sector personnel frequently belonging to the lowest salary categories, and the cutting of expenditures on social services, including health and education, and on basic infrastructure. Access to food has become more difficult for large segments of the population, with the result that malnutrition has increased, particularly among children, infants and pregnant women. . . .

The findings and conclusions of the report entitled *Structural Adjustment in Africa: Insights from the Experiences of Ghana and Senegal*, which was submitted by the staff of the Subcommittee on Africa of the Committee on Foreign Affairs of the U.S. House of Representatives, were equally critical:

> The available evidence strongly suggests that, despite rising per capita growth, structural adjustment has produced little enduring poverty-alleviation, and certain policies have worked against the poor. . . .

The report concluded:

> The international donors and recipients could modify structural adjustment to fully incorporate poverty-alleviation objectives. Reductions in external and internal deficits could be carried out more gradually. "Supply-side" policies could give greater priority to stimulating the production and income of the poor, while "demand-side" policies could better sustain their standard of living. Social sector spending could be directed more efficiently to serve the poor. In addition, foreign decision-makers could be less insulated from national realities and the poor could be given more effective representation in economic policy-making. . . .

With the advent of the 1990s, Africa must achieve the transition from "stabilization and adjustment" to "adjustment with transformation." A process of sustained and sustainable growth and development—which is human-centered, self-reliant and participatory in nature—must be set in motion and must take hold in the coming years. The responsibility for bringing about this socioeconomic revival rests, first and foremost, with the African governments and people themselves. However, unless the international economic environment is made receptive of the efforts of Africa, the continent's socioeconomic revival will remain forever elusive.

Victims of Structural Adjustment

Structural adjustment can have a detrimental effect on the more vulnerable sectors of society, such as women, children, and the aged. Unicef, the ECA, the International Labour Organization, and the IMF and World Bank themselves have conducted a variety of studies documenting serious deterioration in social services, wages, and employment levels associated with structural adjustment.

Ernest Harsch, *Africa Report*, May/June 1989.

The international community has, therefore, the responsibility to create the external conditions that are both necessary and sufficient to enable Africa to realize its objectives. Over the years, the World Bank and IMF have come to wield tremendous—and certainly disproportionate—power over Africa's economic and social destiny, by literally dictating the orientation and pace of economic reforms in the majority of African countries through SAPs. . . .

A generation of SAPs has glaringly revealed the inadequacies of those programmes. To further tie all assistance and debt relief initiatives that favor Africa to SAPs is to mortgage the economic future of the continent to failed policies.

"Washington should restructure its aid programs to Africa, and commit greater resources to democracy-building programs."

Aid to Africa Should Be Tied to Democratic Reforms

Michael Johns

Michael Johns is a policy analyst for The Heritage Foundation, a Washington, D.C.-based public policy research institute. In the following viewpoint, Johns asserts that an increase in political liberty in Africa would make it easier for African governments to effect economic growth in their countries. He argues that in the interest of developing the continent, America should require African nations to initiate democratic reforms before receiving U.S. aid. He also advocates channeling aid to specific programs that develop democracy.

As you read, consider the following questions:

1. According to the author, what specific African programs should America support? Why?
2. How have dictatorships hindered economic growth in Africa, in Johns's opinion?
3. Why does Johns argue that this is a particularly good time to encourage political and economic reforms in Africa?

Michael Johns, "A New Liberation Doctrine for Africa," The Heritage Foundation *Backgrounder*, April 12, 1991. Reprinted with permission.

Aside from the Middle East, Africa is the only region of the world not yet swept by democratic revolution. Deposed are autocratic leaders in Asia, Europe, and Latin America. In their place have emerged democratically elected governments.

But not in Africa. There, political and economic freedom remains virtually unknown. The vast majority of Sub-Saharan Africa's 400 million people cannot speak freely; they often are jailed and killed by African regimes for simply speaking out for democratic change or for questioning existing government policies. And their right to own private property, sell produce at market prices, and trade freely is prohibited throughout much of the continent. The result is that Africa has slipped further and further into poverty. Today, sixteen of the world's twenty poorest nations are in Africa, and some 100 million Africans—roughly one-quarter of the continent—are facing chronic food shortages.

Hope Emerging

Yet, a glimmer of hope at last is emerging that the democratic revolution may yet reach Africa. Political liberty now is making marginal advances there. In the West African state of Benin, the Southern African nation of Namibia, and the Atlantic Ocean island of Cape Verde, governments have been elected in democratic multiparty elections during 1990 and 1991, replacing unrepresentative, autocratic regimes.

More important than the few democratic gains so far is the possibility of more advances on the continent. In Cote d'Ivoire, Gabon, Nigeria, and Zaire, for example, one-party or military dictatorships are now either undergoing or being pressured to introduce democratic rule. And in Angola, Kenya, Mozambique, Zambia, and Zimbabwe strong political movements are challenging non-democratic governments and calling for democracy. Some of these movements are likely to prevail.

The Benefits of a Free Market

The emergence of political freedom in Africa offers hope that free market reforms, too, will take root. If they do, the chronic poverty that plagues Africa could be greatly reduced. In other regions of the world, nations such as Chile and the Republic of China on Taiwan have found that free market reforms preceded the rise of political freedom. Leaders of these nations, while politically autocratic, saw the merits of free enterprise.This has not been, however, nor is it likely to be, the case in Africa. Most African autocrats have a deeply rooted economic and political stake in preserving their control over state-owned agriculture, banking, and manufacturing. Thus, in all but a very few cases, they are dragging their feet on privatizing state-owned enterprises and launching other free market reforms.

With the Cold War receding and the possibility that democracy and economic freedom can blossom in the world's last remaining predominantly undemocratic and economically statist continent, Washington needs to reevaluate its policy toward Africa. Washington was correctly concerned about Soviet advances in Africa during the Cold War, and consequently found it necessary to forge close political relations with dictators like Somalia's Mohammed Siad Barre and Zaire's Mobutu Sese Seko to offset Moscow's expansionism in East and Southern Africa. Washington also had to rationalize South Africa's repressive racism.

Income in Africa

Gross national income per capita in Sub-Saharan Africa and other third world countries, 1970-1987

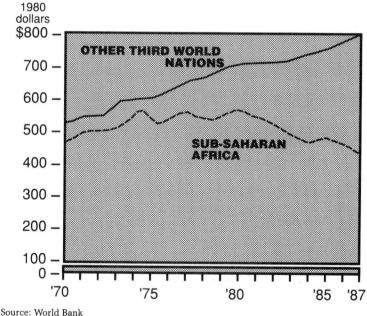

Source: World Bank

While Moscow continues to back pariah, Marxist regimes in Angola and Ethiopia, it is far less likely today than it was during the Cold War that this support will lead to further Soviet expansion on the African continent. This gives Washington the ability to switch its policy toward Africa from containing Moscow to assisting the emergence of political and economic liberties on the continent, which will be Africa's best hope to move beyond its current state of chaos, poverty, and misery. . . .

Washington's traditional objectives in Africa have been noble—to combat starvation, to alleviate poverty, and to expand human rights and liberties. Yet, this policy by and large has failed, except as a onetime Band-Aid to stanch a crisis. The problem has been that America's policy toward Africa generally has been reactive. As a result, Washington has missed opportunities to influence events in Africa, or when things go badly, as in Ethiopia, Liberia, and Sudan, to enter the game in time to have much of an impact.

Washington today has an opportunity to develop a new African policy, at a relatively low cost to American taxpayers, to foster political and economic liberty in Africa. Doing so would help bring lasting solutions to Africa's economic and political crises. While it is true that bitter ethnic divisions and other factors are often to blame for Africa's wars, poverty, and oppression, no factor has contributed to this crisis more than Africa's political authoritarianism. Denying their people political freedom, African regimes generally have faced few impediments in abusing their people.

Encouraging Liberty

Helping foster political liberty in Africa will require a fundamental reevaluation of American policy toward that continent. In place of the old African policy that focused so heavily on assisting dictatorships primarily because they were anti-Soviet, Washington should adopt a new Liberation Doctrine for Africa that will encourage the emergence of political and economic liberty on the continent. The Liberation Doctrine will be rooted in George Bush's declaration, which accompanied the December 20, 1989, American liberation of Panama, that "the day of the dictator is over," and it will seek to advance the emerging trend toward political democratization in Africa.

Exceptions to African Liberty

This doctrine of supporting African liberty will be executed mainly with U.S. diplomatic measures, technical assistance, and public diplomacy. It should be applied across the continent. The possible exceptions are: 1) when there is no indigenous democratic movement, as there now are not in Libya and to a lesser extent Somalia; and 2) when American relations with a non-democratic nation are needed to ensure use of strategic facilities, such as U.S. access to Kenya's ports. But even in these cases, Washington should use diplomatic leverage to convince the non-democratic but friendly governments of the merits of economic and political liberty. . . .

An opportunity now exists for Washington to help Africans in their bid for political freedom. From Zambia to Ethiopia,

Africans are calling on Washington to decide whether it supports the authoritarian rulers or those emerging movements and institutions calling for democratic change. Although Washington has no inherent obligation to expend American resources to promote democracy in Africa, it can now do so with little expense to American taxpayers and little risk that doing so could benefit the Soviet Union.

The spread of political liberty in Africa will make it easier for governments there to correct the many problems created by decades of authoritarianism, like corruption, human rights abuses, famine, and the denial of fundamental economic rights. Without greater political liberty in Africa, Washington will be wasting American money in efforts to help the African economy, expand markets for American goods, and to cooperate more with African governments at the U.N. and other multinational agencies.

Strengthening Democratic Institutions

It is time, therefore, for Washington to overhaul its policy toward Africa and craft a Liberation Doctrine designed to strengthen African democratic movements and institutions. Washington should be careful not to choose sides between competing political parties in Africa. Rather it should contribute to the strengthening of democratic institutions on the continent, such as free press, human rights monitoring groups, and democratic-minded educational organizations. . . .

Whether or not political liberty eventually roots itself in Africa could depend on whether Washington looks anew at Africa, and begins to assist in the emergence of political freedom. This new Liberation Doctrine for Africa should include:

• *Rechanneling at least 15 percent of America's $1.058 billion in annual economic aid to Africa into democracy-building programs.*

American economic aid to Africa has failed to combat African poverty in large part because Africa lacks the democratic political structure that would enable free market economic reforms to take root. Because of this, Washington should restructure its aid programs to Africa, and commit greater resources to democracy-building programs, such as expanded support for National Endowment for Democracy (NED) programs on the continent, and for the creation of a Radio Free Africa. Rechanneling 15 percent of the current $1.058 billion in foreign economic aid to Africa—$159 million—would go far toward funding these Liberation Doctrine projects. (The U.S. also sent $38.73 million in military aid to Africa in 1990.)

NED's budget for African programs for 1990 was around $750,000, spent on democracy-building initiatives in ten African countries—Benin, Botswana, Burkina Faso, Mozambique,

Nigeria, Senegal, Sierra Leone, South Africa, Sudan, and Uganda. In addition, NED funded regional labor groups which, in turn, assisted indigenous labor groups in Guinea, Cote d' Ivoire, Mali, Niger, and Zaire. NED-affiliated groups such as the National Democratic Institute (NDI), the National Republican Institute (NRI), and the Center for International Private Enterprise (CIPE) provided grants to various democracy-building groups and projects in Kenya, Liberia, Namibia, Tunisia, and Uganda. In all, there are 45 non-democratic nations in Africa that potentially could benefit from NED grants.

- *Creating a Radio Free Africa.*

No aspect of a Liberation Doctrine for Africa is likely to be more important than exposing Africans to democratic ideas and values. This approach worked in Eastern Europe, where Radio Free Europe has presented independent news and analysis, and helped build momentum for democratic change. In Cuba, too, Radio Marti, inaugurated in May 1985, is exposing Cubans to alternative news and opinion, which, in turn, is resulting in increased calls for democratic change.

Democratic Radio

Africa will be no different. An American-sponsored Radio Free Africa would broadcast news and democratically-oriented programs, such as those on the mechanics of democracy and the merits of free enterprise. It is estimated by David Sanders, a former staff member of the House Foreign Affairs Committee and an advocate of Radio Free Africa, that by using existing transmitters, Radio Free Africa could be broadcast in five languages for as little as $20 million. Representative Dan Burton, the Indiana Republican, is the leading congressional advocate for Radio Free Africa, though his effort so far has been ignored by the Bush Administration.

- *Putting autocratic African governments on notice that unless American security interests are jeopardized, the continued denial by an African country of fundamental economic and political liberties will result in a reduction or termination of U.S. aid to that country.*

American foreign aid has three purposes—to charitably assist those in need, to protect or advance American security interests, and to promote economic development. The lion's share of American foreign aid to Africa has aimed at the last purpose—to promote economic development. This has failed. In part this is because political and economic freedom is almost always required for economic growth. Without economic and political liberty, most African nations thus have wasted American taxpayers' money. Washington no longer should send foreign aid to African nations with the intention of promoting economic development unless these countries move toward the political and economic liberty necessary for such development.

- *Doubling assistance to the National Endowment for Democracy (NED) for democracy-building programs in Africa.*

Supporting Democracy

(African) countries tending towards pluralism, public accountability, respect for the rule of law, human rights and market principles should be encouraged.

(But) governments who persist with repressive policies, with corrupt management, or with wasteful and discredited economic systems should not expect us to support their folly with scarce aid resources which could be used better elsewhere.

Douglas Hurd, quoted by Baffour Ankomah in *New African*, August 1990.

NED, though small, helps spur democratic change in Africa. Its programs have achieved modest success on the continent so far—particularly in Benin, Botswana, and Nigeria. With further resources it is likely that they can do more. In 1991, NED is spending $750,000 on Africa. A Liberation Doctrine should double this amount by taking an additional $750,000 from the existing $1.058 billion annual Africa foreign aid budget. Although the spread of democracy in Africa is important for U.S. interests, there is no need to expand U.S. foreign aid expenditures to do it.

Unequal Assistance

Yet, there are problems with NED programs in Africa. One is that often money goes to countries needing it least. In 1990, some $715,000 of NED grants, for example, were made to Nigeria and South Africa, even though these countries are among those making the greatest progress toward democratic reform. In very oppressive societies, like Angola and Ethiopia, NED offers no assistance. The reason for this apparently is that few if any eligible democratic organizations exist inside these countries. The authoritarian regimes have jailed, killed, or exiled most leaders of democratic movements; those democratic-minded Angolans and Ethiopians who remain in their country either have joined armed resistance movements or disengaged from politics.

One way to assist the building of democracy in highly oppressive African nations is for NED to assist democratic-oriented exile groups engaged in advancing democracy in their homeland through independent publishing, the hosting of forums, and other such activities. A second way, of course, is by ensuring that Radio Free Africa reaches the people of these repressive nations. As was the case in Eastern Europe, independent communications can play an important role in building momentum for democratic change, even in the most oppressed societies.

At no time since the end of European colonialism a quarter-century ago has the prospect for a fundamental political transition in Africa been so great. Some seventeen of Africa's 45 non-democratic governments are now making moves toward multi-party democracy, and another fourteen may be doing so shortly. Others surely will follow. Africans are making this change because they correctly have come to equate political authoritarianism with economic malaise and human rights abuses. The rise of democracy and free market reforms in Eastern Europe, and Latin America, too, have prompted African leaders and people to look anew at their autocratic political systems.

Washington will not be able, nor should it attempt, to force democracy on Africa. Yet with the Cold War receding and prospects for democratic political change in Africa increasing, America has the flexibility to pursue a nuanced policy towards Africa. . . .

Through this doctrine, Washington can help tip the political balance in Africa toward political freedom. This, in turn, will advance Washington's interests of bringing Africa—one of the world's last remaining bastions of authoritarianism and economic statism—into the growing community of democratic, free market nations.

> *"Linking economic support to broader political liberalization can be a dangerous and destructive approach to forcing desirable changes in African societies."*

Aid to Africa Should Not Be Tied to Democratic Reforms

Carol Lancaster

In the following viewpoint, Carol Lancaster argues that making political reform a precondition for U.S. economic aid would harm African nations. She warns that political liberalization might inflame ethnic conflict, encourage politically powerful groups to oppress weaker groups under the guise of majority rule, and damage current economic reforms. Conditional aid is a form of coercion that allows Western governments to determine the policies and goals of African nations, she concludes. Lancaster is the director of the African Studies Program in the School of Foreign Service at Georgetown University in Washington, D.C.

As you read, consider the following questions:

1. According to the author, why is the idea of conditional aid to Africa appealing to donor countries?
2. What programs does Lancaster suggest might be an alternative to conditional aid?
3. How could reforms of economic governance be effected and encouraged, in the author's opinion?

Carol Lancaster, "Reform or Else?" *Africa Report*, July/August 1990. Copyright © 1990 by the African-American Institute. Reprinted by permission of *Africa Report*.

Should rich countries and international institutions providing concessional assistance and debt relief to sub-Saharan Africa link their aid to political, as well as to economic, reforms? This is the question of the day, raised and debated in the media, in policy discussions within the U.S. government, in public documents by international economic institutions, by African intellectuals, and by development experts.

This question emerges from two rather separate trends in world politics: efforts at structural adjustment in Africa, begun in the 1980s as a result of the deepening economic crisis, the desperate need of African governments for foreign financing, and the increasing tendency of governments, the IMF [International Monetary Fund], and World Bank to condition their assistance on economic stabilization and structural adjustment. Over 30 African countries now have stabilization and/or structural adjustment programs with the IMF and World Bank.

But structural adjustment has yet to produce a clear-cut success in sub-Saharan Africa. Sustained economic reform programs in Ghana and elsewhere have contributed to healthy growth rates (of 5 percent or above in Ghana) over several years. However, an examination of the components of this growth suggests that it is based on an expansion in capacity utilization in agriculture and industry, large aid inflows, some investments in mining—likely to produce quick and profitable gains—and in the informal sector. Significant new investment in manufacturing and agriculture have not yet materialized. Indeed, in Ghana, domestic savings and investment remain among the lowest in the world and disinvestment in industry continues as inefficient firms collapse in the face of import competition. An increase in private, productive investment is a critical element in the success of structural adjustment; without it, there will be no sustained economic growth. The question is why the investment has not occurred and what can be done to encourage it. This is where the problem of governance arises.

The Issue of Investment

Investors, African or foreign, put their resources at risk to make profits. In many lines of investment, particularly in manufacturing, investors will gain profits only over a period of years and so will invest where they have reasonable confidence that business conditions will not alter dramatically. In many of these aspects, Africa remains uncompetitive with other parts of the world. The logistics of doing business in Africa are still difficult, with transport and communications facilities poor and unreliable in many countries. Physical infrastructure is still inferior to that in other parts of the world. African labor is becoming cheaper, but in many places is still uncompetitive with the disciplined, literate, and often skilled labor in much of Asia or, more recently, Eastern Europe.

But above all, investors lack confidence in African governments which say they want private investment, but then act, at times unintentionally, to discourage it or which are riddled with corruption. Perhaps the most important obstacle to private investment and growth in Africa is that everything is open to negotiation. Rules and regulations are frequently implemented by government officials in an arbitrary and capricious fashion. Above all, investors require predictability on the part of their host governments. This is not present for them in much of Africa and so they go elsewhere.

A Poor Solution

A crucial distinction needs to be drawn between political change that evolves from below and free-market economics imposed from outside. A Western-engineered solution to African problems is likely to be booby-trapped from the start: by linking economic policy with political freedoms, the failure of one will almost certainly bring down both.

Josh Mamis, *Toward Freedom*, February 1991.

Without an improvement in governance, sustained growth will not occur, for behind problems of economic mismanagement and corruption are problems of leadership, interest group pressures, patronage politics, a lack of transparency and probity in government decision-making, and an absence of public accountability. The Economic Commission for Africa acknowledged the problem of governance in its report, *An African Alternative Framework to Structural Adjustment Programmes*, as did the World Bank in its long-term study, *Sub-Saharan Africa: From Crisis to Sustainable Growth*. Thus, the problems with structural adjustment and renewed economic growth in Africa raise the question: Should aid be linked to political reform?

The question is also raised as a result of the recent changes in Eastern Europe and the West's response to them. Eastern Europeans have combined their dramatic moves toward economic and political liberalization with appeals to the West for economic help (less concessional assistance than commercial loans, debt restructuring, technical assistance, and private investment). The Western Europeans and the U.S. have responded with some money and some promises, and the conditioning of their help on continuing political liberalization. The fact that democracy could break out in Eastern Europe, where it was least expected, suggests that it could happen elsewhere. Why not encourage it in Africa by conditioning aid on political liberalization there?

In answering this question, there are several important issues to consider. First of all, what is the *objective* of tying aid to political reform? Is it to promote more open, democratic societies as an end, for the good inherent in them? Or is it to promote economic development?

A corollary to this question is *which reforms* are necessary for meaningful political liberalization? What, in the words of Robert Dahl, would it take to ensure that African governments are "responsive to the preferences of their citizens"? To ensure citizens basic political rights, the following conditions are usually regarded as necessary: freedom of expression (implying media, universities, and public fora free to raise and debate political issues and to criticize government) and freedom of assembly; an independent judiciary enforcing the rule of law; and an opportunity on the part of the public to change the political leadership through periodic, free and fair elections. Much of the experience of independent Africa suggests that it may be difficult to fulfill these conditions within the framework of a one-party state. A multi-party state may be unavoidable.

The Hazards of Pluralism

As attractive as the idea of political liberalization is for Africa, there are some potential problems. First, open political competition may center on ethnic, regional, or religious cleavages dangerous to national unity. At independence, the fear of ethnically based politics (far from groundless) was the justification for the one-party state. Is there reason to believe that the dangers of ethnic politics have by now declined in importance or that ethnic politics would be less disruptive of national unity today than at independence? Does the answer to this question differ from country to country? If so, why? The tensions resurfacing in Eastern Europe and the USSR suggest that even when they have been suppressed for decades, ethnic politics do not disappear as potent and often destructive political forces.

Second, is the pluralism so often thought to be necessary for a successfully functioning democracy sufficiently developed in Africa to support democracy? Third, are powerful political groups prepared to abide by democratic rules rather than resort to the use of force to gain or retain political power? Where societies lack powerful, organized groups with diverse and sometimes competing interests, a dominant group or coalition can function as an autocracy, even in democratic camouflage, promoting the interests of its own supporters and depriving others of economic opportunities as well as political rights.

Are Zaire, Liberia, Sudan, or Somalia sufficiently pluralist societies in which powerful groups are willing to play by democratic rules? The answer is clear in these cases. It is less so regarding Kenya, Nigeria, Senegal, or Côte d'Ivoire—although in each of these cases, ethnic or religious-based politics remain a possibility and a threat.

Democracy Could Harm Reforms

Fourth, it is possible that democratization in African societies can harm rather than hurt the success of structural adjustment programs, generally regarded as critical for restoring economic growth in the region. Open political debate would inevitably include the major issue with which so much of the continent is now struggling—structural adjustment. Structural adjustment programs are controversial (not the least because of the foreign involvement in them), painful (particularly for vocal and influential groups), and often emotive and ill-understood by the general public. The largest group benefitting from them—rural farmers—are typically the least articulate, the least well-organized, and among the least politically influential group nationally. Would they organize, articulate, and vote their economic interests in an election where structural adjustment is an issue?

It is very possible that where structural adjustment programs become the subject of open political debate or a major issue in political campaigns, where articulate, powerful groups and individuals are predominant (whose interests are threatened by structural adjustment), these programs will be discarded along with those politicians supporting them. President Babangida of Nigeria has acknowledged this threat by attempting to exclude it from the upcoming national election campaign. It very nearly defeated President Diouf of Senegal. There may well be a trade-off between political liberalization and economic liberalization in sub-Saharan Africa.

A second major issue is *how aid should be linked* to political liberalization. Conditioning foreign aid on political liberalization would add an additional degree of coercion to relationships between African governments and foreign powers, which is already there in conditioning aid on economic reforms. Perhaps a degree of coercion on economic reform in exchange for additional resources is warranted, but there are limits beyond which such conditioning becomes counter-productive, both in terms of short-run relationships between aid donors and recipients, and in terms of the long-run interests of Africans who, in the last analysis, must be responsible for making their own decisions affecting their destinies.

More important, conditioning aid on political reform puts the initiative of deciding which reforms are appropriate and workable in the hands of foreigners, particularly government officials and international civil servants. There are few who are well enough informed to make such decisions about what will work politically in Africa's complex and changing societies.

An alternative to conditioning foreign aid on political liberalization would be for aid donors to deploy a portion of their aid in support of the many changes useful to promote democracy in Africa: training for judges, legislators, journalists, trade unionists; support for non-governmental groups which would be important in a pluralist political system, for example, professional, youth, and women's groups; support for independent public policy research institutions which could develop the alternatives to government policies necessary for open and informed debate.

Dangers of Conditionality

Political economists . . . would condition aid on policy reform, but specifically on political reforms aimed at protecting or expanding democratic and civil rights of African citizens. This approach is, in effect, aimed at empowerment of the poor—using aid to force political changes that will ensure that those now effectively shut out of the political process, including the mass of small farmers, receive an influential voice. Calls for conditioning foreign aid on political reforms generally have been rejected by the development community. They are seen as impractical: Aid donors rarely have sufficient leverage to force political leaders to diminish their own power by transferring political power to others. Such an approach is also far more interventionist than are economic reforms tied to foreign aid and could endanger relations between donors (bilateral governments or international institutions) and the political leadership in recipient governments.

Carol Lancaster, *Coping with Africa's Food Crisis*, 1988.

These would not be new activities for the U.S. government, which has funded similar programs for four decades in Asia and the Far East through the Asia Foundation. It has not financed these sorts of activities in Africa (except in a small way in South Africa). This alternative would not be coercive and would leave decision-making in the hands of the Africans, but it would probably not bring about major political reforms quickly.

A further alternative for supporting democracy in Africa would be for aid donors to provide African governments with additional aid after moves toward democratization had been implemented. This approach would contain a degree of coercion, but would leave decision-making and initiative in the hands of the Africans.

If the objective of linking aid to political reform is to promote the success of structural adjustment, more limited reforms may be sufficient and appropriate. These reforms could be targeted at *economic governance* and would include: transparent government budgeting (no more hidden accounts for the discretionary use of a Mobutu, Doe, or Ahidjo); well-planned investments appropriate to national economic needs and priorities (no white elephants dedicated to the everlasting memory of a particular leader or foreign aid donor); open and competitive bidding for large public investment projects (no more Turkwell dams in Kenya, Inga-Shabas in Zaire or Ivorian sugar projects); and the consistent and fair implementation of regulations governing investment.

Extending the conditions of foreign aid to economic governance implies that foreigners would assume the role of ensuring public accountability by African governments on issues of economic governance through close coordination of their aid and export policies, through monitoring recipient government economic decision-making and policy implementation, and through reducing or raising their aid levels based on the performance of African governments in this area. In theory, this is what is happening now with IMF stabilization and World Bank structural adjustment programs. The conditions of these programs could be formally extended to include economic governance.

Skillfully Avoiding Reforms

An approach linking additional foreign aid to economic governance is not without problems. The most difficult problem may be getting foreign governments to cooperate in their policies vis-à-vis the Africans. There is a considerable degree of informal cooperation now, but many of the failures of implementation of economic reform programs in Africa can be traced to the support of developed countries of their African clients' desires to avoid reforms. President Mobutu of Zaire has demonstrated the most skill in manipulating his three patrons to avoid serious reforms. But he is not alone. Presidents Houphouët-Boigny of Côte d'Ivoire and Traoré of Mali have sought (and obtained) French intervention to avoid painful policy reforms.

Developed countries have their economic and political interests in Africa and are still often willing to put them ahead of their interests in economic reforms. It remains to be seen whether the economic decline in the region and the decrease in East-West tensions will so erode foreign economic and political interests there that they will be willing to center their economic support for African governments largely on progress toward reforms.

Another problem with adding economic governance to the list of aid reforms required by foreign governments and international institutions is operationalizing the concept. What are the policies that should be reformed? How can we tell when they are changed? Should aid be conditioned on a sliding scale of reforms or on attaining an absolute level of reform? These are difficult, but not impossible questions to answer.

The final and most critical question is whether reforms in economic governance would be effective in promoting investment and growth in Africa. There are obstacles to increased investment in Africa, other than problems of economic governance. The question of whether extending structural adjustment lending to include economic governance would be effective in stimulating investment can only be answered in practice. Where other factors (infrastructure, labor costs and productivity, potential profitability of an investment) are favorable, improved economic governance could be helpful and perhaps decisive in encouraging investors. And it may only take one or two large and profitable investments in Africa to re-ignite investor confidence in the region.

In any case, improved economic governance is unlikely to worsen economic conditions in Africa or hurt broader prospects for investment and growth. At a very minimum, it would ensure a more efficient use of existing resources. And something needs urgently to be done to make structural adjustment successful—if initially only in one place. The alternative is further decline.

The Appeal of Conditionality

The linking of concessional resources to economic reforms has been with us for most of the decade of the 1980s. It now appears that governments are beginning to think about linking any additional aid resources to political reforms. This is an attractive notion to Western governments and to many Africans and one strongly suggested by the experience of Eastern Europe. There may be some useful and workable reforms to be achieved through this approach, particularly in the area of economic governance.

But linking economic support to broader political liberalization can be a dangerous and destructive approach to forcing desirable changes in African societies because, thus far, it is so poorly thought out on both sides; because foreign officials are not well-positioned to advise Africans on effective political changes; and because Africans, in their desperation to obtain additional concessional resources, may agree to changes which in reality they cannot or will not implement or which implemented, will prove unsustainable and generate further political and economic instability.

Understanding Words in Context

Readers occasionally come across words they do not recognize. And frequently, because they do not know a word or words, they will not fully understand the passage being read. Obviously, the reader can look up an unfamiliar word in a dictionary. By carefully examining the word in the context in which it is used, however, the word's meaning can often be determined. A careful reader may find clues to the meaning of the word in surrounding words, ideas, and attitudes.

Below are excerpts from the viewpoints in this chapter. In each excerpt, one of the words is printed in italics. Try to determine the meaning of each word by reading the excerpt. Under each excerpt you will find four definitions for the italicized word. Choose the one that is closest to your understanding of the word.

Finally, use a dictionary to see how well you have understood the words in context. It will be helpful to discuss with others the clues that helped you decide on each word's meaning.

1. Africa has not yet been swept by democratic revolution. Many of the *AUTOCRATIC* leaders in Europe and Latin America have been deposed, and the governments are now run by all of the citizens, not just one person.

   AUTOCRATIC means:

   a) tyrannical   c) stupid
   b) helpful   d) proud

2. Because the Tigreans of Ethiopia were not allowed to control their own land and water, they led an *INSURGENCY* to overthrow the nation's government.

   INSURGENCY means:

   a) election   c) conference
   b) strike   d) revolt

3. Despite its recent independence, Namibia will remain *FET-TERED* because multinational corporations control most of the resources of the country, including its valuable land and diamonds.

FETTERED means:

a) free
b) enslaved
c) irresponsible
d) primitive

4. Conditioning foreign aid on political liberalization would add an additional degree of *COERCION* to relationships between African governments and foreign powers. The African governments would have to agree to do everything the donor country wanted.

COERCION means:

a) courtesy
b) closeness
c) domination
d) friendliness

5. It is not enough to just talk about reform programs; African nations must insist on the consistent and fair *IMPLEMENTATION* of reforms. Only when the new programs are actually in place and working will progress and growth be evident.

IMPLEMENTATION means:

a) enactment
b) stalling
c) teaching
d) guarantee

6. The people of Africa are poor because their governments discourage *ENTREPRENEURSHIP*. Most peasants could make enough money to support themselves if they were allowed to start their own businesses.

ENTREPRENEURSHIP means:

a) formal education
b) community discussions
c) private business activity
d) helping others

7. When African nations first began gaining independence, there was no *INDIGENOUS* private sector. Most private firms were controlled by citizens of other countries.

INDIGENOUS means:

a) native
b) law-abiding
c) productive
d) wealthy

Periodical Bibliography

The following articles have been selected to supplement the diverse views presented in this chapter.

Africa News	"A Chance for Africa," May 20, 1991.
Africa News	Whole Issue, December 25, 1989.
George B.N. Ayittey	"Restoring Africa's Free Market Tradition," *Backgrounder*, July 6, 1988. Available from The Heritage Foundation, 214 Massachusetts Ave. NE, Washington, DC 20002.
George B.N. Ayittey	"The End of African Socialism?" *The Heritage Lectures*, January 24, 1990. Available from The Heritage Foundation, 214 Massachusetts Ave. NE, Washington, DC 20002.
Richard J. Barnet	"But What About Africa?" *Harper's Magazine*, May 1990.
R. Stephen Brent	"Aiding Africa," *Foreign Policy*, Fall 1990.
Victoria Brittain	"Africa: Which Way to Go?" *World Marxist Review*, November 1989.
Ernest Harsch	"After Adjustment," *Africa Report*, May/June 1989.
Carol Lancaster	"Economic Reform in Africa: Is It Working?" *Washington Quarterly*, Winter 1990. Available from MIT Press, 55 Hayward St., Cambridge, MA 02142.
Salim Lone	"Challenging Conditionality," *Africa Report*, September/October 1990.
Edwin Meese	"Africa Can Prosper with the Right Policies," *Conservative Chronicle*, September 27, 1989. Available from PO Box 11297, Des Moines, IA 50340-1297.
Colleen Lowe Morna	"Surviving Structural Adjustment," *Africa Report*, September/October 1989.
Newsweek	"A Longing for Liberty," July 23, 1990.
United States Department of State	*Debt Relief Plays Key Role in Helping Sub-Saharan Africa*, Public Information Series, February 1990. Available from the Department of State, Correspondence Management Division, PA/PC Room 5819, Washington, DC 20520.
Nancy E. Wright	"Disastrous Decade: Africa's Experience with Structural Adjustment," *Multinational Monitor*, April 1990.

CHAPTER 4

What Form of Government Would Benefit Africa?

Chapter Preface

In recent years, the world has been swept by democratic revolutions. Throughout Eastern Europe, Asia, and Latin America, autocratic leaders have been overthrown and replaced by democratically elected governments. The two regions untouched by the surge toward democracy are the Middle East and Africa.

In all of Africa, in fact, only seven nations have governments that can be described as democratic. These seven governments all have multiparty political systems, independent legislatures and judiciaries, and guaranteed freedoms. While some other African nations have recently begun leaning toward democracy, most continue to be ruled by authoritarian dictatorships or to be one-party states.

Some analysts believe democracy will eventually come to Africa just as it did to Eastern Europe. Others argue that Africa is unique and may not welcome democracy. They cite several reasons for African nations' reluctance to accept democracy. One, according to many historians, is that African cultures traditionally have a strong respect for leaders and are more comfortable with authoritarian governments than with democracy. April A. Oliver, a reporter for the "McNeil/Lehrer NewsHour," writes of Africa, "Respect for tribal leaders is an honored custom, strengthening authoritarian rulers." This respect for authority, some scholars contend, leads Africans to prefer authoritarian forms of government over democracy.

Other scholars maintain that democracy would be ineffective in a region that needs decisive leadership to bring progress. Democracy is a slow political system, in which laws are passed and decisions made only after much debate between the branches of power. In contrast, authoritarian leaders theoretically have a greater opportunity to make decisions quickly and enact policies efficiently, thereby possibly spurring development without consulting with a parliament or congress. This was one reason why many in the West supported strong African leaders in the post-colonial period, and why many African nations became authoritarian, one-party governments after the end of colonialism. Heritage Foundation scholar George B.N. Ayittey explains: "To initiate development, it was widely held that the state needed wide-ranging powers to marshall resources. Extensive powers were conferred upon African heads of state. . . . In this way, *all* African governments, regardless of their professed ideology, came to assume immense powers."

Africa's fifty-three governments rule people of diverse cultures, languages, resources, and needs. The authors of the following viewpoints present their arguments in support of various forms of government for the nations of Africa.

"A new Africa, with governments truly of, by, and for the people, could rightfully demand a 'New Deal' for the continent."

Democracy Can Solve Africa's Economic Problems

Richard Joseph

In the following viewpoint, Richard Joseph argues that Africa's economic problems are related to the centralized, undemocratic social and political institutions on the continent. Bribery and political corruption make the area unattractive to investors and foreign aid organizations. The author theorizes that Africans must enact democratic economic and political reforms in order to strengthen their economies. Richard Joseph is a professor of political science at Emory University in Atlanta, Georgia.

As you read, consider the following questions:

1. According to the author, how has excessive government involvement hurt the economies of Africa?
2. Why have previous attempts at economic reform and financial management by the International Monetary Fund and U.S. Agency for International Development failed, in Joseph's view?
3. What advantage does Joseph argue democratization would give African countries in dealing with foreign aid donors?

The economic decline that sub-Saharan Africa experienced during the 1980s provoked a sometimes rancorous debate about what should be done. Most of the arguments advanced in that debate are now well-known and have been fully aired in publications of the World Bank and the Economic Commission for Africa. However, before real evidence of economic recovery could be identified in countries undergoing stabilization and adjustment reforms, the continent was swept by a wave of demands for more pluralistic political systems. Single-party rule in particular has come under sustained attack in the streets of many African cities and in the boardrooms of the major bilateral and multilateral donors. . . .

As a general principle, drawing on world-wide experiences, it is clear that the absence of democracy does not mean that economic growth will be stymied. There are nations like South Korea and Taiwan that experienced decades of sustained economic expansion under highly authoritarian systems, and even Japan's "liberal democracy" still retains oligarchic features. Another country now regularly cited in this vein is Indonesia, which has enjoyed a prolonged economic upswing under an autocratic military regime.

A More Complex Paradigm

However, this pattern of reasoning is not fully satisfactory. Some scholars, like Claude Aké, distinguish economic growth from development, the latter which he feels necessitates human-centered qualities that are suppressed in "developmental dictatorships." Equally important is the fact that this issue does not have to be considered abstractly since we now have a good understanding of the dynamics of post-colonial Africa on which any analysis and prognosis should be based.

Virtually all countries in Africa today are hurting economically, including those that adopted socialist strategies of an authoritarian nature, such as Benin, as well as those that used more conciliar approaches, such as Tanzania. They also include countries that have been capitalist in orientation, such as Cameroon, Côte d'Ivoire, and Kenya; those that are led by military as well as by single-party regimes; and even those that are quasi-democratic like Senegal. In brief, a global crisis afflicts most of sub-Saharan Africa and its elements include the weakening of commodity prices, pronounced difficulties in achieving export diversification, the absence of adequate domestic markets and limited access to external ones, and recourse to increasing indebtedness followed by a failure to generate earnings sufficient to service that debt.

A general cycle of impoverishment has therefore taken shape into which the majority of African countries have been gradu-

Democracy in Africa

Source: World Bank.

ally drawn. With an average of nearly 50 percent of external earnings being consumed by debt-servicing, and with commercial investments drying up, African countries have been rendered increasingly dependent on concessional aid and loans. In the short term, one of the major effects of structural adjustment programs is to compel African governments to acknowledge their countries' impoverished status by making sharp reductions in social spending—public employment, education, health, transport, and welfare services.

To adequately address the question of democracy and development in Africa, it is necessary to consider an additional dimension, namely governance. Those countries on the Pacific Rim cited earlier may be undemocratic, or partially democratic, but they have also developed appropriate systems of governance, especially concerning the use of available resources in both the public and private sectors.

Carol Lancaster has advanced the term "economic governance" to refer to practices of decision-making and implementation in the economic realm (*Africa Report*, July-August 1990). Concerned as this perspective is with matters that directly affect public investments and expenditures, her categorization is meant to exclude issues of a more strictly political nature such as the number of political parties, the nature of the electoral system, the structure of the government, and general constitutional provisions.

While there is some overlap between Lancaster's analysis and the one advanced here, one important difference is that I do not believe it is possible in contemporary Africa to achieve the separation she postulates between the economic and the more political dimensions of governance.

In the case of the newly industrialized countries, they succeeded for a few decades in making this separation until their people rejected the suppression of civil liberties and the artificial compression of incomes and living standards. One important reason for the success of these countries in expanding their economies under authoritarian political systems is because an investment climate was fostered characterized by predictability, stability, and productivity. This climate contrasts with the typical African one where, according to Lancaster, "everything is open to negotiation."

The reason why an African economy such as Kenya's began losing its attractiveness to investors, according to human rights lawyer Gibson Kamau Kuria, is because everything became open to negotiation or, put more bluntly, to bribery and political influence: Debts were no longer speedily repaid, official decisions were not based on the relevant legislation and regulations, and judgments of the courts did not reflect a transparent application of the laws. . . .

Growth of Centralization

Most African countries have become characterized by increasing centralization of government operations, by the entrenchment of political monopolies by single parties or military regimes, by the consolidation of what Thomas Callaghy in his writings on Zaire has called political aristocracies, by the relentless increase in presidential and military expenditures, by the bureaucratization and declining efficiency of the state sector, and by the closing-off of democratic routes to the procurement of state-controlled resources and the encouragement of nepotistic networks.

The pervasiveness of what we have termed prebendalism, as state offices are privatized and used to generate income for office-holders and their sectionally defined clients, has often culminated in extensive corruption at the summit of the political order and its replication in subordinate echelons. Students of Africa who many years ago decried Stanislav Andreski's characterization of African urban societies as "kleptocratic" are now forced to acknowledge the contemporary popular adage that "to eat *magendo* you have to earn *magendo*" (*magendo* referring to illicitly obtained goods and income).

In short, the general crisis in governance and the increasingly undemocratic nature of most African political systems have become intertwined. It is no longer possible to tackle one without the other, whether in the USSR and Poland, as is now generally accepted, or in Gabon and Zaire. . . .

The Failure of Current Reforms

Efforts to pursue a series of circumscribed reforms in economic and financial management, as was attempted in Zaire under IMF auspices, and in Liberia under U.S. AID, must now be recognized as impractical. President Gorbachev has learned with difficulty that the Soviet economy and political system must be simultaneously transformed. The Chinese gerontocracy pulled back sharply at the point when its version of perestroika without glasnost was firmly challenged. African countries, with their fragile economies and plural composition, cannot afford either a prolonged re-learning period for their leaders or violent, Ceausescu-like defenses of the decaying order.

It is evident that virtually all African countries must devise appropriate ways of facilitating greater openness, transparency, and accountability in their economic and political life. Attempts to create an economic marketplace without a corresponding political one are no longer credible. It must also be recognized, however, that Africa's predicament does not stop at its shoreline: Increased economic and political pluralism, even if appropriately combined, will not in themselves guarantee economic recovery. What is undertaken domestically will not automatically change the ways in which Africa is marginalized by the operations of the world economy.

Politics of the Future

In exploring new pathways to Africa's resumed development, the political dimension looms large wherever we look. Within African nation-states, unrepresentative and unaccountable governments must give way to ones that enjoy democratic legitimacy. . . .

A new Africa, with governments truly of, by, and for the people, could rightfully demand a "New Deal" for the continent.

"A transplant of Western-style democracy does not address the root causes of conflict and hunger in Africa."

Democracy Cannot Solve Africa's Economic Problems

John Prendergast

John Prendergast is a research associate with the Center of Concern, a group that advises the United Nations by researching social conditions and advocating specific policy reforms. In the following viewpoint, Prendergast predicts the effects of Western democracy on Africa by referring to the experience of Sudan. He argues that democracy cannot strengthen the continent's economies when African nations still face a lack of broad citizen involvement in government, excessive centralization of decision making, and Western involvement in Africa's economic policy-making.

As you read, consider the following questions:

1. According to the author, what internal political conditions in Africa make it virtually impossible for democracy to succeed there?
2. How does the involvement of the World Bank and the IMF in African economies make it unlikely that democracy would help strengthen Africa economically, according to Prendergast?
3. How has attempted democratization affected Sudan, according to the author?

John Prendergast, "Africa: Democracy Misses the Real Problems," *Center Focus*, May 1990. Reprinted by permission of the Center of Concern, Washington, D.C.

More than anywhere else in the world, institutional processes leading to democratic transformation have been conspicuously absent in Africa.

In the thirty years since the "winds of change" swept through Africa and led to the throwing off of the colonial yoke, the institution in most countries which has received the preponderance of government attention and resources has been the military. The political, economic and social institutions of civil society which have formed the backbone of peaceful change in other parts of the globe have been ignored or viciously repressed by most of Africa's governments. And if that isn't enough for the ordinary people of Africa to bear, the old colonial powers, now led by the US and Japan, have maneuvered to regain an enormous amount of control over the economic, trade and resource policies of most of Africa through the World Bank and International Monetary Fund (IMF). Resulting from this extraordinary concentration of political and economic power has been war. Deep-rooted civil wars rage in nearly a quarter of the countries on the continent.

Into this maelstrom have confidently marched the proponents of democracy. Exiled and expatriate Africans, scholars, policymakers and commentators of all stripes have almost unanimously reacted to the events in Eastern Europe by offering democracy as the panacea for Africa's ills. When free, multiparty elections are held, wrote George Ayittey of the Heritage Foundation in the *Washington Post*, "that's when real resolutions will begin to emerge." Richard Joseph of the Carter Presidential Center sounded a similar theme in a *New York Times* op-ed: "If you wish increased assistance for your versions of *perestroika* (restructuring), then give your people *glasnost* (openness)."

Almost hypnotic in its appeal, this simplistic argument for a transplant of Western-style democracy does not address the root causes of conflict and hunger in Africa in three crucial areas:

Little Popular Participation

First, people's participation in the political and economic system would be inadequately addressed by Western-style democracy. At a conference in Tanzania on Popular Participation in Development, an editor of an African magazine noted that the delegates "explicitly identified the lack of participatory processes as the primary cause of Africa's unyielding, decade-long economic catastrophe." With the decision-making apparatus still centralized and biased towards the elite segments of society, popular elections would need to be coupled with the decentralization of administration to local non-governmental institutions, village or neighborhood organizations, credit unions and producer cooperatives to bring about meaningful participation.

156

In Zimbabwe, this would mean that the issue of increasing numbers of landless families would have to be addressed, because their voices would be much louder on the local level. Increasingly resentful northern Ugandans from the Acholi region would no longer have most of their decisions made by a largely southern-based army. In Somalia, the Isaaq clan of the far north may not have taken up arms against the government if they had had more autonomy in their economic affairs.

Democracy Is Not the Solution

Evidence suggests that democracy is not the path to economic salvation in the Third World. Strong, centralized governments have in fact been proven in the Far East to be highly capable of reviving long-dormant economies.

Josh Mamis, *Toward Freedom*, February 1991.

Second, control over the means and aims of development is possibly the critical issue in countries racked by incessant civil strife. This means far more than just the decentralization of political power.

Tigreans in northern Ethiopia want democracy and regional autonomy, but the crux of their insurgency is their demand for control of resources and development processes by Tigreans themselves. Civil strife is on the upswing in Chad and Kenya, where authoritarian governments have recently moved to further consolidate power, and neglected regions and population groups see no alternative to armed insurrection.

Third, economic neo-colonialism makes political liberalization at the national level largely irrelevant. Economic and development policies in many African nations are being increasingly dictated by the IMF, the World Bank, and other multilateral institutions. Namibia will remain fettered despite its recent independence because of control by multinational corporations over most of the resources of the country, including its valuable land and diamonds.

When Nelson Mandela cries for freedom, the international community is obliged to cheer; when he speaks of nationalizing industries and of other measures designed to disperse control of resources, the silence is deafening. Because of the rapidly deteriorating standard of living experienced by Zambians under their IMF structural adjustment program, President Kenneth Kaunda tried to forge his own economic policy independent of donor community "advice". After two years of total isolation from international finance, Zambia returned to the IMF table. President Samuel Doe of Liberia has not always even pretended to run his country's economy: for more than a year he asked a council of American and European economists to develop economic policy.

Sudan: A Case Study

Sudan illustrates many of these issues. Its neo-colonial relationship with the IMF and the World Bank and other economic roots of its authoritarianism have been discussed [but] there are also political roots of Sudan's authoritarianism and political reasons why democracy may not address the reasons for its revolution.

Sudan was a focus for international attention in 1986 not because of famine, but because it held democratic elections to determine national and local leadership—an anomaly in authoritarian Africa. Although the vast majority of the population in the war-torn south did not vote because of the conflict, Sudan's democratic experiment was loudly hailed by Western nations.

By late 1988 the honeymoon with democracy had gone completely sour. Most sectors of Sudanese society were decrying the dominance of sectarianism and the lack of real representation of underdeveloped regions and interests. Former Sudanese Foreign Minister Francis Deng explains further:

> Liberal democracy presupposes a framework characterized by a broad consensus on the fundamental principles of nationhood, the structure of government, and the shaping and sharing of power, wealth, and other natural resources. Where consensus on these fundamentals is lacking, the people lack even a shared sense of belonging to the nation, even the concepts of majority and minority cannot apply. Parliamentarian democracy under those circumstances becomes the rule of a numerical majority imposed on an alienated minority, whether numerically determined or otherwise marginalized. . . .

The three attempts at democracy in Sudan's short independent history (1956-58, 1964-69, and 1986-89) have all ended in military coups. As a workshop of Sudanese scholars concluded, "The Westminster Model of liberal democracy as practiced in Sudan has always served the interests of reactionary forces and paved the way for return to dictatorship."

Many progressive activists and analysts throughout Africa would agree with this vote of no confidence in the ability of Western democracy to address or cure the social conflicts and endemic hunger that continue to plague the people of the continent.

"A number of forces are at work which may . . . generate an improving economic as well as political climate for African capitalism."

Capitalism Would Benefit Africa

Paul Kennedy

For many years, Africans rejected capitalism because they associated it with colonialism. After witnessing the failure of socialism and other forms of government, however, African nations are now ready to establish capitalism, author Paul Kennedy writes in the following viewpoint. Kennedy believes that many factors, including the rise of private business and the emergence of a growing middle class, contribute to the formation of capitalism in Africa. Kennedy is a senior lecturer in the department of social science at Manchester Polytechnic in Great Britain and the author of *African Capitalism*, from which this viewpoint is excerpted.

As you read, consider the following questions:

1. Why have state-controlled economies been discredited in recent years, according to Kennedy?
2. What four long-term changes does the author believe have helped shift African nations to capitalism?
3. Why does Kennedy believe that Africa's political and economic conflicts will wane?

Excerpted from *African Capitalism: The Struggle for Ascendancy* by Paul Kennedy. Copyright © 1988 Cambridge University Press. Reprinted with permission.

A number of forces are at work which may not only compel African governments to become more responsive to national needs as a whole, but which may also generate an improving economic as well as political climate for African capitalism in the years ahead. Indeed, these influences have already been much in evidence in some countries during the last few years.

Statist economic policies have been largely discredited and to some extent are now in retreat. In many instances the wealth extracted by states over the last 25 years or so has not been productively redeployed. Much of it has been misappropriated for private or political purposes, thereby contributing to a situation of growing inequality. Alternatively, it has been invested in different kinds of public-sector enterprise, often on a huge scale. However it is measured—the return on capital outlay, the contribution to government revenue or the ability to supply sufficient goods and services at a reasonable cost—the performance of the various parastatals has often been very poor in relation to the scarce resources they have absorbed. Even some Marxist writers now seem to doubt the wisdom of trying to expand African economies by relying primarily on public enterprise, at least for the foreseeable future. Meanwhile, government attempts at widespread economic regulation and the imposition of various demands on private producers have stifled enterprise and investment.

Expectations Rise, Economies Decline

The result has been economic stagnation, even collapse in the case of some countries. Moreover, this has happened following a long period of rapid economic change and gradually rising living standards from the 1940s to the 1970s which not only helped to raise material expectations among ordinary people but also exposed the rural and urban masses more intensively to the imperatives as well as the inducements of the cash-nexus. Increasing inequality, repression and frustrated aspirations have all generated political tensions. Faced with the dire consequences of statism—economic decline, the threat of increased political instability and a retreat into the 'second' economy— even the most repressive and corrupt regimes have been forced to move some way towards the introduction of an economic climate more conducive to private initiative.

There are also powerful external pressures at work propelling African governments in the same direction. Thus, over the last few years the International Monetary Fund and World Bank have increasingly insisted that the allocation of further financial assistance to African governments—in the form of debt rescheduling and the provision of 'structural adjustment loans' specifically designed to help resuscitate stagnant or crisis-ridden economies—is to be conditional upon government willingness to introduce wide-ranging reforms in economic management. Some Western governments, too, are now insisting that future aid will depend partly on the willingness to place greater reliance on the operation of market forces and the rejection of what a British minister recently referred to as 'fake-socialist solutions'.

Economic Freedom Leads to Prosperity

The solution to Africa's "food problem" lies in solving its "development problem." And the solution to its "development problem" lies in adopting a policy of *laissez faire*. Only through a policy of *laissez faire* is it possible to determine precisely where Africa's natural comparative advantage lies. And allowing individuals the freedom to pursue what is in their comparative advantage is the best and quickest road to economic development. Whether it lies in the production of food for domestic consumption, the production of food for export, or in nonfood production is irrelevant.

If Africans can earn higher incomes by exporting food or other products than they can by growing food solely for domestic consumption, so much the better. For the higher incomes mean that they are in a better position to satisfy their own and their families' needs.

David Osterfeld, *The Freeman*, May 1988.

By the end of 1986 some 22 African countries had accepted reform packages that qualified them to receive special World Bank loan facilities. Included in this group were countries as diverse, in terms of previous political ideology and economic policy, as Guinea, Mali, Ghana, Mozambique, Kenya, the Ivory Coast, Malawi and Senegal. . . .

Changes Bring About Capitalism

But economic necessity and the dangers of political unrest are not the only factors at work. Arguably, a number of important cumulative, long-term changes taking place in the social and institutional structures of most African countries are slowly but surely bringing about a fundamental shift in the crucial relationships between the sphere of private economic activity, on the one hand, and that of state power and politics, on the other:

1. The rise of technocratic/bureaucratic elites imbued with a concern for national as well as personal ambition and whose members are increasingly likely to be directly or indirectly involved in private business activity on their own account.
2. The growing numbers of educated people competing for se-

cure, high-salaried positions in government employment, and this at a time when the public sector may be contracting, may mean that private business appears increasingly attractive as an alternative.

3. The emergence of second- or even third-generation educated middle-class professionals whose families have already established a relatively secure economic base in the ownership of various kinds of wealth, including business (alongside their greater ability to gain access to prestigious avenues of employment), as a result of the inter-generational accumulation and transfer of different kinds of resources.

4. The ability of privileged political insiders and their clients to exploit their proximity to state power and office at different times since Independence in order to amass private wealth, thereby helping to deepen the destructive tendencies towards 'parasitical' or booty capitalism yet also, perhaps, rendering such political beneficiaries less hostile to future private entrepreneurial rivals now that they possess sources of personal wealth that are not dependent solely on the monopolisation of political power.

To the extent that these changes are indeed taking place they offer further prospects of an improving political climate for African capitalism. Thus, the distrust of private as against collective ownership, the feeling that economic enterprise and political or bureaucratic employment were mutually exclusive and opposed avenues for personal success, the perception that an increasingly differentiated society characterised by economic pluralism and political division along class rather than communal lines represented an alien and destructive force undermining African traditions and the unwillingness of political rulers to tolerate the emergence of potentially independent class rivals or share national resources with others outside the state apparatus—all of these polarities and divisions may steadily wane as they become irrelevant as well as counterproductive from the point of view of all emergent classes including political/bureaucratic elites. Instead, the spheres of public and private, politics and economics are increasingly characterised by complementarity and interdependence in just the same way as in other developed and developing capitalist countries. . . .

The Advance of Capitalism

It has become increasingly evident to Western capitalist interests that their ability to anticipate significant and expanding opportunities in African countries in the years ahead depends on the attainment of political stability and competent government but also on the existence of strong domestic bourgeoisies capable of consolidating the conditions for further capitalist advance. . . . Such a 'partnership' arrangement might provide considerable scope for local capitalists to assume a more prominent and determining role than hitherto. In any case, hopefully, African governments have now realised that if extensive investment by foreign interests is to make a useful and lasting contribution to national development programmes then it must be complemented by a strong domestic involvement at the same time. In the final analysis, only powerful and capable local interests—public as well as private—possess a degree of permanent, all-round commitment to national need sufficient to generate the momentum required for a successful onslaught against the condition of dependent, distorted and restricted development.

> *"I see little reason to believe that capitalism . . . would provide any real solution . . . in Africa today. What is needed is rather 'people's power.'"*

Socialism Would Benefit Africa

Lars Rudebeck

Lars Rudebeck, a Swedish social scientist and associate professor of political science at the University of Uppsala, has made several research trips to Africa. In the following viewpoint, excerpted from *The Socialist Ideal in Africa*, Rudebeck argues that Africans need governments based on "people's power," which he describes as power that comes from and addresses the needs of the working class. He maintains that the capitalism established during Africa's colonial period only harmed the working class and created economic inequality. While capitalism benefits only the wealthy, Rudebeck believes that a socialist "people's power" would give Africans control over their governments and their economies.

As you read, consider the following questions:

1. How did the relationship between the "petty bourgeois" and the peasant class change after Africa's colonial period ended, according to Rudebeck?
2. How are democracy and "people's power" related, in the author's opinion?
3. What does Rudebeck believe will lead Africans to demand new governmental structures?

From "Erosion—and Conditions of Regeneration" by Lars Rudebeck, in *The Socialist Ideal in Africa: A Debate*, Research Paper no. 81 of the Scandinavian Institute of African Studies. Copyright © 1988 by Carlos Lopes and Lars Rudebeck. Reprinted with permission.

The struggle for national liberation in [many African] countries . . . was fought basically by an alliance of leaders from the intermediate strata of the colonial society, the *petite bourgeoisie*, and the peasant agricultural producers. The common goal of putting an end to colonialism united people and leaders, it made them mutually dependent upon each other. This necessitated among other things a measure of democracy within the liberation movements as well as in the liberated areas of those countries where there was armed struggle. Through their common struggle, both the "petty bourgeois" leaders and the more or less traditional farming people who had been mobilized for the struggle were radicalized. People's power came to be wielded against colonialism. Democracy and even socialism were put on the political agenda. . . .

In the post-colonial situation, however, the basis is shattered for the previous alliance between those who are now the wielders of state power on the one hand and the potential producers of agricultural surplus on the other. New class contradictions are brought to the fore, exacerbating existing regional and cultural divisions. . . .

The socialist rhetoric of the present wielders of state power is not only an ideological importation, superficially used to legitimize weakly based power. It is rooted also in the historical reality of the independence struggle and the internal processes of transformation then set in motion, however disconnected from today's political practice. The seeds of hope for a life in dignity then sown in people's minds may appear irrelevant in today's contexts of IMF austerity programs. It would be rash, however, to conclude that they have lost their long term historical significance.

Capitalist Colonialism Created Africa's Nation-States

The historical model of nation-states is linked with capitalism. It is, more specifically, a result of European capitalist development, i.e. the very same development that brought about colonialism and the arbitrary splitting up of Africa across existing regional and cultural lines of division. But what good reasons do we have to believe that Africans today would need to, or indeed could, repeat the earlier stages of European history in order to develop their forces of production and raise their levels of living? Why this historical determinism, whether *bourgeois* or marxist?

We know that economic development in Africa today is subjected to the conditions of the world market, mediated to producers and consumers by way of fragile states. So far, the effects have not been very "appropriate" for solving the problems of underdevelopment either under capitalist or socialist-oriented regimes. It is for instance impossible to trace any systematic difference between capitalist and socialist-oriented regimes in Africa with regard to such a basic statistical indicator of "development" as life expectancy at birth (see *World Development Report 1986,* The World Bank). This, in my view, is basically because in post-colonial Africa, under the conditions of the already existing periphery capitalism, regardless of regime orientation, relations of economic and political power are heavily skewed to the disadvantage of ordinary working people. . . .

AFRICA — THE FAT OF THE LAND

©/1988 Ollie Harrington/*People's Daily World*. Reprinted with permission.

I see little reason to believe that capitalism as such would provide any real solution under the conditions at hand in Africa today. What is needed is rather "people's power" in the literal sense once called for by the liberation movements, which goes to show that the experience of those years may after all be more relevant than often assumed under present conjunctures. Growing slowly through people's daily resistance and struggles for a better life, such power may in the long run be able to force both market and state structures to function more equitably.

Democracy and People's Power

In the ideological and theoretical documents of the liberation movements, the democratic goal was more often expressed through the concept of *people's power* (*poder popular* in Portuguese) than through that of *democracy*, although the two were used interchangeably without any serious efforts being made to distinguish them carefully from each other. Trying to do exactly that may, however, still be a worthwhile exercise in the context of our present discussion.

Democracy is about the regulation and organization of the power apparatus of the state and the participation of the citizens in that apparatus. There is no need to confuse the concept beyond the conventional type of definition accepted by most political scientists: *rule based on universal suffrage, guarantees for free discussion and opposition for everybody, the right to associate and organize freely, and safeguards against the arbitrary exercise of power.*

We know that democracy, defined in this way, in reality exists primarily in certain highly developed capitalist societies, where the citizens accept the rule of the market in the economic realm, although having equal rights to vote as well as the right to speak, associate, and organize without being prevented by the state. We also know that democracy in this strict sense gives no guarantees against poverty, misery, social inequality, squandering of resources, war, although making it more possible than under dictatorship to struggle against such ills.

Thus we need concepts also for other types of relations of power than those covered by the strict political science concept of democracy.

People's power is a central such concept, genetically rooted in socialist theory, adopted and developed i.e. by the liberation movements. . . . It is defined theoretically by these movements as an integral part of development for the people, simultaneously a necessary goal and, a necessary condition of such development. The gaps between theory and practice are known.

The following is a simple working definition of people's power, an attempt to sum up the substance of that concept as developed by the liberation movements in the former Portuguese colonies in Africa: *power exercised in close connection with the working people and being legitimized by the fact of meeting concrete and fundamental interests of the people, as experienced by themselves.* Elements of such people's power did develop in practice during the independence struggles, as necessary and natural components of the process of unification against the colonial enemy.

This means that *people's power* and *democracy* ("people's rule" in English) are closely related but not identical concepts, both at the analytical level and at the level of concrete, historical practice. They condition each other mutually, at the same time as they overlap.

In actual historical situations, people's power and democracy do not always appear simultaneously, but still condition each other strongly. It is for instance a good hypothesis, that non-democratic rulers (for example, the former colonial rulers of Africa) only rarely yield to demands for democracy without being forced to do so by mounting people's power at the class level. On the other hand, it is also a good hypothesis that people's power cannot survive for long without being institutionalized as democracy—after the defeat of undemocratic state power through the mobilization of people's power, as during the liberation struggles.

People's power—when translated into scientific language—turns out to be a wider, more sociological concept than democracy. It includes, in the longer run, democracy, without which it cannot survive. But it is not defined institutionally and formally as democracy is, but through its social contents, with regard to actual participation in the exercise of power in society and with regard to actual policies and social relations.

Equal Distribution of Power Is Necessary

In terms of political structure, democracy can be conceived of under varying degrees of power equality/inequality—representative democracy being quite compatible with considerable hierarchy. People's power requires, on the other hand, more equal distribution of political power.

The other major difference between the two concepts is that democracy is primarily political. People's power, on the other hand, is both social, political, and economic, thus not limited to the level of political structure. We may think of people's power as emerging, when or if people jointly assume control of their own living situations. The concrete beginnings are local. The extension of people's power beyond more local levels is, however, inconceivable except in connection with democratization.

In concluding the report on a field study of people's power in northern Mozambique in which I took part in 1983, the collaborating researchers made a point which carries implications far beyond that particular study. Wherever people's power became a reality during the armed struggle, we point out, this resulted from a social process in which the people took active part in discussing and resolving their own problems. Such social relations (relations of power) do not come from the sky, but arise from common goals and common interests. They require concrete efforts on the part of the leadership to listen and act together with the people in order to resolve the various problems of development. The real difficulties come at the moment when party and state officials no longer share the problems of development with the people or when they find ways of resolving them only for themselves.

Africans Will Demand Change

It cannot be excluded that the combination of economic stagnation for the people and political and cultural repression will create strong pressure in many African countries for other kinds of power structures than those provided by the inherited straight-jackets of the post-colonial states: simultaneously more democratic and pluralist and more supra-state.

Under such more democratic conditions, the people would themselves be more able than today to build and extend people's power as discussed above. They would then also be more able than today to influence the choice of policies for their own development, thus moving the choice between capitalist and socialist policies from the levels of ideological rhetoric and academic analysis to the levels of concrete action by those concerned.

"Rights can only be firmly established in a democratic society."

Democracy Would Promote Human Rights in Africa

Bernard Muna

Democracy is the only form of government that can protect Africans' human rights, Bernard Muna argues in the following viewpoint. Democracy would increase political participation in Africa, and would provide a system of checks and balances that would prevent human rights abuses. Muna is president of the Cameroon Bar Association, and has served as president of the Central African Union of Lawyers. He is active in the field of human rights, and was instrumental in developing a model human rights charter for developing nations.

As you read, consider the following questions:

1. What prevented African nations from becoming democratic after the colonial period, in the author's view?
2. Why does Muna believe the notion of one-party democracy is unrealistic?
3. Why are many of Africa's dictators and single-party governments acquiescing to democracy, according to the author?

Bernard Muna, "Africa's Second Independence," *Journal of Democracy*, vol. 2, no. 3, Summer 1991. Reprinted by permission of The Johns Hopkins University Press.

We find ourselves in the midst of an unfinished revolution. This revolution began in Africa soon after the Second World War, when the colonized peoples launched their struggle for freedom. African political leaders of that era were mainly concerned with lifting the yoke of colonialism and gaining political independence. By the beginning of the 1960s, most of the countries in West and Central Africa had gained political independence in one form or another and the rest of Africa was not far behind. A revolution had begun; it has not yet been completed.

It was a revolution that started with calls for the liberation of the African peoples from colonial exploitation and slavery, and expressed their aspirations to self-government and independence. Self-government and independence were granted to the new nations, but the revolution was hijacked by the new indigenous leaders. The African people were never handed their full sovereignty. In the name of national unity and rapid economic development, many basic human rights and democratic freedoms were sacrificed. Dictatorships, minority governments, and single-party regimes became the order of the day. The peoples of Africa watched helplessly as their own countrymen became the new oppressors. Country after country suffered as oppression, tribalism, and gross injustice ran rampant.

Ironically enough, the retreating colonial powers had left most of these young nations with the necessary structures of democratic government: multiparty parliaments, independent judiciaries, and strong executive branches. Before long, however, most of Africa's multiparty parliaments and independent judiciaries had been done away with. Rulers preferred strong central governments without checks and balances to limit their power.

New Rulers, Old Structures

The revolution also remained unfinished in another respect. During the colonial period, the European-imposed governments had their own administrative structures, tailored to serve the aims and needs of colonialism and the colonial power. At no time did these aims include the development of the colony for the benefit of its people. Yet the new indigenous governments that took over after independence did little or nothing to change the administrative structures that they had inherited; the new rulers found in these structures a convenient means of consolidating their power and oppressing their fellow citizens. Even if all of Africa's postcolonial rulers had nothing but good intentions, however, the colonialist structures that passed into their control could never have proven themselves suitable for serving a sovereign people and developing the nation for their benefit. Hence, the need to reform these structures is another aspect of the unfinished revolution.

What, then, are the prospects for multiparty democracy in Africa today—or rather for democracy simply, since I do not believe that there can be any other kind? The notion of one-party democracy in Africa was at best an empty dream, and for the most part nothing but sheer hypocrisy. One-party democracy can work only with an angel as president and saints as members of the central committee. Even in heaven, the existing order was challenged by Satan, and we all know that today he is still in the opposition.

The second phase of Africa's revolution—what General Olusegun Obasanjo has called the second independence of Africa—now seems to be underway. The leaders who hijacked the revolution and trod upon the sovereignty of the people are now being called to account. Thirty years of dictatorship, minority government, and one-party rule have brought neither national unity nor economic development. Africa is still ravaged by civil wars and ethnic conflicts, as well as by ignorance, poverty, hunger, and disease.

The Triumph of Democracy

Issues of democratization and human rights are increasingly dominating the world's interest in Africa, overcoming a legacy of indifference to the fate of democracy on the continent. . . .

The reforms in Eastern Europe have contributed to this change of heart by providing the West with a dramatic vindication of its own values and a sense of the historical inevitability of the triumph of democracy. The aggressive vacuity of the Cold War has been replaced by the mission of democratization, a mission which, it is widely believed, will firmly consolidate the hegemony of Western values all over the world. Thus the West has come to regard democracy as an important item on the African agenda. This change in attitude also reflects the fact that the long struggle for democracy in Africa is beginning to show results, results too impressive and too widespread to be ignored.

Claude Ake, *Journal of Democracy*, Winter 1991.

Today, thankfully, respect for human rights and the establishment of a democratic society are coming to be seen as the true means to unity and development. But this view is not universally shared. Some ask whether democracy is not a luxury for Africa, and wonder if truly democratic governments can be maintained in the midst of ignorance, poverty, and hunger. Others suspect that democracy might impede development, or fear that it will merely exacerbate intertribal tensions and make the task of government that much more difficult.

It must be admitted that in Third World countries today, development must be brought about under political conditions far different from those which prevailed in Europe and North America at the onset of the Industrial Revolution. Today the philosophy of human rights has become popular politics, while the economics of the private-enterprise system have become much tempered by the concept of an equitable society whose government will devote itself to solving the problems of mass illiteracy, hunger, poverty, and ignorance. In Africa, the need to deal with such problems plays a key role in shaping the choices that democrats must make. Are there really any choices? The temptation to sacrifice certain freedoms in the name of economic development is one to which Africans must not yield, for we would only be repeating old mistakes.

The Power of the Silent Majority

I believe that in Africa, as elsewhere, there exists a large silent majority. It is this majority that has risen today against the corrupt and oppressive practices of the ruling elites. The members of this majority have risen against the pillage of their nations by tiny and selfish minorities. They ask for a fair and equitable society; a society that is just and respects the rule of law; a society in which they are free to choose their political leaders and to hold them accountable for their actions. Many African countries contain dozens, and in some cases, hundreds of different tribes and ethnic groups. Yet in no case does the survival of any of these tribes depend upon the conquest or exploitation of any neighboring tribe. Today all Africans recognize the need to keep their nations together; most tribes recognize their dependence on one another. Single-party rule and minority dictatorship, not democracy, have fueled the tribal conflicts of these last few decades.

In a democratic Africa, the majority would govern but the rights of the minority would be respected. The second independence of Africa will require not only the introduction of true popular sovereignty, but also the complete transformation of the old colonial-era administrative structure into one that serves rather than oppresses the people. Decision making at both the local and national level must be opened to popular participation. This must include an educational effort that will teach the people of Africa how to understand democratic and human rights, and how to defend them against violation. Freely elected parliaments and truly independent judiciaries are also needed in order to check abuses of executive power.

It is in light of these changes that we can talk of the prospects of multiparty democracy in Africa. The African people understand that the defense of their rights and freedoms rests in their own hands. They also realize that these rights can only be firmly established in a democratic society, and that the defense of these rights is a continuing process.

Today, many sons and daughters of Africa are dying or being jailed in fights for these rights. Because democracy and human rights are not being handed to them on a platter, the people of Africa know their true value and are ready to defend them. It is this new spiritedness on the part of the African people that has put the fear of God, or rather the fear of the people, into the hearts of dictators and single-party governments throughout the continent. A few are still resisting democratic reform, but their days are numbered.

I would say, then, that the prospects for multiparty democracy in Africa are quite promising. The people of Africa must keep up the fight until their second independence has been achieved, until the revolution is finished.

"Socialism . . . has the potential for establishing a more rational human social order."

Socialism Would Promote Human Rights in Africa

Osita Eze

Socialism ensures that basic human rights—food, education, health care, housing—are provided, Osita Eze asserts in the following viewpoint. He believes that once these needs are met, Africans will be able to fight for their civil and political rights. While some experts support capitalism as the key to human rights, Eze maintains that capitalism excessively emphasizes the importance of the right to private property and consequently favors the wealthy and hinders the progress of human rights for all. Eze is a professor and dean of the college of legal studies at Iwo State University in Okigwe, Nigeria, and the author of *Human Rights in Africa: Some Selected Problems*.

As you read, consider the following questions:

1. What are some of the socioeconomic and cultural rights Eze believes are vital to sustain life?
2. Why does the author believe access to legal assistance is not always beneficial to underprivileged Africans?
3. How does Eze criticize the media in capitalist societies?

Reprinted by permission of Greenwood Publishing Group, Inc., Westport, CT, from *Emerging Human Rights: The African Political Economy Context*, edited by George W. Shepherd Jr. and Mark O.C. Anikpo. Copyright © 1990 by George W. Shepherd Jr. and Mark O.C. Anikpo.

Most African constitutions embody provisions on human rights. . . . Some of the preambular provisions refer to the French Declaration of Rights of Man and Citizen, and other provisions are similar to those elaborated in the Universal Declaration of Human Rights. Since all independent African states are members of the United Nations and other relevant institutions, it is assumed that they accept the foundations for human rights promotion and protection elaborated therein.

But there is selective emphasis on protected human rights, depending on whether the underlying philosophical value system is capitalist or socialist or even Islamic. The secular capitalist states emphasize civil and political rights along with the right to private property. Civil and political rights include the right to life; prohibition of torture or inhuman and degrading treatment or punishment, slavery or the slave trade; the right to liberty and security of persons to freedom of movement, to equality before the law, privacy, and freedom of thought; the right to opinions, peaceful assembly, and freedom of association; and the right to take part in the conduct of public affairs and to vote and be elected at genuine periodic elections.

The Dominance of Private Property

Invariably, all are entitled to enjoy these rights without distinction as to race, sex, color, language, religion, political or other opinion, national or social origin, birth or other status. Yet the role of the dominance of private property, even in the developed welfare states, in perpetuating inequality and injustice is often glossed over on the basis of the primacy of individual freedom to pursue goals in a free enterprise system with minimal state intervention and control. Nearly everywhere, whether in secular Christian or in Islamic states, discrimination exists based on sex, religion, and political opinion. Racism and ethnic-based discrimination persist. Chad, Sudan, Kenya, Uganda, and to some extent Nigeria represent instances of ethno-based or racial discrimination.

If we consider certain categories of human rights, the situation is nearly the same. In most cultural and religious traditions the right to life is accepted as fundamental and sacrosanct. Yet the manner in which it is guaranteed empties it of its substance. The right is conceived primarily in a technistic manner. Everyone has the right to life, and life may not be taken except in certain specified circumstances according to due process, in self-defense or defense of property, or in the course of lawful arrest, even when the force used may be reasonable. Hardly any distinction is made between loss of life where only private property is the object of defense. Somehow primacy is given to private property over life, thereby confirming the thesis that the major task of the capitalist state is to protect private property by force or war if necessary.

More fundamentally at the institutional level, no provision is made for the socioeconomic and cultural rights needed to sustain life: the right to work, to obtain social security, fair wages, and equal remuneration for work of equal value without distinction of any kind, to enjoy an adequate standard of living, freedom from hunger, to get an education, to form trade unions, to enjoy the highest attainable standard of mental and physical health, to take part in cultural life, and to enjoy the benefits of scientific progress and its application. In nearly all African countries, at most 20 percent of the population can claim to enjoy in varying degrees these privileges without which the right to life is reduced to a mere palliative. Without life there can be no society and no rights. Yet the manner in which that right is conceptualized and applied raises serious doubts as to the commitment of most ruling classes to human rights generally.

The inability to guarantee socioeconomic rights is a factor of underdevelopment, resulting from neocolonial development strategies. Nearly everywhere this inability has led not only to stagnation but also to regression and the increasing impoverishment of a growing majority of African peoples. Even though the principle of self-determination which encompasses both civil and political as well as social and economic rights has been progressively accepted by African countries, its implementation in various countries has varied immensely. The right implies that all peoples have the right to self-determination by virtue of which they freely determine their political status and pursue their economic, social, and cultural development. It also implies that all peoples may for their own ends freely dispose of their natural wealth and resources without prejudice to any obligations arising out of international economic cooperation based on the principle of mutual benefit and international law. Subject to these reservations, the African Charter on Human and Peoples' Rights also stipulates that this right shall be exercised in the exclusive interest of the peoples and that in no case shall a people be deprived of it. In case of expropriation, the dispossessed people shall have the right to the lawful recovery of its property as well as to an adequate compensation. Not only shall all peoples have the right to development, but all states have the duty, separately or in cooperation with others to ensure they exercise the right of development.

Rights of the Ruling Class

The rights to self-determination and development represent the core of the problem and a point of departure for African performance in the field of human rights. . . . The right of self-determination and development has ceased to be taken seriously.

This tendency is reflected internally by increasing poverty and inequality. In this context one is better able to appreciate the limited efficacy of the civil and political rights guaranteed in most African constitutions.

To begin with, despite pretensions to the contrary, the basic laws (constitutions) are invariably made not by the people but by vested interests, lawyers, bankers, industrialists, merchants, and other elite, and in some cases traditional rulers as well. Consequently, these rights reflect a bias favorable to these groups. The right to life has already been examined.

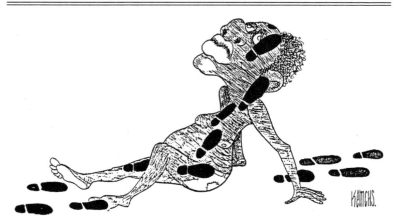

© 1985 Kemchs/Rothco. Reprinted with permission.

What can be said about the democratic right to participate in public affairs, which should not only ensure that the majority participate in shaping the political economy but also that they are in a position to effectively control the rulers? Most constitutions invariably provide for periodic elections whether under multi- or uniparty systems. There is invariably general franchise and adult suffrage. The elections are expected to be free and fair. How does an ignorant population with a low level of consciousness achieve these objectives, when they do not understand the issues involved? When they are alienated from the mainstream of governance and are manipulated, intimidated, or blackmailed into voting, and in many cases both the electoral register and the voting are rigged and votes and offices bought and sold, with the result that the same class is elected into office to continue oppressing and exploiting the masses? It does not make much sense, therefore, to wave the constitutions and declare that African constitutions guarantee the right of citizens to participate in governance.

What about the notion of equality before the law and equal

protection of the law? Access to the law implies knowledge of the law even when bourgeois law insists that ignorance of law is no excuse. Most of the population is indeed ignorant of the law. They see the legal institutions and the law which they apply as alien and do not have the economic means to pursue claims before the courts, even when they are aware that their rights have been infringed. . . .

What about the principle of separation of powers—between the legislature, the executive, and the judiciary—which should minimize arbitrariness and be conducive to the impartiality and independence of the judiciary? Does it make much sense when the same class enacts the laws, interprets them, and enforces them? Is it not logical that the laws and their implementation should promote and sustain productive relations favorable to this class? The law itself is arbitrary with respect to the majority, and its interpretation and execution are not likely to be different. When you add to this the principle of the rule of law implying respect for fundamental human rights, democracy, and the imperative of obedience to the law, it becomes clear what end it is intended to serve. In the circumstances, disobedience to unjust laws amounts to breach and the imposition of sanctions that are enforced with all the instruments of coercion a state possesses. In the end it serves to preempt a radical transformation of the inequitable socioeconomic system in place. Any attempt in this direction might amount to a crime against the state and may lead to the death penalty and harassment by security officers. What then for the right to life, freedom of expression, and so on? Even when judges have taken the oath to uphold the constitution, both the executive and the legislative may interfere when the ruling class feels threatened or angered by judicial decisions. President Kenneth Kaunda of Zambia once declared, with regard to the independence of the judiciary, that such independence would be maintained "on the condition that its criticisms were constructive.". . . In Uganda under Idi Amin, the judiciary was so terrorized that it ceased to act as an arbiter.

In some instances the courts have insisted on their guaranteed independence. But there is always the danger that in the prevalent fluid situation that exists in most African countries, the independence of the judiciary could be threatened, since it emphasizes the interpretation and application of the law, whether just or unjust.

The Rights of Labor

If the right to work remains a luxury, the right of workers to organize and promote their interests is still precarious. In many cases, not only are trade union rights circumscribed, but also the leadership is often coopted into the ranks of the ruling classes. . . .

What about the freedom of expression which includes freedom of the press as well as the right to receive information? To begin with, the practice of hoarding information by most African governments makes it difficult for the ruled to assess and inform government decisions. Routine information is often clearly marked "secret," and publications reactivate the secrecy laws found in the statute books of most African states. Publication of material embarrassing to government may lead to sanctions. No doubt there is need to protect certain information, the exposition of which might threaten national security or lead to disaffection or imminent breach of the peace. But who decides on these sanctions, the courts or the government? Whereas in many cases the courts of law have the last say, there might be some respite. They might be subject to prior restriction in which the granting of licenses might be used discriminately or they might be censored. But these derogations must be seen in their proper context. In capitalist-oriented states the media are invariably owned or controlled by the bourgeoisie, both public and private, and censorship exists (1) to ensure conformity with the government policies generally accepted by the ruling classes or (2) to prevent the exposure of government or political leadership malpractices. In some of the countries the media might even be controlled by foreign capital, and in nearly all countries they are influenced by foreign media.

We could go on and on, not because one is necessarily cynical or pessimistic, but because our concrete material and psychic conditions are what they are. They have become more precarious.

Human Rights and Socialist States

What about the socialist-oriented states? They too are plagued by the problems of underdevelopment, and as a consequence they too have increasingly come within the grip of imperialism. There are some differences, however. They proffer an anti-imperialist posture. They have attempted in varying degrees to abolish private property and to extend the participation of the masses in the decision-making process. . . .

While the adoption of a socialist option does not signify the enthronement of socialism, it does by and large point to the rejection of exploitation inherent in a free enterprise system. Realizing that private property stands in the way of effective human rights promotion and protection, every effort is being made to enthrone the social ownership of the means of production. . . .

Failures to achieve these objectives have nothing to do with the merits of socialism which has the potential for establishing a more rational human social order. The failure to make much progress should not be equated with the failure of socialism per se, but rather should be regarded as resulting from a lack of clarity in the goals sought and the adoption of wrong tactics and strategies to overthrow nascent local capitalism and imperialism.

From a certain perspective, the difference between the capitalist and socialist concept of law and human rights is that in the capitalist view basic contradictions exist between declaration and objective conditions to achieve them. In the socialist view, private property and imperialism are seen as the main causes of underdevelopment and as obstacles to the enjoyment of human rights. . . .

A Discouraging Human Rights Record

The record of violations of human rights in Africa remains very discouraging. Some progress might have been made since independence, but the increasing impoverishment of the African peoples, together with the growing reach of imperialism in the African countries with the active collaboration of the local ruling classes which has increasingly undermined the capacity of these classes to take the initiative and to make autonomous decisions in matters of national development, leaves little room for consolation. If the African masses are to gain from the national and world movements in the field of human rights they must be at the center of development. They must participate in that process on the basis of self-reliance. They must also be in the forefront of national liberation which can only be achieved on the basis of anti-imperialist struggle. In effect, what is needed is a socialist transformation of African countries which alone will ensure that the majority decree laws are protective and promotional of their human rights and not violative of them. This, in our view, is the central problem of human rights protection or violation.

a critical thinking activity

Ranking Concerns for the Ethiopian Government

This activity will allow you to explore the priorities you think should be important for Ethiopia's government. While your answers may differ from those of other readers, these disagreements mirror the complexity of Ethiopia's problems and the consequent difficulty of creating government policies that address these problems.

Ethiopia is a nation plagued by turmoil. In addition to civil wars that have been waged for decades, the country has suffered numerous famines. These famines have been exacerbated by the civil wars and by the policies of dictator Mengistu Haile Mariam, whose rule began in 1977. Neglect, corruption, and poor management by Mengistu's autocratic socialist regime impoverished the nation. While millions of Ethiopians starved, Mengistu used foreign aid money to purchase weapons rather than food. International food aid was often sold or left to rot rather than given to the people.

In May 1991, Tigrean rebels stormed the Ethiopian capital, Addis Ababa, and seized control of the government. Mengistu fled to Zimbabwe. This event ended years of civil war. While war has ended, however, Ethiopia still faces overwhelming problems. The new government is young and inexperienced and lacks the support of many Ethiopians. The nation is still torn by deep ethnic divisions in regions such as Eritrea and Tigre that sought independence from Ethiopia. In addition, famine once again threatens the land. International relief officials estimate that without substantial rains up to seven million Ethiopians will need emergency food.

People's opinions concerning how the Ethiopian government can strengthen the nation may vary according to their understanding of the problems and their relationship to the government. For example, a rebel from one of Ethiopia's provinces may favor independence for the province, while the president of Ethiopia may support keeping the nation united.

The authors in this chapter discuss government policies they believe would benefit Africa. In this activity, you will rank the government priorities you believe would benefit Ethiopia.

Part I

Imagine that you are the new president of Ethiopia. Below is a list of priorities that your government advisors may consider to be important. Working individually, rank the priorities. Decide what you believe to be the most important priorities for Ethiopia and the Ethiopian people. Be ready to defend your answers. Use number 1 to designate the most important concern, number 2 for the second most important concern, and so on.

_____ holding talks to further understanding between rival ethnic groups within Ethiopia

_____ protecting human rights

_____ extraditing Mengistu from Zimbabwe for trial in Ethiopia

_____ protecting Ethiopia's endangered species

_____ establishing a democratic government

_____ granting independence to all provinces that seek it

_____ protecting Ethiopia's native traditions and customs

_____ teaching Ethiopians new agricultural methods to help prevent future famines

_____ using the military to end rebel activities in provinces

_____ promoting free enterprise and private ownership to invigorate the economy

_____ encouraging Western nations to provide economic and food aid to starving Ethiopians

Part II

Step 1. After each student has completed his or her individual ranking, the class should break into groups of four to six students. Students should compare their rankings with others in the group, giving reasons for their choices. Then the group should make a new list that reflects the concerns of the entire group.

Step 2. In a discussion with the entire class, compare your answers. Then discuss the following questions:

1. Did your individual rankings change after comparing your answers with the answers of others in the group?

2. Why did your reasons differ from those of others in the group?

3. Consider and explain how your opinions might change if you were:

   a. a rebel leader

   b. a starving Ethiopian farmer

   c. Mengistu Haile Mariam

Periodical Bibliography

The following articles have been selected to supplement the diverse views presented in this chapter.

Africa News	"Africa: A Turning Point?" October 22, 1990.
Claude Ake	"Rethinking African Democracy," *Journal of Democracy*, Winter 1991. Available from the National Endowment for Democracy, 1101 15th St. NW, Suite 200, Washington, DC 20005.
George B.N. Ayittey	"The End of African Socialism?" *The Heritage Lectures*, January 24, 1990. Available from The Heritage Foundation, 214 Massachusetts Ave. NE, Washington, DC 20002.
Lisa Beyer	"Continental Shift," *Time*, May 21, 1990.
J. Leo Cefkin	"Africa: Brighter Prospects," *Freedom Review*, vol. 22, no. 1. Available from Freedom House, 48 E. 21st St., New York, NY 10010.
Herman J. Cohen	"Africa: Democracy and U.S. Policy," *Mediterranean Quarterly*, Summer 1991.
Herman J. Cohen	"African Political Changes and Economic Consequences," *U.S. Department of State Dispatch*, September 9, 1991. Available from Superintendent of Documents, U.S. Government Printing Office, Washington, DC 20402-9325.
Robert Fatton	"Liberal Democracy in Africa," *Political Science Quarterly*, vol. 105, no. 3, 1990.
Jon Kraus	"Building Democracy in Africa," *Current History*, May 1991.
Colleen Lowe Morna	"A Luxury No More," *Africa Report*, November/December 1990.
Herman Nickel	"Democracy or Disaster for Africa," *The Wall Street Journal*, January 31, 1990.
April A. Oliver	"Transplanting Democracy in a Forgotten Continent," *In These Times*, February 20-26, 1991.
Dan Quayle	"African Democracy and the Rule of Law," *U.S. Department of State Dispatch*, September 23, 1991.
Richard Sandbrook	"Taming the African Leviathan," *World Policy Journal*, Fall 1990.
Abdoulaye Wade, interviewed by Margaret A. Novicki	"Abdoulaye Wade: Democracy's Advocate," *Africa Report*, March/April 1991.

How Will the Dismantling of Apartheid Affect South Africa's Future?

Chapter Preface

For more than forty years, the policy of apartheid oppressed South Africa's black majority. Under the system, which was established by the minority white population, blacks and other nonwhites were forced to live in designated tribal homelands, or *bantustans*, and were denied the economic and political benefits given to whites.

The 1989 election of reformer Frederik W. de Klerk, however, brought sudden, dramatic changes to South Africa. In January 1990, de Klerk released political activist Nelson Mandela, lifted the ban on the African National Congress (the nation's most powerful opposition group), and began talks with opposition leaders. Then, in June 1991, de Klerk led the parliament to repeal the 1948 Population Registration Act, which had required all South Africans to be registered at birth as white, colored, or black, and had enabled the government to control where nonwhites lived, worked, and traveled. With the repeal of this act, many observers proclaimed the end of apartheid.

However, while official apartheid may be ending, many observers question whether racism itself will end. Many experts are hopeful that social change will follow the change in government policy, and that gradually the races in South Africa will unite as one people. They believe that white South Africans want to put an end to the nation's racist past, and that this is the first step to ridding the nation of racism. As evidence of the whites' good intentions, these experts cite the fact that the white majority supported de Klerk's reforms. As Michael Johns, an African expert with The Heritage Foundation, states, "These reforms were made politically possible by a white electorate that now clearly rejects the apartheid system." Johns and others believe that if the whites continue to support reforms in government and society, South Africa's future will be one without racism.

Other observers are less optimistic that racism is decreasing in South Africa. For while officially apartheid may be disappearing, the cultural and social barriers between blacks and whites still exist and may be difficult to tear down. South Africans became accustomed to separate societies in which blacks and whites did not share beaches, or schools, or neighborhoods. Because of this, South Africans may find that racism and separatism are so entrenched that they will be impossible to eradicate.

Those who doubt that racism will end point to the United States as an example of a nation that has ended official discrimination but that still struggles with racism. In America, more than two centuries of slavery ended in 1863 with Lincoln's

Emancipation Proclamation, but it was not until the 1960s—one hundred years later—that American blacks were granted civil rights. Even today many Americans argue that racism in the U.S. is still pervasive. If racism in South Africa is as tenacious as it has been in the U.S., it will be decades before all South Africans are truly equal. As *New York Times* writer Christopher S. Wren comments, "Apartheid was so intricately constructed over four decades and has created such economic disparity between blacks and whites that many South Africans might find their separate lives little changed by the reforms."

The dismantling of apartheid has brought about unprecedented changes to South Africa, but whether the changes will continue and how they will affect the nation is unknown. The authors in the following chapter debate these issues and debate the results of the declared end of apartheid.

"Our principal goal is to ensure peace, prosperity, progress and participation for all South Africans."

The End of Apartheid Benefits All South Africans

F.W. de Klerk

F.W. de Klerk was elected president of South Africa in 1989. In 1990, he freed long-time political prisoner Nelson Mandela and legalized the formerly outlawed African National Congress. In June 1991 he persuaded the South African parliament to repeal the Population Registration Act of 1948, which required all South Africans to be classified by race. By repealing this law, the parliament officially ended apartheid, a system which separated the races and permitted discrimination. In the following address to the parliament after the decision, de Klerk maintains that the end of official discrimination will result in equality for all South Africans.

As you read, consider the following questions:

1. What does de Klerk believe is required if South Africans are to build a safe and secure future?
2. What actions has the government taken to create opportunities for all South Africans, according to the author?
3. How does de Klerk respond to critics of his reforms?

F.W. de Klerk, "The Removal of Statutory Discrimination," speech delivered to parliament, June 17, 1991.

Today, the vast majority of our population are rejoicing. They are rejoicing because they know there is no turning back. They are rejoicing because they accept the inevitability of an irreversible process of liberation from racial discrimination. They are rejoicing because they see that we keep our word and fulfil our promises.

Only a small minority of our population, led by the Conservative Party and a few extra-Parliamentary splinter groups, are negatively disposed and hostile to the removal of discrimination and the vision of a new and just South Africa. They are attempting to turn this moment of truth in our history into a basis for resistance and even revolt. With contemptuous disregard of reason and reality, they are exploiting the uncertainty of change and the anxiety it brings with it.

To all who still feel uncertain and are still seeking their security in restrictive and discriminatory legislation, I wish to say today:

Do not let yourselves become the victims of inciting right-wing politicians and agitators.

Think for yourselves. Look about you and realise that you cannot build a safe and secure future on a denial of the rights of the permanent and irremovable majority of the population. That which is dear to you can be protected only if there is full recognition of the human dignity and basic rights of all South Africans, regardless of their race or colour.

One cannot build security on injustice and there is no doubt that the Group Areas Act and the other laws that determined the tenures of land, as well as the Population Registration Act, did lead to injustice.

Instead of allowing your talents and energies to be misused for negative resistance and even revolt, you should use them far rather to serve the community.

Take a leaf out of the book of the many communities in our country and elsewhere that have succeeded so well in retaining themselves and in retaining that which is important to them without the protection of legislation. That will be possible in a new and just South Africa. . . .

International Reaction

I wish to emphasise that the Government, in removing every form of discrimination and in taking its initiatives of reform and renewal, desires only to serve the best interests of South Africa and all its people. We are not doing it to gain international recognition. We are not working to the agendas of the United States, Africa or Europe in order to have sanctions lifted or to gain favour.

We wish to do that which is right for South Africa. The fact that this has led already to international breakthroughs is a bonus. Similarly, one may expect further international developments to follow if anything like morality exists in international politics.

That too, will be welcome, but it is not our primary objective. Our principal goal is to ensure peace, prosperity, progress and participation for all South Africans. In the pursuit of these goals we have made impressive progress in the period after September the 6th, 1989—progress which goes far beyond the comprehensive repealing of discriminatory legislation. In that period there were other positive developments in various fields that hold out hope for the future.

Allow me to give a brief overview without its claiming to be complete in any way.

In the field of terminating discrimination, not only the Group Areas Act, the Land Acts and the Population Registration Act have been repealed, but the Separate Amenities Act as well. With that, statutory racial discrimination has been removed honestly and completely and any assertions to the contrary are without any substance.

The political playing field has been made equal by the removal of the restrictions on organisation and parties such as the ANC and others, as well as by the lifting of the State of Emergency.

Freedom of speech and of organisation have been recognized by allowing protest marches to be held, subject only to reasonable measures of control.

The release of prisoners was commenced at the Government's own initiative in 1988 already with the release of Messrs. Sisulu, Mbeki Snr and others, followed by that of Mr. Mandela in February 1990. Together with this, the Government took the initiative by proposing legislation to make indemnity possible for exiled South Africans. . . .

Positive Steps

In many other areas, the initiative was taken to eliminate adverse conditions and backlogs, to create opportunities and to promote a positive climate. They include:

• the adoption of eighteen important acts for reforming the law and the process of law;

• the bill directed at fundamental changes to the security legislation to obviate any inhibition of the democratic process;

• legislation directed at aiding the victims of violence under certain circumstances;

• proposals and an exciting debate on a new strategy for education renewal and for health;

• good progress with the elimination of the last remaining disparities in respect of pensions and allowances;

190

• the extraordinary allocation of a total of R4,000 million, over and above the normal budgetary provision, for education, housing and special projects designed to improve the quality of life;

• the White Paper on Land Ownership and the concomitant legislation to make land more easily affordable and accessible to everybody.

Bob Gorrell *Richmond News Leader*. Reprinted with permission.

In the field of negotiation, the Government has gone out of its way to remove obstacles. Good progress has been made and continues to be made. Dialogue is still being conducted over a wide spectrum.

The three principal agreements reached with the ANC were of decisive importance. Contrary to what is being suggested in some of the media, discussion and dialogue are continuing. . . .

A New South Africa

Taken together, all of this does, indeed, constitute a comprehensive picture of progress and dynamic change. The new South Africa is on the march. Nothing can stop it any more. The whole process has developed its own dynamics which are greater than the will or recalcitrance of any participant.

It is easy for any party, and for critics and observers at home and abroad, to find fault here and point to a weakness there if they prefer to look at single trees instead of at the wood. Such an attitude, however, makes no contribution. If anything, it has a negative effect. What is needed now, is constructive involvement and encouragement by all who are able to make a contribution. Then the new and just South Africa, which can no longer be stopped by anyone, will become a reality sooner.

Naturally, there are deficiencies and difficulties occurring now and then. However, problems of that kind are there to be solved. Everybody should know that the Government has the will to do it.

We are not playing games. The peaceful future of our country and all its people is at stake. Petty politics and trying to be clever will get us nowhere. The best place for the removal of obstacles is at the negotiating table itself. . . .

Do we realise how close we are to the final breakthrough? All who desire peace desire of all the actors that they should begin performing in respect of the negotiating process. They are even impatient. The vast majority of South Africans want to see action now. They are tired of words.

The Government stands ready to play its part. We have kept our word on every promise we have been able to fulfill already. We will also keep our word about that which still has to be done.

Enough has happened to convince even the most skeptical participant or observer that we are irreversibly on the road to a new, negotiated and just constitutional dispensation. No one need doubt any longer that it will happen. The big question now is merely how it will look in detail and when it will be achieved.

Creative Thinking Is Required

Humanly speaking, the answer to this lies in the hands of the leadership corps in South Africa. My call to them is:

Let us do it now.

The time is ripe for strong, rational and considered leadership.

The time has passed for a broad, general and climate-creating dialogue.

The times demand of us to proceed to creative thinking and actions.

For that the National Party and the Government are ready and prepared.

"The end of legal apartheid will have very little real effect on the conditions facing the vast majority of Azanian people."

The End of Apartheid May Not Benefit Black South Africans

Michael Slate

In June 1991, South African president F.W. de Klerk led the South African parliament to repeal the Population Registration Act of 1948, which classified South Africans by race. Many people believe this marked the end of official apartheid. Michael Slate disagrees. The repeal of the act is a minor event that will do little for the oppressed black majority of South Africa, Slate declares in the following viewpoint. Slate argues that blacks continue to be discriminated against socially and economically. He proposes that only through revolution will blacks gain power in South Africa. Slate is a correspondent for *Revolutionary Worker*, the weekly newspaper of the Revolutionary Communist Party. He is the author of a series of articles describing his experiences in South Africa.

As you read, consider the following questions:

1. Why did South Africa's white rulers repeal the apartheid laws, in Slate's opinion?
2. What evidence does the author give to show that the repeal of the apartheid laws will not expand the rights of black South Africans?

Michael Slate, "Apartheid Abolish Itself? Don't Believe the Hype," *Revolutionary Worker*, the weekly newspaper of the Revolutionary Communist Party U.S.A., June 30, 1991. (Greenhaven editors have changed some subheads, retitled the article, and added inserts).

Editor's note: Slate refers to South Africa as Azania, *the traditional African name for the country, and calls native South Africans* Azanians.

Every time I hear another news item about how the South African regime is taking steps to end apartheid I think about a conversation I had with a young Azanian comrade during my last visit to South Africa. We were sitting inside a shack in the Eastern Cape squatter camp known as Soweto by the Sea discussing this comrade's views on whether it was possible to somehow end the oppression of the Azanian people through reform and the repeal of racist legislation. The young comrade stamped his foot on the patch of linoleum covering the dirt floor, sort of like he was killing a cockroach, as he told me, "It is system that you have to deal with. And, like everything that is system, you have to smash it, kill it dead. If you don't, it will kill you dead."

On June 17, 1991, the South African Parliament repealed the notorious Population Registration Act. This law, enacted at the beginning of the apartheid regime, classified everyone born in South Africa into racial categories based on their background and skin color. There were four major racial categories—white, Indian or Asian, Colored or mixed race, and African. From the very moment of birth, literally, everything about a South African's life—where they live, where they work, where they go to school, who they talk to and how, who they love, who they marry, how they travel, where they play sports, where they dance, where they piss, what hospitals they go to, what political rights they had, and where they could be buried—was determined by the racial category assigned. Under apartheid, whites occupy the top of the society, and that position and everything that goes along with it is based on the systematic oppression of the rest of the Azanian people—especially the Africans who are the vast majority of the population and the indigenous people of the country.

Acts of Parliament

The Population Registration Act was the last major legal pillar of what is called "grand apartheid" in South Africa—the four key laws of the apartheid setup. Earlier in June 1991 the Group Areas Act, which set up segregated living areas, and the Land Acts, which legally enforced white ownership of 87 percent of the land in South Africa, were repealed. In the Fall of 1990 the Separate Amenities Act, which legalized segregated public facilities, was taken off the books. When the South African Parliament repealed the Population Registration Act, F.W. de Klerk declared that apartheid, and all of the oppression based on it, was a thing of the past. Addressing a special joint session of the white, "Col-

"Welcome! Welcome!"

ored" and Indian Houses of Parliament, de Klerk stated, "Now everybody is free of it. Now everybody is free from the discouragement and denial . . . and from the moral dilemma caused by this legislation, which was born and nurtured under different circumstances in a departed era."

Classifications Remain in Force

But the apartheid constitution still stands—black people have no political rights and are still not even allowed to vote in South Africa. And even with the repeal of the Population Registration Act, only the newborn babies will not be classified—everyone in South Africa will remain classified in a racial category on their national I.D. until a new constitution is adopted. Also, all of the security legislation, the Internal Security Act, the preventive detention laws, the right to ban individuals and organizations, and the whole repressive apparatus used to keep black people down are still in force.

Imperialist governments around the world applauded de Klerk and praised the birth of a new South Africa. Olympic officials are discussing the possibility of South Africa once again participating in the Olympics, possibly as soon as the 1992 Summer games. In the U.S. the Bush administration and the Congress immediately began talking about rewarding South Africa by lifting the economic sanctions that had been placed against South Africa in 1986. And on top of this, Gatsha Buthelezi, the head of the Zulu bantustan and a notorious collaborator with the apartheid regime, not only met privately with George Bush but was also received throughout official Washington with all of the fanfare normally reserved for a visiting head of state.

The repeal of the apartheid legislation was not an insignificant act by the racist rulers of South Africa. But the significance of these actions lies mainly in the fact that the white minority rulers were forced to do it at all. Just a few years ago no one would have dreamed that all of these laws would be repealed by the apartheid regime itself.

There were a number of factors that played into the South African rulers' decision to get rid of the apartheid laws. For one thing, the collapse of the Soviet imperialist bloc and the consequent effects on the African National Congress (ANC), including their rush into trying to work out some kind of negotiated settlement with the regime, gave the apartheid government an opening it wasn't quite expecting. But mainly, it was the struggle of the Azanian people themselves and the threat of that struggle developing into something with the potential of bringing down the whole apartheid setup that motivated the government to act while it still could. The repeal of all these racist laws and the whole attempt to negotiate out a new form of government in South Africa is not the result of some sudden enlightenment of the oppressors in South Africa. Instead, these are desperate maneuvers of a vulnerable regime attempting to maintain its rule over the black people of Azania.

Few Benefits

Some of the Azanian people will get a few benefits as a result of these changes. This is particularly true for the small but growing black middle class. But even that will be limited, as many of these black middle class people will find out when they attempt to move into white neighborhoods or send their kids to all-white schools. When you get right down to it, though, the end of legal apartheid will have very little real effect on the conditions facing the vast majority of Azanian people. This is true even on the surface of things. The repeal of this legislation isn't just a trick, but it is not a sudden blossoming of integration, equality and acceptance on the part of the white settlers and their government.

I was in Azania when the Separate Amenities Act was repealed. It was big news that black people could no longer be barred from using public facilities simply because they were black. However, most black people who tried to begin exercising these rights—like going to libraries or public swimming pools in white areas—very quickly found out that they had to come up with hundreds and sometimes thousands of Rand to buy a membership in the libraries and pools. Likewise, the move by the regime to grant release of political prisoners showed what these reforms really mean for the people. Of the 15,000 political prisoners, only 1,000 were released. More than 90 percent who applied for release from prison were denied political prisoner status and were kept in jail classified as "common criminals."

What difference is the repeal of the Land Acts going to make to the millions and millions of Azanian peasants whose land was long ago stolen from them? While it is no longer the law that black people can only own land in 13 percent of the country, the fact is that 87 percent of the land is now owned by whites and this is the most fertile and valuable land in the country. By law black people will now have access to the land if they can buy it and if they can find someone to sell it to them. But what difference will this make to the peasants I spoke to in KwaZulu, who were literally slaves on white-owned plantations? And what about the black peasants I spoke to who were forcibly removed from their ancestral farms and dumped in the Ciskei bantustan 15 years ago? The farms that once belonged to these peasants have been turned into valuable white farms while these peasants are starving out in the remote and barren areas of Ciskei. And what difference will it make to the youth I spoke to in squatter camps all over the country who, with the repeal of the Group Areas Act, are now free to buy a house in a white suburb or a white section of the city—that is, if they meet the "norms and standards" required by the white neighborhood? These people aren't living in tin and cardboard shanties just because of a few apartheid laws. The Azanian people are forced to live in these squatter camps—often in defiance of the law—because they have absolutely nothing and this is the result of the super-exploitation and oppression that comes from a whole system based on the oppression of African people, not just a few laws. This system is backed up and enforced by the armed power of the regime and their army and police. As Mao Tsetung said, "political power grows out of the barrel of a gun."

Little Change

No one is more aware of this reality than the rulers of South Africa. The South African authorities themselves have unwittingly admitted that not all that much is going to change for the majority of the Azanian people. Hernus J. Kriel, the Minister of Planning and Provincial Affairs, recently talked about the real effect of the repeal of the Group Areas Act. According to Kriel, black townships and squatter camps will not only remain on the scene but will increase due to a combination of strict housing codes enforced in white areas, economic factors, and a shortage of housing built for black people. While Kriel stressed that this situation will have "nothing to do with race," he predicted a growth in black "informal housing" around the major cities. In the middle of all the talk about the birth of a "new South Africa," the South African government also made it clear that the bottom line of brute military force maintaining their rule and the oppression of the Azanian people still remains—and will remain—in effect. Just a couple of weeks before the repeal of the Population Registration Act, South African paratroopers launched a mock invasion of Soweto as part of a military exercise.

For the Azanian people the bottom line also remains the same. No matter how many laws the South African regime repeals, this maneuver will not bring about the liberation of the Azanian people. Neither will the hammering out of a new constitution—that grants black people some form of political rights—bring an end to the oppression of the Azanian people. This oppression is rooted in and serving the interests of the imperialist system and the white South African settler state allied to it. There is only one solution to the oppression of the people of Azania and only one path to genuine liberation—the path of a Maoist people's war and all-the-way revolution. Only a "new democratic revolution"—to overthrow the apartheid regime, break free from imperialism, and move on to build a genuine socialist society—can bring national liberation to the Azanian people.

"Our people demand democracy. "

South Africa Will Be a United, Democratic Nation

Nelson Mandela

Nelson Mandela is the leader of the African National Congress, South Africa's most powerful anti-apartheid organization. After serving twenty-seven years as a political prisoner, he was released in 1990 after his supporters throughout the world pressured the South African government for his freedom. Mandela has since led the ANC in negotiations with the white South African government. In the following viewpoint, Mandela asserts that democracy is the only form of government that will protect the rights of all South Africans. He envisions a South Africa without racism, where all citizens are equal.

As you read, consider the following questions:

1. What kind of economic reforms does Mandela propose?
2. What must happen for a political settlement and democracy to survive, in the author's opinion?
3. How can South Africans help to eradicate racism in the world, according to Mandela?

Nelson Mandela, address to the U.S. Congress, June 26, 1990.

Our people demand democracy. Our country, which continues to bleed and suffer pain, needs democracy. It cries out for the situation where the law will decree that freedom to speak of freedom constitutes the very essence of legality, and the very thing that makes for the legitimacy of the constitutional order.

It thirsts for the situation where those who are entitled by law to carry arms as the forces of national security and law and order will not turn their weapons against the citizens simply because the citizens assert that equality, liberty, and the pursuit of happiness are fundamental human rights which are not only inalienable, but must, if necessary, be defended with the weapons of war.

We fight for and visualize a future in which all shall—without regard to race, color, creed or sex—have their right to vote and to be voted into all elective organs of state. We are engaged in struggle to ensure that the rights of every individual are guaranteed and protected through a democratic constitution, the rule of law, and an entrenched bill of rights, which shall be enforced by an independent judiciary as well as a multiparty political system. . . .

What we have said concerning the political arrangements we seek for our country is seriously meant. It is an outcome for which many of us went to prison, for which many have died in police cells, on the gallows, in our towns and villages, and in the countries of southern Africa. Indeed, we have even had our political representatives killed in countries as far away from South Africa as France. . . .

To deny any persons their human rights is to challenge their very humanity. To impose on them a wretched life of hunger and deprivation is to dehumanize them, but such has been the terrible fate of all black persons in our country under the system of apartheid. The extent of the deprivation of millions of people has to be seen to be believed. The injury is made the more intolerable by the opulence of our white compatriots and the deliberate distortion of the economy to feed that opulence.

A New Economy

The process of the reconstruction of South African society must and will also entail the transformation of its economy. We need a strong and growing economy. We require an economy that is able to address the needs of all the people of our country, that can provide food, houses, education, health services, social security, and everything that makes human life human, that makes life joyful and not a protracted encounter with hopelessness and despair.

We believe that the . . . enormous and pressing needs of the people make it inevitable that the democratic government will intervene in this economy, acting through the elected parliament. We have put the matter to the business community of our country that the need for a public sector is one of the elements in a many-sided strategy of economic development and restructuring. That has to be considered by us all, including the private sector.

Another wall

Dennis Renault/*The Sacramento Bee*. Reprinted with permission.

The ANC [African National Congress] holds no ideological positions which dictate that it must adopt a policy of nationalization. But the ANC also holds the view that there is no self-regulating mechanism within the South African economy which will, on its own, insure growth with equity.

At the same time, we take it as a given that the private sector is an engine of growth and development which is critical to the success of the mixed economy we hope to see in the future South Africa. We are accordingly committed to the creation of a situation in which business people, both South African and foreign, have confidence in the security of their investments, are assured of a fair rate of return on their capital, and do business in conditions of stability and peace.

We must also make the point, very firmly, that the political settlement and democracy itself cannot survive unless the material needs of the people, the bread-and-butter issues, are addressed as part of the process of change and as a matter of urgency. It should never be that the anger of the poor should be the finger of accusation pointed at all of us because we failed to respond to the cries of the people for food, for shelter, for the dignity of the individual. . . .

. . . [T]his complex South African society, which has known nothing but racism for three centuries, should be transformed into an oasis of good race relations where the black shall to the white be sister and brother, a fellow South African, an equal human being, both citizens of the world. To destroy racism in the world, we together must expunge racism in South Africa. Justice and liberty must be our tools, prosperity and happiness our weapon.

. . . [P]eace is its own reward. Our own fate, borne by a succession of generations that reach backwards into centuries, has been nothing but tension, conflict, and death. In a sense, we do not know the meaning of peace, except in the imagination. But because we have not known true peace in its real meaning, because for centuries, generations have had to bury the victims of state violence, we have fought for the right to experience peace. . . .

The Will of All South Africans

The day may not be far when we will borrow the words of Thomas Jefferson and speak of the will of the South African nation. In the exercise of that will, by this united nation of black and white people, it must surely be that there will be born a country on the southern tip of Africa which you will be proud to call a friend and an ally because of its contribution to the universal striving towards liberty, human rights, prosperity, and peace among the peoples.

"We . . . reject the naive concept of democracy
for all races and nations in South Africa."

South Africa Will Never Be a United, Democratic Nation

Andries P. Treurnicht

The many diverse races and cultures in South Africa will prevent it from ever becoming a united democracy, Andries P.
Treurnicht asserts in the following viewpoint. The author believes that South African president F.W. de Klerk's attempts to
give more power to the black majority will not unify the country but will result in the oppression of the white minority.
Treurnicht predicts that de Klerk's policies will increase violence and unrest in the nation. Treurnicht is the leader of South
Africa's Conservative party. The party favors partitioning South
Africa into separate areas for blacks and whites.

As you read, consider the following questions:

1. What distinction does Treurnicht make between a "state" and
   a "nation"?
2. What comparison does the author make between the Soviet
   Union and South Africa?
3. Why does Treurnicht reject the concept of democracy for all
   South Africans?

Andries P. Treurnicht, "South Africa Will Never Be One Nation," *Los Angeles Times*, May 20,
1991.

The idea of a "new South Africa" is not new. Seventy years ago, Prime Minister Daniel Malan announced a new South Africa. And recently, Oliver Tambo, leader of the African National Congress, envisaged a different new South Africa.

Tambo and President Frederik W. de Klerk share a similar vision of renewal, that is, the surrender of white rule and the introduction of black rule over all of the peoples of South Africa. De Klerk denies any intention of surrendering power; he is prepared to share it. He does not explain how power can be shared without losing control, or how white people can avoid being dominated by a black majority in government posts and in the security forces.

De Klerk's idea of building a new nation out of disparate nations is not new either. Soviet leaders have tried and failed. That was also the mistake of colonial powers in 19th Century Africa. While a "state" can be any population ruled from one center, a "nation" consists of people who feel that they belong together and who demand that the power by which they are governed is their own.

Not One Nation

De Klerk should be aware that South Africa's 13 peoples and racial groups are not one nation and will never be. However, he plans to "reform," or transform, them into one nation. He apparently disregards the violent clashes between the Zulu and the Xhosa (4,000 killed), or the cultural, political and even religious differences—the clashing loyalties and antipathies that cause the deaths of dozens of blacks every week. We have also seen the beginning of violent conflict between blacks and whites.

The modern trend in political development elsewhere in the world will tell de Klerk that his idea of a unitary state composed of various nations is outdated and against the trend. (Margaret Thatcher referred to the idea of one sovereign parliament for the various European nations as "airy fairy".)

In the Soviet Union, the attempt to build a supernation from the peoples of 15 republics failed miserably. Even the race-related Walloons and Flemish of Belgium confirm the folly of forcing disparate communities into one political system.

I can speak on behalf of the majority of the white nation when I say we are not prepared to accept domination by any other nation or its allies. We do not harbor any death wish. We demand recognition of our right to govern ourselves and to protect our value system.

The current conflict will only escalate if de Klerk forces his ideal of a nonracial new nation on us.

This conflict is also not conducive to investment from abroad. Every right-minded South African would welcome increased in-

vestment in our country. But it is obvious that the political uncertainty created by the so-called reform policies, the prospect
of black rule and economic decline will lead to an ungovernable
state if the present conflict and unrest continue.

LURIE'S WORLD

"Finally we're all together!"

De Klerk's intended land reform will enable black tribes to retain their land and even expand by purchasing more land. But
what has been considered white land will be free for all who
can pay, thereby depriving the white nation of its own geopoliti-
cal basis. This is discrimination in the reverse.

There is an increasing impatience among whites against
American and European pressure for majority rule for the
whole of South Africa and their refusal to recognize the independence of the black homelands. We seriously object to the
double standards by which self-determination is granted to all
peoples but denied the whites in South Africa.

Democracy as Tyranny

We also reject the naive concept of democracy for all races and
nations in South Africa. Such democracy would be tyranny. We
suggest that such advocates try to establish a French-German-
Dutch-Swiss democracy in one undivided Europe. The very idea
is absurd. So why demand it of South Africa's peoples?

I fully agree with those who say that it is over-optimistic to think that for the first time in history, the wisdom of the poor masses and their leaders will find a way to bring together different races, tribes, cultures and classes, and to find a straight way to heaven without detrimental effects.

It is not only over-optimistic, and more than a little stupid, it is somewhere between idiotic and criminal to neglect all historical facts in the whole world.

De Klerk talks much about the irreversibility of his reforms. We maintain, however, that it would be the biggest irreversible error if the white nation thinks that it can retain control over the economy and the security forces under a black-dominated government.

It is a true maxim that you either rule or are ruled. It is a myth to think that you can share power and still be in control.

"We firmly believe in the future of socialism."

A Post-Apartheid South Africa Should Be Socialist

Joe Slovo

Because the South African Communist party (SACP) and the African National Congress have been closely linked for decades, many experts have predicted that if the ANC comes to power in South Africa, it will establish a socialist state under the guidance of the SACP. At the same time, however, the fall of socialism in Eastern Europe has led many experts to question socialism's viability. In the following viewpoint, Joe Slovo defends socialism and offers it as a solution to South Africa's economic and political problems. Slovo, the general secretary of the SACP, was forced to live in exile for nearly thirty years because of his political beliefs.

As you read, consider the following questions:

1. What statistics does Slovo cite as evidence that socialism is a successful economic system?
2. What role does the working class play in Slovo's vision of a socialist South Africa?
3. How has capitalism failed Africa, in the author's opinion?

Joe Slovo, "Has Socialism Failed?" *Africa News*, February 26, 1990. Reprinted with permission.

Socialism is undoubtedly in the throes of a crisis greater than at any time since 1917. The last half of 1989 saw the dramatic collapse of most of the communist party governments of eastern Europe. Their downfall was brought about through massive upsurges which had the support not only of the majority of the working class but also a large slice of the membership of the ruling parties themselves. These were popular revolts against unpopular regimes; if socialists are unable to come to terms with this reality, the future of socialism is indeed bleak.

The mounting chronicle of crimes and distortions in the history of existing socialism, its economic failures and the divide which developed between socialism and democracy, have raised doubts in the minds of many former supporters of the socialist cause as to whether socialism can work at all. Indeed, we must expect that, for a time, many in the affected countries will be easy targets for those aiming to achieve a reversion to capitalism, including an embrace of its external policies.

Shock-waves of very necessary self-examination have also been triggered off among communists both inside and outside the socialist world. For our part, we firmly believe in the future of socialism; and we do not dismiss its whole past as an unmitigated failure.

(Among other things, statistics recently published in *The Economist* (UK) show that in the Soviet Union—after only 70 years of socialist endeavour in what was one of the most backward countries in the capitalist world—there are more graduate engineers than in the U.S., more graduate research scientists than in Japan and more medical doctors per head than in western Europe. It also produces more steel, fuel and energy than any other country.)

The Nobility of Socialism

Socialism certainly produced a Stalin and a Ceaucescu, but it also produced a Lenin and a Gorbachev. Despite the distortions at the top, the nobility of socialism's basic objectives inspired millions upon millions to devote themselves selflessly to building it on the ground. And, no one can doubt that if humanity is today poised to enter an unprecedented era of peace and civilized international relations, it is in the first place due to the efforts of the socialist world.

But it is more vital than ever to subject the past of existing socialism to an unsparing critique in order to draw the necessary lessons. To do so openly is an assertion of justified confidence in the future of socialism and its inherent moral superiority. And we should not allow ourselves to be inhibited merely because an exposure of failures will inevitably provide ammunition to the traditional enemies of socialism.

The commandist and bureaucratic approaches which took root during Stalin's time affected communist parties throughout the world, including our own. We cannot disclaim our share of the responsibility for the spread of the personality cult and a mechanical embrace of Soviet domestic and foreign policies, some of which discredited the cause of socialism. We kept silent for too long after the 1956 Khrushchev revelations. . . .

The implications for socialism of the Stalinist distortions have not yet been evenly understood throughout our ranks. We need to continue the search for a better balance between advancing party policy as a collective and the toleration of on-going debate an even constructive dissent.

We do not pretend that our party's changing postures in the direction of democratic socialism are the results only of our own independent evolution. Our shift undoubtedly owes a prime debt to the process of *perestroika* and *glasnost* which was so courageously unleashed under Mikhail Gorbachev's inspiration. Closer to home, the democratic spirit which dominated in the re-emerged trade union movement from the early 1970s onwards, also made its impact.

But we can legitimately claim that in certain fundamental respects our indigenous revolutionary practice long ago ceased to be guided by Stalinist concepts. This is the case particularly in relation to the way the party performed its role as a working class vanguard, its relations with fraternal organizations and representatives of other social forces and, above all, its approach to the question of democracy in the post-apartheid state and in a future socialist South Africa.

Leading the Workers

We have always believed (and we continue to do so) that it is indispensable for the working class to have an independent political instrument which safeguards its role in the democratic revolution and which leads it toward an eventual classless society. But such leadership must be won rather than imposed. Our claim to represent the historic aspirations of the workers does not give us an absolute right to lead them or to exercise control over society as a whole in their name. . . .

This approach to the vanguard concept has not, as we know, always been adhered to in world revolutionary practice and in an earlier period we too were infected by the distortion. But, in our case, the shift which has taken place in our conception of 'vanguard' is by no means a post-Gorbachev phenomenon. The wording on this question in our new program is taken almost verbatim from our Central Committee's 1970 report on organization.

The 1970 document reiterated the need to safeguard, both in the letter and the spirit, the independence of the political expressions of other social forces whether economic or national. It rejected the old purist and domineering concept that all those who do not agree with the party are necessarily enemies of the working class. And it saw no conflict between our understanding of the concept of vanguard and the acceptance of the African National Congress as the head of the liberation alliance.

The Possibility of Socialism

The principal issue in South Africa is not the demise of apartheid, which everyone except the Far Right recognizes to be washed up. Nor is it the timing of this demise, though the strength of reactionary forces guarantees a complex, drawn-out and bloody process. No, the main issue in South Africa concerns the nature of post-apartheid society. What will emerge once the monster is dismantled?

Needless to say, nobody knows the answer to this one. But quite the most remarkable thing I learned during my stay in the country was that thinking about the future of South Africa requires taking into account the possibility of socialism—as in workers' power over the means of production and the state.

If socialism is now on the agenda it is because South Africa has one of the most active, militant, and highly conscious working classes in the world. More, its strength is rapidly increasing.

Joel Kovel, *Z Magazine*, November 1989.

Despite the inevitable limitations which illegality imposed on our inner-party democratic processes, the principles of accountability and electivity of all higher organs were substantially adhered to. Seven underground Congresses of our party have been held since 1953. The delegates to Congress from the lower organs were elected without lists from above and always constituted a majority. The incoming Central Committees were elected by a secret ballot without any form of direct or indirect 'guidance' to the delegates. In other words, the Leninist concept of democratic centralism has not been abused to entrench authoritarian leadership practices.

Our structures, down to the lowest units, have been increasingly encouraged to assess and question leadership pronouncements in a critical spirit and the views of the membership are invariably canvassed before finalizing basic policy documents. Our 7th Congress, which adopted our new program, "The Path to Power", was a model of democratic consultation and spirited debate. . . .

As we have already noted, one of the most serious casualties in the divide which developed between democracy and socialism was in the one-sided relationship between the ruling parties and the mass organizations. In order to prevent such a distortion in a post-apartheid South Africa, we have, for example, set out in our draft Workers' Charter that:

'Trade unions and their federation shall be completely independent and answerable only to the decisions of their members or affiliates, democratically arrived at. No political party, state organ or enterprise, whether public, private or mixed, shall directly or indirectly interfere with such independence.'

The substance of this approach is reflected in the way our party has in fact conducted itself for most of its underground existence. . . .

Respect for Unions

We do not regard the trade unions or the national movement as mere conduits for our policies. Nor do we attempt to advance our policy positions through intrigue or manipulation. Our relationship with these organizations is based on complete respect for their independence, integrity and inner-democracy. In so far as our influence is felt, it is the result of open submissions of policy positions and the impact of individual communists who win respect as among the most loyal, the most devoted and ideologically clear members of these organizations.

Old habits die hard and among the most pernicious of these is the purist concept that all those who do not agree with the party are necessarily enemies of socialism. This leads to a substitution of name-calling and jargon for healthy debate with non-party activists. As already mentioned, our 7th Congress noted some isolated reversions along these lines and resolved to combat such tendencies.

But, in general, the long-established and appreciable move away from old-style . . . sectarianism has won for our party the admiration and support of a growing number of non-communist revolutionary activists in the broad workers' and national movement. We also consider it appropriate to canvass the views of such activists in the formulation of certain aspects of our policy. For example, we submitted our preliminary conception of the contents of a Workers' Charter for critical discussion not only in our own ranks but throughout the national and trade union movements.

Our party's program holds firmly to a post-apartheid state which will guarantee all citizens the basic rights and freedoms of organization, speech, thought, press, movement, residence, conscience and religion; full trade union rights for all workers including the right to strike, and one person one vote in free and democratic elections. These freedoms constitute the very essence of our national liberation and socialist objectives and they clearly imply political pluralism.

Both for these historical reasons and because experience has shown that an institutionalized one-party state has a strong propensity for authoritarianism, we remain protagonists of multi-party post-apartheid democracy both in the national democratic and socialist phases. . . .

It follows that, in truly democratic conditions, it is perfectly legitimate and desirable for a party claiming to be the political instrument of the working class to attempt to lead its constituency in democratic contest for political power against other parties and groups representing other social forces. And if it wins, it must be constitutionally required, from time to time, to go back to the people for a renewed mandate. The alternative to this is self-perpetuating power with all its implications for corruption and dictatorship.

People, Not Profit

We dare not underestimate the damage that has been wrought to the cause of socialism by the distortions we have touched upon. We, however, continue to have complete faith that socialism represents the most rational, just and democratic way for human beings to relate to one another. . . . The all-round development of the individual and the creation of opportunities for every person to express his or her talents to the full can only find ultimate expression in a society which dedicates itself to people rather than profit.

The opponents of socialism are very vocal about what they call the failure of socialism in Africa. (They conveniently ignore the fact that most of the countries which tried to create conditions for the building of socialism faced unending civil war, aggression and externally-inspired banditry; a situation in which it is hardly possible to build any kind of stable social formation—capitalist or socialist.)

But they say little, if anything, about Africa's real failure; the failure of capitalism. Over 90% of our continent's people live out their wretched and repressed lives in stagnating and declining capitalist-oriented economies. International capital, to whom most of these countries are mortgaged, virtually regards cheap bread, free education and full employment as economic crimes. . . .

The way forward for the whole of humanity lies within a socialist framework guided by genuine socialist humanitarianism and not within a capitalist system which entrenches economic and social inequalities as a way of life.

"The main obstacle to black social modernization in the future may well be the belief in socialism."

Socialism Would Destroy a Post-Apartheid South Africa

Francis Fukuyama

Francis Fukuyama, a consultant to the Rand Corporation in Los Angeles, California, is a frequent contributor to political journals such as *The National Interest*. In 1989, Fukuyama wrote a controversial essay arguing that socialism had died and would be replaced throughout the world with capitalism. In the following viewpoint, Fukuyama writes that South Africa alone is seriously considering establishing a socialist economy. Such a move would be disastrous, Fukuyama argues, and would threaten South Africa's economic stability. Socialism would not promote the economic growth that the nation needs to thrive and to bring blacks out of poverty, Fukuyama states.

As you read, consider the following questions:

1. What comparisons does Fukuyama make between Eastern Europe and South Africa?
2. What main concern does the author have about the African National Congress?
3. How would capitalism strengthen South Africa, in the author's opinion?

From "The Next South Africa" by Francis Fukuyama. Reprinted, with permission, from *The National Interest*, No. 24, Summer 1991.

Most of the former communist world has one advantage not enjoyed by South Africa: an almost universal revulsion of elites and popular masses alike to the old socialist system, and a broad consensus on the need ·to replace it with the democratic free market system of the West. The winds of perestroika, so strong in Eastern Europe, have not reached South Africa's shores: according to Joe Slovo, head of the South African Communist Party (SACP), the Soviet Union's problems were due to "pilot error" rather than to the plane's design and direction. Eastern Europe, which has just overcome the socialist stage of history and is now ready to build capitalism, is in different respects both behind and ahead of South Africa. . . .

Much of the ANC [African National Congress] advocates policies that, if enacted in their presently articulated form, would be an utter disaster for South Africans, both black and white. . . .

The ANC's left is anchored by its close alliance with the South African Communist Party. It remains the case that the executives of the two organizations are closely intertwined, with officials like Joe Slovo, Chris Hani, and Ronnie Kasrils serving on both. Moreover, the SACP constitutes what one observer called the "competent half" of the ANC, with the organizational ability and manpower to staff and control the ANC's central bureaucracy and executive. To the extent that the ANC is able to institutionalize itself effectively as a political party, it will be due in no small measure to the efforts of the communists within its ranks.

The SACP was called by one liberal editor in Johannesburg the "last communist party on earth," a title it must share with those in Havana and Pyongyang. . . . Slovo claims now to believe in multiparty democracy, but suspicions of continuing Leninism are fed by the fact that his party (like the ANC) has not democratized internally, and continues to veil its activities in secrecy. His objective, moreover, remains constant: socialism, which has failed everywhere else, will finally be built correctly in South Africa. . . .

The Danger of Communism

The real danger that the South African communists represent lies in the kinds of economic policies that they will advocate as close allies of a governing ANC. They will be a consistent voice in favor of strong state control of economic life and of the most radical forms of wealth redistribution. . . .

The main problem with the ANC as a governing party is its own strong continuing attachment to socialism. As with the communists, much of the ANC's economic thinking appears to have been placed in a deep freeze for several decades. What is now thawing is not necessarily doctrinaire Marxism, but the Fabianism of postwar Britain, or even a kind of 1950s Keynesianism, as reflected in the slogan "growth through redistribution." Much of this thinking does not reflect knowledge of economics so much as the moral conviction, quite understandable in South Africa's case, that property is unjustly distributed. The liberal economic revolution now sweeping Eastern Europe and Latin America, which maintains that wealth must be created before it is redistributed and favors privatization and liberalization of trade policy, has passed the ANC by. While Mexico, Brazil, and Argentina are busily selling off state companies and negotiating free trade pacts, the ANC is steadfastly opposed to the further privatization of South African parastatals, which are regarded as family heirlooms or, less gracefully, milk cows for future public-sector employment once a black government is in power. . . .

Three Scenarios

In thinking about future scenarios for South Africa once a new government, based on one man, one vote, is in place, it is useful to think in terms of analogous futures. The first, and most optimistic scenario, is that the future South Africa will be like Germany—that is, the developed part of the country will peacefully absorb the less developed part and, while suffering a temporary drop in living standards, will ultimately bring it up to its level. At the opposite end of the spectrum is the nightmare of Lebanon: the current township violence will spread and become the future of the country as a whole as increasingly it is partitioned between different ethnic and racial communities that have taken up arms to defend themselves. In between is the Latin American model where decline is not so much political as economic: massive increases in public spending followed by hyperinflation, leading to a situation like that of Brazil (if one is optimistic) or Peru (if one is not). . . .

If a future South Africa will resemble neither Germany nor Lebanon, and if its economy remains too strong for it to sink into African poverty in the short-run, the question then becomes which Latin American country it will take after. For if it seems just possible that South Africa can skirt a political maelstrom of instability and violence, it is hard to see how it can avoid a long-term economic deterioration. The starting point for this deterioration is the evident need for the redistribution of wealth within the country. To a much greater degree than in other developed countries, it is possible to say that the rich in South Africa got their wealth at the expense of the poor and that it is important to remedy the situation.

The problem is that any large-scale attempt to right these wrongs over a short period of time would be self-defeating in that it would wreck the economy, and thereby undermine the basis for wealth creation that is the only hope for black South Africa itself. It is here that the evolution of the ANC's economic thinking over the next few years will be critical. Both the ANC and SACP have asserted that they want to preserve a "mixed economy," but the precise mixture of public and private could spell the difference between "muddling through" and total disaster. . . . A necessary condition of success is that the ANC drop its socialist agenda, and internalize concepts of pluralism and civil society. . . .

Capitalism Will Modernize

Unfortunately, the main obstacle to black social modernization in the future may well be the belief in socialism on the part of the ANC and its communist allies. Capitalism, if left to itself under a system of truly equal political rights, will tend to modernize South African society and bring about what Tocqueville called an "equality of condition." Unplanned and without resort to coercion, capitalism fosters an enormous social revolution, tearing people away from traditional attachments and forms of authority and bringing about a new order in which education, skill, and work rather than race or tribe determine a person's status.

The Goal: A Market Economy

In a future South Africa, we hope to see an economic system that is open, competitive, and capable of generating growth on the order of at least 5 percent a year, which will be required if the country is to meet the social needs of its growing population. International experience, confirmed by recent events in Eastern Europe, shows that only a strong market economy can create opportunities that will allow greater numbers of South Africans to share in the wealth of an increasingly prosperous country.

Julian Ogilvie Thompson, *Journal of Democracy*, Fall 1990.

Socialism has always presented itself as a higher and more progressive form of social organization than capitalism. But in the contemporary world, socialism has been revealed to be an obstacle to social and economic modernization—the hallmark of a certain kind of backwardness that needs to be overcome, just like illiteracy and superstition. The countries of Eastern Europe are now moving rapidly backward into the future, undoing the legacy of forty years of dictatorship and socialist planning. Let us hope that South Africa, as it makes the necessary transition to democracy, does not move forward into the past.

Distinguishing Between Fact and Opinion

This activity is designed to help develop the basic reading and thinking skill of distinguishing between fact and opinion. Consider the following statement: "Blacks comprise 70 percent of South Africa's population." This is a fact and could be checked by looking at South African population statistics in an almanac or encyclopedia. But the statement "Because blacks are in the majority, they should control South Africa" is an opinion. While some South Africans agree with this statement, others believe that blacks and whites should share power or that whites should continue to control the government.

When investigating controversial issues it is important that one be able to distinguish between statements of fact and statements of opinion. It is also important to recognize that not all statements of fact are true. They may appear to be true, but some are based on inaccurate or false information. For this activity, however, we are concerned with understanding the difference between those statements that appear to be factual and those that appear to be based primarily on opinion.

Most of the following statements are taken from the viewpoints in this chapter. Consider each statement carefully. *Mark O for any statement you believe is an opinion or interpretation of facts. Mark F for any statement you believe is a fact. Mark I for any statement you believe is impossible to judge.*

If you are doing this activity as a member of a class or group, compare your answers with those of other class or group members. Be able to defend your answers. You may discover that others come to different conclusions than you do. Listening to the reasons others present for their answers may give you valuable insights into distinguishing between fact and opinion.

> *O = opinion*
> *F = fact*
> *I = impossible to judge*

217

1. The laws of apartheid led to injustice.

2. South Africa's Group Areas Act, the Land Acts, and the Population Registration Act have been repealed.

3. A new constitution will not bring an end to the oppression of black South Africans.

4. There is only one solution to the oppression of the people of Azania and only one path to genuine liberation: the path of a Maoist people's war.

5. The Population Registration Act classified all South Africans into racial categories based on their background and skin color.

6. The whites took South Africa with guns and the blacks must do the same to take it back.

7. When the South African parliament repealed the Population Registration Act, F.W. de Klerk declared that apartheid and all of the oppression based on it was a thing of the past.

8. The reforms are desperate manuevers of a vulnerable regime attempting to maintain its rule over black South Africans.

9. The new and just South Africa will soon be a reality.

10. Governments around the world applauded de Klerk and praised the birth of a new South Africa when the reforms were announced.

11. Eighty-seven percent of South Africa's land is owned by whites.

12. South Africa is comprised of thirteen racial and ethnic groups.

13. The prospect of black rule and economic decline will lead to an ungovernable state.

14. The African National Congress has for years been allied with the South African Communist Party.

15. It is overly optimistic to think that for the first time in history, the wisdom of the poor masses and their leaders will find a way to bring together different races, tribes, cultures, and classes.

16. The South African government desires only to serve the best interests of South Africa and all of its people.

17. Discrimination in South Africa has been completely eliminated.

18. Both the ANC and the SACP have asserted that they want to maintain a mixed capitalist and socialist economy.

Periodical Bibliography

The following articles have been selected to supplement the diverse views presented in this chapter.

George J. Church "A Black-and-White Future," *Time*, July 22, 1991.

Joseph Contreras "Poor, White, South African," *Newsweek*, August 26, 1991.

Peter Duignan "The Record on Sanctions," *The World & I*, September 1991.

W.G. Eaton "South African Destiny," *The Futurist*, January/February 1991.

Anton Harber "Looking Beyond Apartheid," *Africa News*, June 24, 1991. Available from PO Box 3851, Durham, NC 27702.

Michael Johns "Preparing for a Post-Apartheid South Africa," *Backgrounder*, December 31, 1990. Available from The Heritage Foundation, 214 Massachusetts Ave. NE, Washington, DC 20002.

Journal of Democracy "South Africa's Future," special section, Fall 1990. Available from PO Box 3000, Dept. JD, Denville, NJ 07834.

Scott MacLeod "Crisis of Confidence," *Time*, August 5, 1991.

Nelson Mandela, interviewed by *New Perspectives Quarterly* "South Africa: Bleak Predictions, Prophetic Prescriptions," Summer 1991.

Steven Mufson "Toward a Civil Society," *The New Republic*, July 23, 1990.

The Nation "Beware the Recon Man," August 5, 1991.

New Dimensions "South Africa: Time Bomb," special section, February 1991. Available from Subscription Dept., PO Box 811, Grants Pass, OR 97526.

The New Republic "South Africa's Window," August 5, 1991.

Randall Robinson "We Lost—and de Klerk Won," *Newsweek*, July 29, 1991.

John S. Saul "Free at Last? The Next Round in South Africa," *Monthly Review*, August 1990.

Khehla Shubane "Civil Society in South Africa," *Journal of Democracy*, Summer 1991.

Ralph Slovenko "The Destiny of South Africa," *The World & I*, July 1991.

John Train "The Other Perestroika," *The American Spectator*, March 1991.

Chronology of Events

1413	Prince Henry the Navigator leads a Portuguese conquest of the Moroccan city of Centa, inaugurating the era of European conquest in Africa.
1493	Portuguese explorer Pedro de Covilhão reaches Ethiopia and presents a letter from King John II addressed to Prester John. The legendary Prester John, who was believed to rule over a fabulous kingdom in central sub-Saharan (south of the Sahara) Africa, inspired many European explorers to search through uncharted African territory for him.
1497	Under Vasco da Gama, three Portuguese ships sail completely around Africa, including the Cape of Good Hope.
1497-1500	In an effort to monopolize East African trade, the Portuguese, including da Gama, conquer centuries-old East African city-states.
1518	A Spanish ship brings the first cargo of Africans to South America, starting 350 years of slave trading.
1652	The Dutch East India Company builds a depot for provisions at the cape. This colony, which later became Cape Town, is the first *Boer* (Dutch for farmer) colony in South Africa.
1738-56	A severe drought is recorded in sub-Saharan Africa.
1781-1881	The Boers crush the Xhosa and Zulu peoples in the Nine Wars of Dispossession. Tens of thousands of natives are killed while others are enslaved.
1795	The British, fearing that Holland and France may try to cut off trade to India around the cape, send a military force to South Africa and force the Dutch governor to capitulate.
1806	The British annex the Cape Province.
1828	French explorer René Caillié enters the fabled city of Timbuktu, located just south of the Sahara in modern-day Mali. He is the first European to do so and return to tell about it.
1830	British explorers John and Richard Lander find the mouth of the Niger River at a delta long known as Oil Rivers. Their discovery ends a search that had taken the lives of a number of Europeans.

1833	Slavery is abolished in Britain and its colonies, including South Africa.
1837	The Boers, or *Afrikaners*, as they called themselves, march into the interior of South Africa and settle there in protest of British domination and the loss of slave labor. This march is called the Great Trek, and those who marched are called *Voertrekkers*.
1847	The Republic of Liberia is established on Africa's northwest coast for former American and European slaves.
1854	South Africa is divided into four provinces, with the two coastal provinces going to the British and the inland provinces to the Dutch.
1863	President Abraham Lincoln issues the Emancipation Proclamation, ending slavery in the United States.
1871	The flamboyant Anglo-American explorer and journalist Henry Stanley meets Scottish missionary and river explorer Dr. David Livingstone on the banks of Lake Tanganyika (in Tanzania) in what is probably the most famous moment in white exploration of Africa. Stanley's first words, "Dr. Livingstone, I presume," have become part of European and American legend.
1873	The British stop the last of the slave trade, after 20 million to 30 million Africans have been kidnapped and enslaved.
1884-85	At the Berlin Conference, the colonial powers of England, France, Germany, Belgium, Italy, Portugal, Spain, and Holland formally divide the African continent. Present-day South Africa is apportioned to England and Holland.
1888-1900	De Beers Consolidated, a British mining company, obtains control of all the diamond fields and most of the gold fields in Boer South Africa. The tension between the British and Dutch settlers increases.
1899-1902	The British defeat the Boers in the Boer War and South Africa becomes part of the British Commonwealth.
1910	The British and Afrikaners form the Union of South Africa. Africans, "coloreds," and Asians are excluded from Parliament.
1912	The African National Congress (ANC), representing blacks, "coloreds," and Asians, is formed to protect and increase their rights in South Africa.

1913	The Natives Land Act is instituted in South Africa, limiting African land ownership.
1915	South African troops occupy South West Africa (Namibia), a German colony, on behalf of the Western European allies in World War I.
1920	South Africa begins administration of Namibia in accord with a United Nations mandate.
1929	Emperor Haile Selassie begins his reign in Ethiopia.
1930	The Rhodesian legislature passes the Land Apportionment Act, which, like the Natives Land Act in South Africa, gives the white minority the best land.
1934	South Africa gains independence from Great Britain.
1936	In South Africa, Africans are removed from the common voters' roll by the introduction of the Representation of Natives Act.
1943	The French colonial government in Madagascar kills eighty thousand natives who are fighting for independence.
1945	World War II ends.
1948	In South Africa, the primarily Afrikaner National party comes to power and enforces its policy of *apartheid*. This party has won every election in South Africa since then. Twenty-nine protesters are killed in the "Gold Coast" (Ghana) by British soldiers. This begins the struggle for independence led by Kwame Nkrumah.
1952-58	The Mau Mau War begins in Kenya when Kenyan leader Jomo Kenyatta demands that each Kenyan have a vote and be free to vote for whomever he or she chooses. Thirty-two whites and 1,812 Africans are killed. Kenyatta spends the war in prison.
1954-62	Algerian nationalists fight a guerrilla war against the French occupying army. Thirteen thousand French troops and 145,000 Algerians are killed. This uprising leads France to abandon its colonial policy.
1957	Ghana becomes the first of many black African countries to gain its independence from colonial rulers. Kwame Nkrumah leads the fledgling government.
1958	Guinea gains its independence from France. Sekou Toure is its first president.

1959	War breaks out in Portuguese Angola; thousands die.
1960	A.J. Luthuli, a leader in the black civil disobedience campaign in South Africa, wins the Nobel Peace Prize.
	Sharpeville massacre: South African police gun down sixty-nine antipass law demonstrators. This convinces some ANC leaders that nonviolent, Gandhi-style protest cannot be effective in South Africa.
	The newly independent Congo (later Zaire), led by Joseph Kasavubu and Patrice Lumumba, asks for United Nations' assistance in expelling the remaining Belgian army. When the UN forces prove ineffective, Lumumba states that he "will take aid from the devil or anyone else" as long as they get the Belgian troops out. The USSR sends supporting troops soon after. President Kasavubu dismisses Lumumba.
1961	Tanganyika (later Tanzania) gains its independence from Britain. Julius Nyerere, an advocate of a distinctly African brand of socialism, leads the government.
	In response to the Sharpeville massacre, Nelson Mandela and other nationalist leaders form *Umkhonto we Sizwe* (Spear of the Nation), the military wing of the ANC. This marks the first time the ANC formally advocates the use of organized violence.
	Soviet premier Nikita Khrushchev pledges support for Angolan revolutionaries.
	Kasavubu and Joseph Mobutu, co-leaders of the Congo and allies of the Belgians and Americans, deliver Lumumba to his tribal enemy, "King" Albert Kalongi, who kills him.
1962	Ahmed Ben Bella is named president of the newly independent Algeria. France recognizes the new government.
	Uganda becomes independent, with Milton Obote as prime minister.
1963	Kenya's independence is secured. Jomo Kenyatta is the first president.
	Nelson Mandela and other ANC leaders are imprisoned under the Suppression of Communism Act.
1964-65	Che Guevara, a charismatic Cuban revolutionary, tours most of the independent African countries with Marxist leanings, hoping to join Africa

223

and South America in a union of Third World nations. Within one year, Cuba begins to provide arms and troops to revolutionary movements in Angola, Cape Verde, and Mozambique.

1964	White Rhodesians, worried that moderate and liberal governments in other African nations are making too many concessions to blacks, elect hard-line racist Ian Smith prime minister.
1966	Jonas Savimbi organizes UNITA, an Angolan liberation group supported by the Portuguese.
1969	After a successful coup, Col. Mu'ammar Qaddafi becomes president and prime minister of Libya.
1971	Idi Amin takes over the government of Uganda.
1972-74	A severe drought strikes the Sahel region of Africa. This region, always arid, stretches along the southern border of the Sahara. More than 200,000 die in Ethiopia alone.
1973	After a forty-five year reign, Emperor Haile Selassie is deposed by the Ethiopian military.
1975	Samora Machel, a Marxist, heads the government of newly independent Mozambique.
	Angola gains its independence, but its leadership is contested.
1976	Millions of dollars in American assistance are filtered through the CIA to anticommunist factions in Angola. Jonas Savimbi's UNITA is the largest beneficiary.
	The MPLA (Popular Movement for the Liberation of Angola), led by Agostinho Neto, defeats its rivals and forms the government of Angola.
1977	Mengistu Haile Mariam, a self-proclaimed Marxist, formally becomes chief of staff in Ethiopia. Mengistu and his radical leftist government expel U.S. troops and court the Soviets.
	Steve Biko, president of the South African Students' Organization and a strong proponent of black consciousness, is killed while in police custody.
1978	Kenyan president Jomo Kenyatta dies and vice president Daniel arap Moi succeeds him.
	The UN Security Council adopts Resolution 435, a plan for a peaceful transition to Namibian independence from South Africa. South Africa, still occupying Namibia, refuses to abide by the plan.

1979	An army of Tanzanians and exiled Ugandans occupies Uganda's capital city, Kampala, forcing dictator Idi Amin out of the country and ending his violent rule.
	Ian Smith holds an election in Rhodesia in which blacks are allowed to vote. Bishop Abel Muzorewa wins. The majority of Rhodesians consider the election and government system flawed. Civil war continues.
1980	Rhodesia's name is changed to Zimbabwe as it formally gains its independence. Robert Mugabe wins 71 percent of the vote over Muzorewa and another long-time rebel leader, Joshua Nkomo.
	Milton Obote is elected president of Uganda.
1984-85	The second major drought in the Sahel region in fifteen years leads again to hundreds of thousands of deaths. The combination of this drought, the drought of 1972-74, and the decreased rainfall since 1968 is considered the worst drought of the century.
1984	Bishop Desmond Tutu, general secretary of the South African Council of Churches, is awarded the Nobel Peace Prize for his nonviolent opposition to apartheid.
	A new constitution granting "coloreds" and Asians limited participation in the South African parliament inflames the black segment (73 percent) of the population left out of the reform. Violent resistance spreads through the townships. President P.W. Botha's reform plan eliminating some "petty apartheid" laws (bans on interracial marriage, segregation in sports, beaches, and, in some areas, movie theaters) appeases few people.
July 1985	In the face of rising resistance, P.W. Botha declares a state of emergency in thirty-six districts. This gives his government greatly expanded police power. In the week following this announcement, one thousand people are detained and sixteen killed.
August 1985	In Nigeria, Maj. Gen. Ibrahim Babangida overthrows the twenty-month-old government of Maj. Gen. Mohammed Buhari in a bloodless coup.
September 1985	U.S. president Ronald Reagan orders limited trade and financial sanctions, and eleven European nations impose trade, cultural, and military sanctions against South Africa.

October 1985	Military ruler Gen. Samuel Doe wins Liberia's first multiparty election.
November 1985	Tanzanian president Julius K. Nyerere voluntarily gives up office to his hand-picked successor Ali Hassan Mwinyi.
1985-86	The U.S. Agency for International Development distributes $135 million in aid to Africa.
January 1986	Lesotho prime minister Leabua Jonathan is overthrown in a bloodless coup led by Gen. Justin Lekhanya. Ugandan rebel group, National Resistance Army, overthrows the six-month-old government of Maj. Gen. Tito Okello. Yoweri Mouseveni becomes president.
February 1986	Libyan-backed Chadian rebels revolt. French air force bombs rebel airfield, and French commandos arrive to guard Chad's main airport. France plans to send planes and five hundred servicemen to Chad.
March 1986	The state of emergency in South Africa is officially lifted. The total of those killed is more than 750.
April 1986	Sadiq al-Mahdi elected prime minister of Sudan in the first multiparty election in eighteen years.
May 1986	Reagan administration orders expulsion of South Africa's senior military attaché in Washington and recalls U.S. military attaché from South Africa after South African military forces attack alleged ANC strongholds in Zimbabwe, Botswana, and Zambia.
June 1986	South African government declares nationwide state of emergency. Security forces are given authority to arrest, search, interrogate, and detain citizens. Media are forbidden to record any conflicts without police approval.
August 1986	More than seventeen hundred people die after a cloud of toxic gas arises from a volcanic lake in Cameroon.
September 1986	U.S. Senate and House override presidential veto and approve legislation banning new U.S. investment in South Africa and increasing sanctions.
October 1986	Mozambican president Samora Machel dies in plane crash. Foreign minister Joaquim Alberto Chisano named president.
December 1986	U.S. State Department announces that Reagan authorized $15 million in military aid for the Chadian army fighting Libyan forces. Somalia's president, Mohammed Siad Barre, is elected to a new seven-year term in an uncontested election.

February 1987	Ethiopians approve a new constitution that provides a one-party communist civilian government.
July 1987	Nigeria's president, Ibrahim Babangida, announces a timetable for his nation's transition from military rule to civilian democracy by 1992.
August/September 1987	Chadian government troops clash with Libyan troops in several battles. France shoots down a Libyan bomber over Chad. Kenneth Kaunda, chairman of the Organization of African Unity, arranges a cease-fire. Maj. Pierre Buyoya takes leadership of Burundi after Pres. Jean-Baptiste Bagaza is overthrown in a bloodless coup.
October 1987	Blaise Compaore overthrows and executes Thomas Sankara, president of Burkina Faso.
November 1987	Nigerian president Seyni Kountche dies in Paris of a brain tumor. Armed forces chief of staff Ali Seybou is named acting president.
December 1987	Zimbabwean opposition leader Joshua Nkomo merges his party with the ruling party of prime minister Robert Mugabe. Mugabe becomes the nation's first executive president, and Nkomo is named one of two vice presidents.
February 1988	Abdou Diouf is elected to a second five-year term as president of Senegal.
June 1988	South African president Botha renews two-year-old state of emergency for another year. Government increases media restrictions.
December 1988	Angola, Cuba, and South Africa sign agreement calling for Namibia's transition to independence and for a phased withdrawal of Cuba's fifty thousand troops from Angola. South Africa agrees to withdraw its sixty thousand troops from Namibia after UN-supervised elections.
January 1989	U.S. fighter aircraft are approached by two Libyan jets north of Libyan coast; Libyan jets are shot down. Libya claims jets were unarmed, but U.S. Department of Defense film reveals jets were armed. UN Security Council resolution condemning downing of jets is vetoed by U.S., Britain, and France.
May 1989	Attempted military coup to overthrow Ethiopian president Mengistu Haile Mariam fails. Coup leaders kill defense minister. After regaining power, Mengistu executes leaders of coup and imprisons several hundred military officers.
June 1989	Omar Hassan Ahmed al-Bashir overthrows Sudanese prime minister Mahdi in bloodless military coup.

August 1989	U.S. congressman Mickey Leland (D-TX) killed with fifteen others in plane crash in Ethiopia. South African president Botha resigns after ministers demand he step down. National party chairman Frederik W. de Klerk becomes acting president.
September 1989	De Klerk is elected president of South Africa.
October 1989	De Klerk orders release of ANC leader Walter Sisulu and seven other leading black political prisoners.
November 1989	President of Comoros, Abdullah Abderemane, is assassinated by presidential guard in attack led by French mercenary Bob Denard. Denard and followers turn over authority to French naval commandos.
February 1990	De Klerk legalizes ANC, the South African Communist Party, the Pan-African Congress, and other opposition groups. Nelson Mandela is released after twenty-seven years in prison.
March 1990	Namibia gains independence after seventy-five years of control by South Africa. Sam Nujoma becomes president. In Zimbabwe, Robert Mugabe wins landslide victory and calls the results "a mandate to create a one-party state."
April 1990	Zaire's president Mobutu Sese Seko announces plan to end one-party rule and create a new constitution. U.S. advises Americans in Liberia to leave because of mounting violence between government and rebels. U.S. Defense Department orders amphibious task force of more than two thousand marines to sail to Liberia and evacuate Americans. Task force arrives in June.
June 1990	De Klerk lifts four-year-old nationwide state of emergency in all provinces except Natal, the site of conflict between rival black organizations.
July 1990	Liberian National Patriotic Front (NPF) rebels attack Monrovia, Liberia's capital. Rebel Yormie Johnson announces intent to take American hostages. U.S. Marines fly into Monrovia, evacuate U.S. embassy, and eventually rescue at least 125 people.
August 1990	In talks between the ANC and the South African government, the ANC announces a cease-fire and the government pledges to release political prisoners and to allow political exiles to return home. The Economic Community of West African States sends peacekeeping force of three thousand to Liberia; the force captures large sections of Monrovia.

September 1990	Liberian president Samuel Doe is killed by rebels.
October 1990	Ivory Coast president Félix Houphouet-Boigny wins nation's first contested presidential election.
December 1990	Zambian president Kenneth Kaunda legalizes opposition political parties.
May 1991	Tigrean rebels storm Addis Ababa, Ethiopia, and overthrow the government of dictator Mengistu Haile Mariam. Mengistu flees to Zimbabwe. The new government promises to form a multiparty transitional government.
June 1991	South African president F.W. de Klerk leads parliament to repeal the Population Registration Act of 1948, which had required all South Africans to be registered according to their race. De Klerk promises further reforms and states that the law's repeal is the beginning of the end of apartheid.
July 1991	U.S. president George Bush lifts sanctions against South Africa. It is revealed that the South African police secretly channeled funds to the Inkatha Freedom party beginning in early 1990 in an effort to prevent Inkatha from merging with the ANC. Inkatha, headed by Chief Mangosuthu Gatsha Buthelezi, is the primary rival opposition movement to the ANC. The revelation increases support for the ANC and leads to demands that de Klerk step down and allow an interim government to manage the transition to a post-apartheid, democratic South Africa.
November 1991	It is estimated that approximately three thousand South Africans have been killed in tribal violence since summer 1990.

Organizations to Contact

The editors have compiled the following list of organizations that are concerned with the issues debated in this book. All have publications or information available for interested readers. The descriptions are derived from materials provided by the organizations. This list was compiled upon the date of publication. Names and phone numbers of organizations are subject to change.

Africa Faith and Justice Network
198 Broadway
New York, NY 10038
(212) 962-1210

The network is comprised of religious groups concerned with oppression and injustice in Africa. It analyzes how U.S. foreign policy affects Africa and challenges policies it believes are detrimental to Africans. The network publishes the bimonthly *AFJN Newsletter* and quarterly *Documentation Pamphlets*, in addition to other materials.

Africa News Service
PO Box 3851
Durham, NC 27702
(919) 286-0747

The Africa News Service provides information to the media and the public concerning events and issues in Africa. The service also researches the effect of U.S. policies in Africa. In addition to its library of books, documents, and newspaper clippings related to Africa, the service publishes the biweekly magazine *Africa News*.

Africare
440 R St. NW
Washington, DC 20001
(202) 462-3614

Africare works to assist the villagers of sub-Saharan Africa to develop water, agricultural, health, and environmental resources. The organization has offices in twenty-two African nations to assist in the development of rural Africa. It publishes pamphlets such as *Food in Africa, African Development: The Big Picture,* and *Homeless in Africa.*

American Committee on Africa (ACOA)
198 Broadway
New York, NY 10038
(212) 962-1210

The ACOA is dedicated to ending apartheid and racism in South Africa. It sponsors the Africa Fund, a nonprofit organization that supports U.S. sanctions against South Africa. ACOA educates Americans concerning the conflict in South Africa and aids victims of apartheid, including South African political prisoners and refugees in Africa and the U.S. The committee publishes the quarterly *ACOA Action News* newsletter in addition to books, fact sheets, and videos concerning South Africa.

Amnesty International
322 Eighth Ave.
New York, NY 10001-4808
(212) 627-1451

Amnesty International is an independent, worldwide movement that works for the release of all political prisoners. It supports fair and prompt trials for political prisoners and an end to torture and executions. Amnesty publishes reports on human rights violations in Africa and other regions of the world.

The Hunger Project
1 Madison Ave. 8A
New York, NY 10010
(212) 532-4255

The project is committed to eliminating world hunger by the year 2000. It educates the public concerning hunger and starvation in Africa and other regions. The project publishes *World Development Forum*, a semimonthly report of facts, trends, and opinion on international development.

Institute for Food and Development Policy (Food First)
145 Ninth St.
San Francisco, CA 94103
(415) 864-8555

Food First conducts research and educates the public concerning world hunger. It opposes foreign aid to impoverished regions such as Africa and believes that world hunger would be eliminated if developed nations such as the U.S. would allow the people of the Third World to control their own food production with traditional, native techniques and crops. The institute publishes books, pamphlets, study guides, and the quarterly newsletter *Food First News*.

International Monetary Fund (IMF)
700 Nineteenth St. NW
Washington, DC 20431
(202) 623-7000

The IMF's purpose is to promote international economic cooperation, to help maintain a balance of trade, and to lend its members money. It publishes the semimonthly *IMF Survey* and brochures including "Helping the Poor: The IMF's New Facilities for Structural Adjustment," which explains IMF strategies concerning Africa and other impoverished regions.

The Population Institute
110 Maryland Ave. NE
Washington, DC 20002
(202) 544-3300

The Population Institute is dedicated to decreasing the rate of population growth in the Third World. It encourages leaders and the media to draw the public's attention to the problems of overpopulation. To promote its cause, the institute publishes the bimonthly newsletter *Popline*.

Population Renewal Office
36 W. 59th St.
Kansas City, MO 64113
(816) 363-6980

The office advocates increased world population growth and opposes population control in Africa and other regions. It believes that people are a resource and that the world will benefit from a growing population. The group publishes brochures and articles such as "Out of Africa: Some Population Truths."

TransAfrica
545 Eighth St. SE, Suite 200
Washington, DC 20003
(202) 547-2550

TransAfrica, founded in 1976, lobbies the U.S. Congress to influence U.S. foreign policy in Africa. It has staged protests at the South African embassy in Washington, D.C., and worked to maintain U.S. sanctions against South Africa.

United Nations Center Against Apartheid
United Nations Plaza, Rm. S-3275
New York, NY 10017
(212) 963-5511

The United Nations Center Against Apartheid was established in 1976 to help eliminate apartheid in South Africa. The organization monitors events in South Africa and prepares studies and reports concerning apartheid and the people of the nation. It consults with governments and organizations that can influence public opinion against apartheid. The center publishes reports, pamphlets, films, posters, and other materials.

Washington Office on Africa (WOA)
110 Maryland Ave. NE
Washington, DC 20002
(202) 546-7961

The Washington Office on Africa is a national, nonprofit organization supported by churches and labor movements. It lobbies the U.S. Congress to pass legislation to help end apartheid and racism in South Africa and to benefit the people of Africa. WOA opposes U.S. intervention in Africa and supports continued sanctions against South Africa. It publishes numerous pamphlets and books concerning issues related to Africa and U.S. policies in the region. It publishes the quarterly newsletter *Washington Notes on Africa*.

The World Bank
1818 H St. NW
Washington, DC 20433
(202) 477-1234

The World Bank is an international financial organization that loans money to members of the bank for the purpose of economic development and progress. The bank has published many books and reports on the economies of Africa, including *Sub-Saharan Africa: From Crisis to Sustainable Growth*.

Zero Population Growth (ZPG)
1400 Sixteenth St. NW, Suite 320
Washington, DC 20036
(202) 332-2200

ZPG is concerned with population growth throughout the world. It supports population control measures in Africa and other regions and believes that such measures would help decrease poverty and famine. It publishes the bimonthly newsletter *ZPG Reporter* and the quarterly bulletins *ZPG Activist* and *Action Alerts*.

Bibliography of Books

Adebayo Adedeji and Tariq Husain	*The Leadership Challenge for Improving the Economic and Social Situation of Africa.* New York: Africa Leadership Forum, 1988.
Ibrahim B. Babangida and Olusegun Obasanjo	*Africa in Today's World and the Challenges of Leadership.* New York: Africa Leadership Forum, 1988.
Panos D. Bardis	*South Africa and the Marxist Movement: A Study in Double Standards.* Lewiston, NY: Edwin Mellen Press, 1989.
P.T. Bauer	*Equality, the Third World, and Economic Delusion.* London: Weidenfeld and Nicholson, 1981.
Nsekuye Bizimana	*White Paradise: Hell for Africa?* Berlin, Germany: Edition Humana, 1989.
Paul Bohannan and Philip Curtin	*Africa and Africans.* 3d ed. Prospect Heights, IL: Waveland Press, 1988.
Karl Borgin and Kathleen Corbett	*The Destruction of a Continent: Africa and International Aid.* New York: Harcourt Brace Jovanovich, 1982.
Denis Boyles	*African Lives.* New York: Grove-Weidenfeld, 1988.
Michael Cassidy	*The Passing Summer: A South African's Response to White Fear, Black Anger, and the Politics of Love.* Ventura, CA: Regal Books, 1990.
Fantu Cheru	*The Silent Revolution in Africa: Debt, Development, and Democracy.* London: Zed Books, 1989.
Peter Collins, ed.	*Thinking About South Africa: Reason, Morality, and Politics.* Hemel Hempstead, Hertfordshire, England: Harvester/Wheatsheaf, 1989.
Stephen Commins, ed.	*Africa's Development Challenge and the World Bank.* Boulder, CO: Lynne Rienner, 1988.
Catherine Coquery-Vidrovitch	*Africa: Endurance and Change South of the Sahara.* Berkeley: University of California Press, 1989.
Basil Davidson	*Modern Africa: A Social and Political History.* 2d ed. London: Longman Group, 1989.
Francis M. Deng and I. William Zartman, eds.	*Conflict Resolution in Africa.* Washington, DC: Brookings Institution, 1991.
Alexander de Waal	*Famine That Kills.* Oxford: Clarendon Press, 1989.
Larry Diamond, Juan J. Linz, and Seymour Martin Lipset, eds.	*Democracy in Developing Countries: Volume 2, Africa.* Boulder, CO: Lynne Rienner, 1988.
Nicholas Eberstadt	*Foreign Aid and American Purpose.* Lanham, MD: Freedom House, 1989.
L.H. Gann and Peter Duignan	*Hope for South Africa?* Stanford, CA: Hoover Institution Press, 1991.
Richard W. Franke and Barbara W. Chasin	*Seeds of Famine.* Montclair, NJ: Allanheld, Osmun & Co. Publishers, 1980.
Julie Frederikse	*The Unbreakable Thread: Non-Racialism in South Africa.* Bloomington: Indiana University Press, 1990.
Harvey Glickman, ed.	*The Crisis and Challenge of African Development.* New York: Greenwood Press, 1988.

Kofi Buenor Hadjor	*Africa in an Era of Crisis*. Trenton, NJ: Africa World Press, 1990.
Blaine Harden	*Africa: Dispatches from a Fragile Continent*. New York: Norton, 1990.
Donald L. Horowitz	*A Democratic South Africa? Constitutional Engineering in a Divided Society*. Berkeley: University of California Press, 1991.
Robert D. Kaplan	*Surrender or Starve: The Wars Behind the Famine*. Boulder, CO: Westview Press, 1988.
Paul Kennedy	*African Capitalism: The Struggle for Ascendency*. New York: Cambridge University Press, 1988.
Carol Lancaster	*U.S. Aid to Sub-Saharan Africa: Challenges, Constraints, and Choices*. Washington, DC: The Center for Strategic and International Studies, 1988.
Pierre Landell-Mills, Rampopal Agarwala, and Stanley Please	*Sub-Saharan Africa: From Crisis to Sustainable Growth, A Long-Term Perspective Study*. Washington, DC: The World Bank, 1989.
Aklilu Lemma and Pentti Malaska, eds.	*Africa Beyond Famine*. London: Tycooly Publishing, 1989.
Stephen R. Lewis Jr.	*The Economics of Apartheid*. New York: Council on Foreign Relations, 1990.
Azzam Mahjoub, ed.	*Adjustment or Delinking: The African Experience*. London: Zed Books, 1990.
Nelson Mandela	*Nelson Mandela: Speeches 1990*. New York: Pathfinder Press, 1990.
Fatima Meer	*Higher than Hope: The Authorized Biography of Nelson Mandela*. New York: Harper & Row, 1990.
Mokgethi Motlhabi	*Challenge to Apartheid: Toward a Moral National Resistance*. Grand Rapids, MI: Eerdmans, 1990.
Olusegun Obasanjo	*Africa in Perspective: Myths and Realities*. New York: Council on Foreign Relations, 1987.
Bill Rau	*From Feast to Famine: Official Cures and Grassroots Remedies to Africa's Food Crisis*. London: Zed Books, 1991.
Diana E.H. Russell	*Lives of Courage: Women for a New South Africa*. New York: Basic Books, 1989.
Richard Sandbrook	*The Politics of Africa's Economic Stagnation*. New York: Cambridge University Press, 1986.
Robert A. Schrire, ed.	*Critical Choices for South Africa: An Agenda for the 1990s*. Oxford: Oxford University Press, 1990.
Allister Sparks	*The Mind of South Africa*. New York: Knopf, 1990.
Lloyd Timberlake	*Famine in Africa*. New York: Gloucester Press, 1986.
Jennifer Seymour Whitaker	*How Can Africa Survive?* New York: Council on Foreign Relations, 1988.
Walter E. Williams	*South Africa's War Against Capitalism*. New York: Praeger Publishers, 1989.
John A. Wiseman	*Democracy in Black Africa: Survival and Revival*. New York: Paragon House, 1990.

Index

DATE DUE

MR 2 0 '93			
APR 3 0 1994			
MR 2 1 1995			
DEC - 6 1997			
JY 23 '00			
OCT 07 '01			

HIGHSMITH 45-220

WITHDRAWN